Race, Law, and "The Chinese Puzzle" in Imperial Britain

Race, Law, and "The Chinese Puzzle" in Imperial Britain

Sascha Auerbach

palgrave
macmillan

RACE, LAW, AND "THE CHINESE PUZZLE" IN IMPERIAL BRITAIN

First published in hardcover in 2009 by PALGRAVE MACMILLAN® in the United States—a division of St. Martin's Press LLC, 175 Fifth Avenue, New York, NY 10010.

Where this book is distributed in the UK, Europe and the rest of the world, this is by Palgrave Macmillan, a division of Macmillan Publishers Limited, registered in England, company number 785998, of Houndmills, Basingstoke, Hampshire RG21 6XS.

Palgrave Macmillan is the global academic imprint of the above companies and has companies and representatives throughout the world.

ISBN: 978-1-137-28197-5

Library of Congress Cataloging-in-Publication Data

Auerbach, Sascha.
Race, law, and "the Chinese puzzle" in imperial Britain / Sascha Auerbach.
p. cm.
Includes bibliographical references and index.
ISBN 978-0-230-60949-5
1. Chinese—Great Britain—History. 2. Chinese—Great Britain—Social conditions—20th century. 3. China—Emigration and immigration—History—20th century. 4. Great Britain—Race relations—History—20th century. I. Title.

DA125.C5A84 2009
305.895'104109041—dc22 2008042810

A catalogue record of the book is available from the British Library.

Design by Scribe

First PALGRAVE MACMILLAN paperback edition: January 2013

10 9 8 7 6 5 4 3 2 1

Transferred to Digital Printing in 2013

For Norbert Theo Auerbach, 1922–2009,
un gentilhomme de vieille Europe

Contents

Maps and Figures

Maps

Figures

Acknowledgments

This book began as one aspect of a larger study of law and culture in modern Britain. Its completion would have been impossible without the generous contributions of colleagues, friends, and family. I would first like to thank Virginia Commonwealth University and Emory University for supporting my research. The awarding, by VCU, of a Career Scholarship Enhancement Grant at a crucial juncture in the project's development was invaluable, and my special gratitude goes to Robert Holsworth, Catherine Ingrassia, and Bernard Moitt for their encouragement. In the VCU History Department, particular thanks are due to Wanda Clary, Leigh Anne Craig, Samantha Giles, John Kneebone, Gary Marquardt, Sarah Meacham, George Munro, Kathleen Murphy, Laura Ping, and Karen Rader. I am also grateful for the extraordinary hospitality shown to me by Bruce and Roberta Stover during my research trips to England.

It has been my great pleasure to work with a remarkable cohort of scholars who have guided me through every step of the research and writing process. Antoinette Burton, Anne Clendinning, Leigh Anne Craig, Paul Deslandes, Margot Finn, Dane Kennedy, Patrick McDevitt, Zachary Morgan, and Gail Savage all read portions of the manuscript and shared generously of their expertise. In England, Robert Bickers, Kelly Boyd, Janet Nelson, and Kirsty Reid kindly provided forums for me to present my work. In the United States and Canada, Leonard V. Smith and Stephen Heathorn did the same. Thanks are due for the comments and advice offered by the faculty and students who attended my papers and seminars at the Centre for the Study of Colonial and Post-Colonial Societies (University of Bristol), the Capitol Hill Gang, the Institute of Historical Research, McMaster University, the Mid-Atlantic Conference on British Studies, the North American Conference on British Studies, Oberlin College, the Pacific Coast Conference on British Studies, the University of Buffalo, and the Honors College of VCU. Along the way, I also received invaluable input and encouragement from Kathryn Amdur, Andrew August,

Anna Clark, Carolyn Conley, Dina Copelman, Anna Davin, Nadja Durbach, Heide Fehrenbach, Michael Fisher, Rick Jobs, Lara Kriegel, Philippa Levine, Matthew Payne, Susan Pennybacker, Elizabeth Prevost, Ellen Ross, Kevin Siena, John Soister, and Laura Tabili. Zane Bevan at the VCU Graphics Lab helped prepare the images for the book. Chris Chappell, Allison McElgunn, Rosemi Mederos, Henry Whitney and the other editors and staff at Palgrave Macmillan and Scribe have been terrific to work with, and I appreciate all the time and energy that they have devoted to bringing *The Chinese Puzzle* to fruition.

The helpful staffs of various archives and libraries in Britain and the United States patiently endured even my most relentless and obscure inquiries. I am particularly thankful to the staffs of the British Library, the Colindale Newspaper Library, the JUSTIS legal archive, the Library of Virginia, the London Metropolitan Archives, the National Archives, the Tower Hamlets Local History Library and Archive, and the Trades Union Congress Library of London Metropolitan University. The help provided by Kevin Farley and the staff of VCU's James Branch Cabell Library was above and beyond the call of duty, as was that of Anne Benham and the staff of the Alderman Library at the University of Virginia.

To my friends, my appreciation for your patient support is unbounded. Just a few who deserve special mention are Cennydd Bowles, William Carrigan, Amy Enright, Larissa Smith Ferguson, Sabo Gil, Gianni Masotto, Darren Morris, Todd Mustard, Aaron and Renee Fichtelberg, and Godfrey Uzoigwe. To my family, who kept me going from the first word to the last—Mom, Dad, Adam, Martin, David, Maia, Abbie, and the Sprout—thank you for believing that all who wander are not lost.

My most profound gratitude goes to the two people who were, respectively, the finest mentor and the best friend anyone could wish for. Margot and Colin, thanks for always being there, especially in the rough weather.

Chapter 1

Introduction

"The Chinese puzzle" was a metaphor employed by British commentators to sum up the difficulties of dealing with the Chinese and with the complexities of their society, culture, and politics.[1] It was used as the title of a British play, first performed in London in 1918, about a diplomatic scandal involving a Chinese ambassador, his Caucasian wife (played by Lillian Braithwaite), and their associates.[2] Arthur Ransome, the noted British journalist, similarly titled his book on China *The Chinese Puzzle* (1927).[3] David Lloyd George endorsed the book and wrote its preface. Although Ransome's experience in China was limited to a few weeks, *The Chinese Puzzle* was acknowledged as an important contribution to the subject. As one reviewer commented, unwittingly highlighting a persistent trend in Britain, an author did not need to possess extensive knowledge *of* the Chinese in order to be publicly recognized as an authority *on* them.[4]

The concept of "the Chinese puzzle" was employed not only by journalists, diplomats, playwrights, and scholars of international relations, but also more prosaically by political leaders and union officials in Britain and the empire. For them, the phrase aptly portrayed the challenges of regulating Chinese immigration and dealing with the social and cultural incompatibilities of Chinese immigrants and white residents. Like many other aspects of Anglo-Chinese relations, "the Chinese puzzle" appeared first in imperial discourse and was later replicated in a domestic context. In 1877, Sir Archibald Michie, the former Attorney-General of Victoria, used the phrase to describe the legal problems posed by Chinese immigration to Australia. "The two people can never amalgamate," he declared, and nowhere was this more evident than when Chinese men appeared as witnesses, defendants, or plaintiffs in courts of law.[5] Thirty years later, the editors of

The Seaman printed an article titled "Solving the Chinese Puzzle," wherein Joseph Havelock Wilson, Member of Parliament (Middlesbrough, Liberal) and founder of the National Amalgamated Sailors' and Firemen's Union, addressed the controversial issue of race and labor law aboard British ships.[6] As the comments made by Michie and Wilson suggested, law and legal forums played a pivotal role in constructions of race and in the management of race relations across British society and throughout the empire during this period. Those who opposed or supported Chinese labor and immigration often argued that legal regulation was the most effective response to the moral, economic, and social challenges presented by Chinese communities in Britain and the empire. Trials and their public retellings also provided opportunities for all of those involved, including Chinese residents themselves, to affirm or contest racial stereotypes.

"The Chinese puzzle" proved particularly difficult for Britons to resolve as the issues of Chinese labor and immigration rose to prominence in political discourse, law, labor relations, and popular culture in the opening decades of the twentieth century. From a historian's perspective, perhaps the most intriguing aspect of Anglo-Chinese relations in Britain during this period is the contrast between the small size of the Chinese immigrant community and the considerable attention they received in law, press, and literature.[7] The rapid evolution, in British public discourse, of Chinese residents and London's "Chinatown" from an exotic curiosity at the turn of the century to a dire threat to society in the interwar period is especially confounding. The timing of this changeover provides part of the explanation, hence the situation of this study chronologically between two periods of heightened racial awareness in Britain, the vociferous debate over "Chinese labour" in South Africa in 1903–6 and the race riots of 1919. The most determined attempts to regulate Chinese immigration and Chinese immigrants through law, and the most negative portrayals of them in press and literature, came to a head as Britain confronted military and economic challenges abroad. The rise of chauvinistic nationalism, labor tensions, sensationalized journalism, and anti-immigrant sentiment in this period were significant factors as well.

The growth of the Chinese population in the metropolis also intensified public concerns with their labor and residency. But timing and numbers alone are insufficient to explain the public controversy over London's "Chinatown" and its residents. Even at its highest point, the Chinese population of the metropolis never numbered more than a few thousand, and anti-Chinese sentiment reached its zenith in the interwar period, when their numbers were declining from a wartime apex. Viewing negative portrayals or treatment as an inevitable response to the increasing numerical presence of Chinese immigrants in Britain is unhelpful in any case, since it naturalizes racial antipathy as an undifferentiated and ahistorical phenomenon. Further explanation for the rapid rise in anti-Chinese sentiment lies in its articulation across a broad spectrum of British society. Chinese residents became a concern for union leaders, journalists, police, magistrates, politicians, Home Office officials, playwrights and authors, and the working-class residents of London and other cities in Britain. Anglo-Chinese relations were also mutually constituted at the local, national, and imperial levels.[8] Many of the issues that came to dominate metropolitan race relations first rose to prominence in the empire. And the perceived threat of the Chinese to white communities was often based on the imagined potency of their race and the purported coherence of their international community as compared to the permeability of Britain and the vulnerability of the British race to corruption and demoralization. In sum, Chinese immigration and labor became significant issues in public discourse because they were intimately bound up with the economic, cultural, political, social, and legal development of British society as a whole in the early twentieth century.

The multiple points of contact between Chinese and Britons, however, were not accompanied by any recognition of shared interest or character. On the contrary, the fundamental incompatibility of the Chinese and Anglo-Saxon "races" was the single most persistent and prominent element of British public discourse on the Chinese and on Anglo-Chinese relations. The supposed opacity of the Chinese made them an ideal racial foil for a broad spectrum of British society, from British seamen struggling to maintain their economic viability, to judicial officials combating crime and demoralization in the East End, to demobilized veterans adjusting to interwar gender relations. Chinese laborers, for example, were portrayed by British union leaders as being immoral, feminized, mutinous, sexually deviant, and mercenary, whereas their British counterparts were described as masculine, virtuous, and patriotic. For all the supposed impossibility of assimilation, however, British commentators' portrayals of the Chinese and of their own countrymen often had much in common. This helps explain why observers from a variety of perspectives described the Chinese as challenging the British in ways that almost no other non-European cohort did. Both peoples had a long history of complex law, culture, and government; both were resistant to political or legal subjugation by other nations; they were both seen to be imperial, commercial, acquisitive, ambitious, hard-working and legalistic; both were globally mobile; and, like British communities in Asia and Africa, the Chinese were often perceived as voluntarily segregating themselves, socially and culturally, from those around them.[9] It is a testament to the intimate distance between the two groups that the designation of the Chinese everyman as "John Chinaman" paralleled the popular sobriquet of the British everyman, "John Bull."[10]

But there was no singular, unvarying image of "the Chinese," any more than there was a static interpretation of "white," "Anglo-Saxon," or "the British," nor was there an undifferentiated response to Chinese labor and residency in Britain and the empire. The development of Anglo-Chinese relations and the defining of race as a category itself in Britain and the empire were fundamentally fragmented, contested, unstable, and incomplete processes. In the case of the Chinese, these processes were further complicated by the diverse interests of those groups that sought to define them and by the speech and actions of Chinese residents themselves. The complexities and contradictions of Chinese stereotypes in Britain and the empire were particularly apparent in discussions of the alleged willingness of Chinese men to work harder, and for less remuneration, than their white counterparts were. As active participants in the imperial mining and maritime labor force, Chinese workers were a key component of Britain's imperial trade and industry.[11] "Chinese labour" was touted as a boon to British employers at the same time that it was condemned as a curse to the white workingmen of Australia, South Africa, Canada, and Britain. When the members of Ernest Shackleton's 1908–9 South Pole expedition—a venture that challenged man and beast alike to survive arduous labor under harsh conditions with the promise of little monetary reward—nicknamed one of their pack ponies "Chinaman," few in Britain would have failed to get the joke.[12] Was this not, after all, the perennial lot of the Chinese "coolie?"[13] Naming a hard-working animal after a figure that was sometimes viewed, and treated, as being little better typified the mixture of respect and derision that often characterized British attitudes toward Chinese immigrants. The obvious contradictions in these stereotypes—that Chinese men were both dependable and conniving, savage and civilized, degenerate but powerful, deprived and yet wealthy—were resolved by the supposition that their calm outward visage often belied a vastly different interior. This sense of "the Chinese world as profoundly hidden" also helped British observers reconcile the banal physical appearance of Chinese neighborhoods in Britain with the deviance, corruption, and villainy that supposedly pervaded them.[14] Such assumptions, and the tendency to reduce "the Chinese" into a homogenous, undifferentiated mass, were exacerbated by the persistent inability (or unwillingness) of Britons to distinguish between individuals. The habits, characteristics, and character of one (whether observed, constructed, or simply assumed) thus became that of the whole, and every individual became equally accountable for the sins of his race.

Map 1.1. London's East End, 1883. (*Baedecker's London and its Environs*. London: Dulau, 1883. Courtesy of the Library of Virginia.)

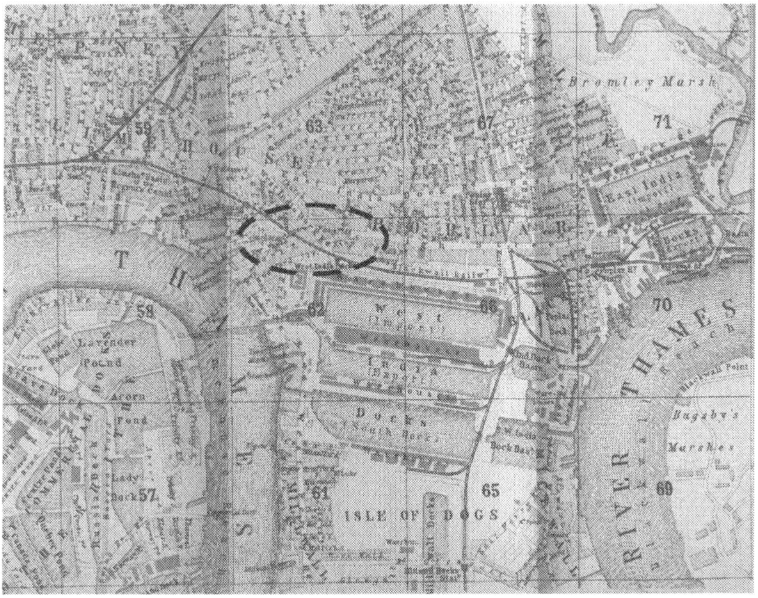

Map 1.2. Limehouse and the West India Docks, 1883. Dotted line encompasses Pennyfields and Limehouse Causeway, a.k.a. "Chinatown" or "Limehouse Chinatown." (*Baedecker's London and its Environs*. London: Dulau, 1883. Courtesy of the Library of Virginia.)

Although Chinese men did not become a serious concern in London law, press, and literature until the early twentieth century, they had been living in the East End since the late eighteenth century. Among the earliest residents were seamen who had been discharged from East India Company ships.[15] Chinese men began appearing in London coutrooms as early as 1800, when Awing, a resident of Ratcliff Highway, testified in a burglary case heard in the Old Bailey.[16] More detailed descriptions of Chinese East End residents dated to the mid-nineteenth century, when they appeared in the accounts of social investigators and journalists such as Henry Mayhew, J. Ewing Ritchie, Joseph Charles Parkinson, and Charles Dickens.[17] By the 1890s, the China-born population of the metropolis numbered roughly three hundred.[18] London writers were regularly referring to the area encompassed by Pennyfields and Limehouse Causeway—two streets that ran east and west, respectively, from the West India Dock Road—as "Limehouse Chinatown" or simply as "Chinatown" (Map 1.2).[19] These early accounts focused on subjects that would remain central to almost all subsequent discussions of Chinese residents. Chinese contact with the white community, internecine violence, interracial relationships, the success or failure of Chinese attempts to assimilate, the racially cosmopolitan character of Chinatown, its poverty, and Chinese "vices"—especially gambling and opium smoking—all figured prominently in them. With the exception of opium smoking, however, similar concerns were often expressed in the descriptions of other immigrant groups that appeared in journalism and literature.[20]

What made these nineteenth-century descriptions of London's Chinese residents most notable was the dramatic contrast in tone—but not substance—between them and those written in the interwar period. Henry Mayhew, in *London Labour and the London Poor* (1861), nonchalantly depicted the relationship between Chinese Emma, an Irishwoman, and Appoo, her absent Chinese husband.[21] J. Ewing Ritchie and Joseph Charles Parkinson were similarly unfazed by the opium smoking they encountered (and, in Ritchie's case, experienced firsthand) in their East End explorations. Decades later, both Count E. Armfelt, in his contribution to George R. Sims's edited collection, *Living London* (1902), and George Wade, who wrote a long expository piece on "The Cockney John Chinaman" for the *London Illustrated Magazine* (1900), described interracial marriages and their offspring in equally nonjudgmental terms.[22] Walter Besant's visit to an opium den in 1899 left him disappointed. Earlier literary depictions had led him to expect a "dreadful place" that would cause "a creeping of the flesh."[23] Instead, he encountered merely a handful of Chinese men smoking peaceably, the only "horrible" thing there being a discordant musical instrument.

Although these accounts generally portrayed the Chinese as orderly and law-abiding, the writers were often far from complimentary in their descriptions of the district, its inhabitants, and their practices. They commented on the squalor they witnessed, the insalubrious environment of the "opium dens" they visited, and the chaotic admixture of races, cultures, and languages that made these areas seem alien to their eyes. Parkinson warned of opium's potential to make "slaves" of those who used it and described one opium dealer as the "high priest" of the drug.[24] Mayhew was particularly alarmed by "the disease communicated by the Malays, Lascars, and Orientals" to white women, which, along with the opium habit they sometimes acquired, destroyed such women physically and spiritually.[25] From its initial entry into public discussions in press and literature, London's Chinatown was portrayed as a space dominated by Chinese men and devoid of Chinese women, and as a neighborhood that fit, at best, uneasily, and often not at all, with the popular views of what constituted healthy, moral domesticity.[26] While opinions differed on the moral and physical consequences of interracial marriage in this period, white women who attached themselves to Chinese men or to other Asian immigrants, or who immersed themselves in their culture, often did so at risk to their own racial status. Their liminal racial identity was reflected in the nicknames they acquired, such as "China Emma," "Lascar Sal," "Canton Kitty," and "Mother Abdallah."[27]

But Chinatown was only one in the long list of demoralized East End districts that were a perennial source of public concern in late Victorian London. And beyond the possible moral and physical repercussions for the few white women who chose to marry Chinese men—women who were often described as already being immoral, debauched, or otherwise incapable of making a respectable match to a white man, in any case—Chinatown and its Chinese residents seemed to pose little threat to the broader community. Armfelt, in his piece written for Sims, was quite explicit in this regard. The Japanese, he wrote, "will never rest until they have built an Empire of the West that shall rival the power and the grandeur of Great Britain," but all that the Chinese desired, as a people and a nation, was "to be left alone."[28] According to Parkinson, the policeman he interviewed warned him that the danger of the Chinese neighborhood was not its Chinese residents. It was, rather, "an uncommon rough crew of English hangin' in and about there" that he should fear.[29] Wade, in a similar vein, insisted that "the Chinaman in Limehouse is a most peaceable, inoffensive, harmless character," and even that the white residents of Limehouse were "rather proud of the honour done it by [the Chinaman] being where he is."[30]

It is worth noting that these innocuous descriptions persisted even after the British press circulated dire accounts of Chinese "atrocities" against Westerners during the Boxer Rebellion.[31] Tales of the conflict that filtered back to London certainly reinforced the stereotype of Chinese men as being violent and bloodthirsty, but the event itself was rarely mentioned in connection with London's Chinese population. Most observers assumed that the dynamics of British settlement in China operated quite differently from those of Chinese settlement in Britain, nor, in the twentieth century, were the Chinese commonly conflated in Britain with the Japanese, and it would be more accurate to speak of "Yellow Peril(s)" in British public discourse than of a singular, undifferentiated "Asian" threat. Public opinion on Chinese labor and residency in Britain would remain sharply divided well into the war years, with some praising Chinese workers and asserting that they were orderly residents of the metropolis while others heaped calumny upon them. By 1920, however, both public opinion and official policy toward Chinese labor and residency had hardened considerably. The same practices that had been dismissed as exotic but inoffensive by earlier commentators were prompting mass arrests and mass deportations, interracial sexuality had been deemed "moral and physical suicide" by the most prominent East End magistrate, and Chinese residents were being depicted in the London popular press as a dire threat to both the white race and the British nation.

Popular perceptions and portrayals of the Chinese were usually shaped by those with legal, political, or cultural authority in Britain and the empire, authority to which Chinese residents themselves could rarely lay claim. But their efforts to establish for themselves—often against fierce resistance—a place in the economy, society, and culture of their adopted homes were nonetheless central to the shaping of Anglo-Chinese relations in Britain and the empire.[32] Reassembling the full history of Chinese immigrants in Britain—who were a small population that left only limited written records of their experiences—is an immensely challenging and worthwhile task. Hopefully, a new volume by Terence Gomez and Gregor Benton will fill this crucial lacuna in the historical record.[33] The London Metropolitan Archives, working in cooperation with the Chinese residents of London, is also helping to preserve the living memory of the Chinese community for posterity. Chinese residents remain very much subjects, and not objects, in the following chapters, but *The Chinese Puzzle* is not meant to be a comprehensive social history of the Chinese experience in Britain. My focus is on the meaning of race, race relations, and immigration as the Chinese in Britain became a prominent issue in law, culture, and public discourse, rather than on the historical narrative of their life and labor. This is a necessary step toward understanding the broader history and significance of the encounters between the peoples and cultures of Britain and China in both the metropole and the empire, and it will hopefully encourage further investigation. But what follows is as much a study of those Britons who interacted with Chinese immigrants, who formulated and implemented policy toward them, and who wrote about them in newspapers, plays, and popular fiction, as it is a study of such immigrants themselves.

This broad perspective on Chinese immigration and Anglo-Chinese relations addresses a number of major themes in modern British history. First and foremost, it speaks to the history of race. By "race," I mean that constellation of attributes thought to be intrinsic to a certain group with assumed origins in a common cultural (i.e., historic), geographic, and physical heritage. Racial identity can be imposed, assumed, declared, or rejected by both groups and individuals. It is a highly unstable and contested category whose meaning and significance emerge from their particular historical contexts. Race is thus subjectively determined, but its impact on society is objectively measurable, particularly in law and public policy. With the notable exception of work on Irish and Jewish immigrants, the advance of scholarship on race in Britain has lagged well behind the scholarship on other aspects of identity such as class and gender.[34] The most important recent development has been the interpretation of race as a constructed, historically contingent category that, in the nineteenth century, most commonly emerged in conjunction with the ideologies and practices of imperialism, colonialism, and nationalism.[35] Historians have only recently turned their attention to race, race relations, and racism as they related to non-European communities in pre-World War II Britain.[36] Recent work on this subject has tended to focus on residents of Indian, African, or Afro-Caribbean origin.[37] While there is still great deal to be learned about these groups, historians have at least established a solid foundation for future study.

The Chinese, meanwhile, remain "Britain's least understood racial minority," according to immigration historian Colin Holmes.[38] Historians' elision of the differences between the Chinese and other Asian residents—a practice that was increasingly uncommon among Britons themselves in the early twentieth century—has further obscured the unique features of Anglo-Chinese relations in Britain and the empire. Despite important common elements in the experiences of different cultural, national, and ethnic groups in Britain and the empire, any attempt to ascribe British prejudices against these groups simply to "racism" runs the risk of conflating their unique historical features. In approaching how the category of race operated in public discourse, it is more accurate to speak of "races," and therefore of "racisms," than it is to speak of one overarching designation or dynamic that applied to all peoples and all situations. This caveat for specificity must also be made with regards to Orientalism as a theoretical model. Edward Said himself has emphasized the vast differences between "the Orient" and the "Far East" in European discourse.[39] Orientalism, although still quite useful in this context, thus provides only one of many possible starting points for understanding the complex debates over Chinese labor and immigration.[40]

The focus of analysis here is on Chinese immigrants and Anglo-Chinese social relations. But my broader goal is to explore what race itself meant in British society, to what degree it was an autonomous category of identity and identification, and, conversely, how it accrued meaning from its associations with other social, economic, gender, political, and cultural dynamics.[41] I emphasize the depth, breadth, and persistence of both negative and positive portrayals of the Chinese by carefully tracing their evolution chronologically, horizontally (across geographic distance), and vertically (throughout British society) and by anchoring them in the concrete expressions of racial prejudice in law and public policy.[42] The significance of race, however, goes far beyond the negative consequences of stereotyping for those who were being stereotyped. Race has no *a priori* existence, and the act of defining it in public discourse is a reciprocal process for all those who participate.[43] Although I argue that constructions of race and the meaning of race relations were specific to time, (social) place, and (geographic) space, my research highlights how manifestations of race in different periods, regions, or groups in Britain and the empire related to one another. In identifying "the Chinese," "Celestials," or "Asians," politicians, labor leaders, magistrates, journalists, police, and popular authors, as well as Chinese residents themselves, were also defining what it meant to be "white," "Anglo-Saxon," "British," and "European." The latter categories were all themselves constructed in relation to one another as well as in relation to the racial other.[44]

Race also evolved in constant dialogue with other aspects of identity, and with class, gender, and nationalism in particular. Any exploration of race tells us much about the shifting definitions of masculinity and femininity, about the constitution of working-class identity, and about the constructions of "British" as an identity, "Britain" as a nation, and

"Britons" as a people.[45] As unstable categories, all of these designations were open to construction and contestation. Whenever possible, I have highlighted the flexible employment of racial terms to intentionally include certain cohorts and to exclude others, usually for the purpose of garnering political support or of justifying legal regulation. In British public discourse, "Asians" could refer to Chinese, Japanese, and Indians; "British" could be used synonymously with "English"; and "white labour" could include the entire working-class male European populations of Britain, Australia, Canada, and South Africa.[46] Conversely, Chinese defendants in court could claim to be "English" or "British" by virtue of their long residency and their marriage to British women, while magistrates or journalists could argue not only that such men remained invariably "Chinese," but also that their wives had become more so by association.

This study, besides examining the many implications of race, speaks to a number of other major themes in British history. It addresses the relationship between the empire and the metropole by demonstrating how images of race generated in and by the empire were integrated into race relations in the capital.[47] I examine both discursive and concrete exchanges, looking not only at how Chinese stereotypes originated and spread, but also at how the same methods employed to monitor and control Chinese residents in the empire were reproduced in the metropolis. My investigation of the imperial dimension of metropolitan race relations in law and public discourse has been aided by recent scholarship that seeks to combine the rich historiography of London with the "new imperial history."[48]

The Chinese Puzzle also contributes to the historiography of London itself, and to that of immigration, law, culture, and social relations in the East End most especially.[49] Even though, for most of the nineteenth and early twentieth century, Liverpool had a larger Chinese community than London did, there are compelling reasons for focusing on the metropolis.[50] Just as the capital occupied a unique position in the cultural, political, and economic structure of both the nation and the empire, the Chinese community in the East End was at the center of public discussions of Chinese immigration, labor, and residency. The prominent role of the metropolis as a nexus of contact between Britons and immigrants from Europe, Asia, and Africa was one reason for this. The proliferation of the popular press in the capital also contributed to the centering of London's "Chinatown" and its residents in the broader public discourse about Chinese immigration and race relations in Britain. The focus of literary descriptions on East End Chinese residents; the publicity attracted by metropolitan scandals involving violence, "vice," and interracial contact; and the centrality of the East End in public discussions of morality, class, gender, and race did as well. For novelists, magistrates, journalists, union officials, and many others who helped shape public perceptions, London's Chinatown was not just one of several Chinese neighborhoods in the nation but was rather "the Chinese quarter of England."[51]

The role that race played in the execution of law and public policy in the metropolis is another essential aspect of this study. Although British historians have successfully incorporated gender into their examination of law and legal discourse, the same cannot be said of race. [52] One explanation for the latter's absence lies in the dearth of overt references to race in British law, though the impetus to legally regulate the "Asiatic" population of London dates back at least to the early nineteenth century, when this cohort made its first prominent appearance in domestic political discourse.[53] Interracial contact was a key concern of officials who commented on the matter, and the regulations put in place drew their precedents from imperial policies in urban India (especially Madras and Calcutta) that separated Europeans from indigenous residents.[54] In the early twentieth century, the contested legal status of Chinese immigrants, some of whom were British subjects, and some of whom claimed to be British subjects but were actually resident aliens, only complicated matters further during their encounters with the law and its representatives. Unlike the United States, South Africa, Canada, and Australia, however, in the late nineteenth and early twentieth century, Britain did not deploy a constellation of domestic laws that applied specifically to certain racial groups or that *explicitly* segregated different races from one another. Although the laws of Britain did not officially differentiate between races, the organization of peoples into racial categories and the arrangement of these categories into a hierarchy based on "advancement" was a prominent aspect of Victorian discourse.[55] In the nineteenth century, public figures from John Stuart Mill to Lord Palmerston articulated a system of racial classification that placed Anglo-Saxons above other European races and Europeans (with the exception of the Irish) well above the peoples of Africa, Asia, and the Middle East.[56] During the period of "new imperialism," the expansion of British authority in Asia and Africa, racial tension and violence in the empire, and the influx of immigrants to Britain raised the significance of racial and ethnic distinctions in parliamentary debates, in electoral campaigns, and in a wide variety of other public forums.

The prominence of racial stereotypes in public discourse and the sensitivity of those with legal authority in London to the issues of race and immigration meant that even a legal system that was *officially* "race-blind" often treated people very differently depending upon their race. Trials themselves could also become forums for the construction, dissemination, and contestation of racial stereotypes. Examining the reciprocal relationship between the cultural manifestations of race (in newspapers, fiction, and theater) and the racial biases of magistrates, police, and other government officials is therefore essential to understanding the impact of race on the execution of law in the metropolis. [57] U.S. historians' study of the institutionalization of racial bias against the Chinese in law and public policy provides useful insights into this process, and there were noteworthy parallels in the articulation of negative Chinese stereotypes in London, New York, and San Francisco.[58] But the considerable contrasts in the size and composition of the Chinese communities there, along with variations among the social, legal, political, and cultural structures of these cities and their respective nations, often make direct comparisons problematic. Significant differences in the history of British and American society with regard to immigration, imperialism, labor, and race also encourage us to view institutionalized racism in Britain and the United States as distinct phenomena, albeit as ones with important shared aspects.[59]

Each of the following chapters examines the complex links between representation and practice in the interactions between Chinese residents and union officials, magistrates, police, journalists, popular authors, and the white, working-class residents of the East End, London, Britain, and the empire. I have focused on sources that highlight the mutual constitution of law, public policy, and culture with regard to race and race relations. Newspaper articles (local, metropolitan, and national), parliamentary debates, political speeches, government documents, public demonstrations and protests (both formal and informal), transcripts of court cases, novels, plays, cartoons, and autobiographies all reveal different perspectives on these issues.[60] The chapters themselves are organized chronologically in order to highlight the evolution of race relations over the course of the early twentieth century. The tensions over Chinese immigration, labor, and residency in Britain and the empire did not follow an undisturbed upward trajectory. They waxed and waned across this period in relation to other cultural, social, economic, and political dynamics and as a result of specific events, statements, actions, their portrayals, and their interpretations. Chapters 2 and 3 explore the growth of anti-Chinese sentiment in the empire, how that sentiment was transmitted to Britain, its relationship to class tensions in British society, and the popularization of negative stereotypes of Chinese immigrants in British culture through the prewar period. Chapter 4 discusses the effect of World War I on race relations in London and the first concerted legal campaigns conducted against East End Chinese residents. In Chapter 5, I analyze several prominent postwar court cases and the public scandals that they generated, which helped focus public attention on the alleged threats that Chinatown and its Chinese residents posed to white Britons. Finally, Chapter 6 examines how official concern, negative stereotypes, and popular hostility against the Chinese residents of London coalesced in the tumultuous interwar period, prompting both widespread mob violence and a concerted campaign of arrests, prosecutions, and deportations.

These chapters make no claim to exhaust the topics of Chinese immigration and labor in Britain or to reveal their full significance in the dynamics of law, culture, and society. But they do tell us much about the role played by race in the relationship between genders, between classes, between the empire and the metropole, between morality and policy, between law and literature, between discourse and practice, and ultimately, about the meaning and consequences of race itself in British society. Discussing race and law is a delicate process, however, and the danger of being misunderstood as replicating past prejudices by labeling one group or another as particularly prone to crime or immorality is ever present. But if we ignore the significance of race, we overlook a central element in the development of modern British society and do a grave disservice to those who experienced the consequences of racial stereotypes firsthand in the courts, culture, and communities of imperial Britain.

Chapter 2

"Chinese Labour" and the Imperial Dimensions of British Racial Discourse

The initial public debates over Chinese immigration and labor highlighted the interrelationship between high politics and popular opposition and between empire and metropole in the evolution of race relations in Britain. In these debates, the term "Chinese labour" rapidly accrued powerful symbolic meanings that extended well beyond the measurable economic impact of Chinese workers. "Chinese labour" served as a foil to the image of a pan-imperial "white labour" interest that politicians and union leaders employed to justify Chinese exclusion across the British Empire. In Britain, public discussions of race, law, and the protection of "white labour" against the encroachment of "Chinese labour" in Australia and South Africa popularized two specific arguments concerning Chinese immigrants. The first was that they were fundamentally incompatible with white communities and could therefore never assimilate with them. The second was that since Chinese immigrants represented the vanguard of an almost limitless population, they were threatening out of all proportion to their numbers in any given region. Law and the use of legal authority were central to these debates, which combined elements of the "scientific racism" of Anglo-Saxonism with economic opposition and moral concerns. Both those who opposed "Chinese labour" and those who supported it agreed that legal restrictions were necessary to protect the economic and political position of working-class white men in Australia, South Africa, and Britain.

The debate over Chinese immigration to Australia laid the initial groundwork for subsequent portrayals of Chinese men as threats to white communities, but the first major contest in Britain itself pitted the Trades Union Congress and other supporters of "white labour" in South Africa against the advocates of free trade and a globalized labor market. The public contest over "Chinese labour" in South Africa was crucial to the Liberal victory in the general election of 1906, which changed the course of British politics. By then, the rhetoric of union leaders and politicians seeking working-class support had made "Chinese labour" synonymous with the cynical exploitation of British workingmen by industry magnates and their advocates in government.

But the disputes over the Chinese and their impact on white communities hardly ended there. Following the 1906 general election, public opposition to "Chinese labour" in British shipping, which drew strongly on the South African debate for its precedents, was led by Joseph Havelock Wilson MP (Middlesbrough, Liberal) and other representatives of the National Sailors' and Firemen's Union. Of particular significance in this period was the growing hostility against Chinese workers themselves in Britain rather than against their employers and the politicians who supported them. Although British labor leaders' demands for the exclusion of Chinese workers were not accommodated in the short run, in London, the acrimonious debate over Chinese labor in British shipping helped draw the attention of the press, the public, and local officials toward Chinese residents. The assertion made by Wilson and his allies that Chinese immigrants were active, willing agents in the demoralization of white communities and in the marginalization of "white labour" would, in subsequent years, come to dominate negative Chinese stereotypes in British law, press, and literature.

"No Peace between the Races": Anglo-Saxonism and the "White Australia" Debate in Britain

Prior to the South African debate of 1903–6, despite the prevalence of British portrayals associating Chinese men with violence or the use of opium, Chinese immigrants were rarely considered to be a serious threat to the nation. Britain's repeated military victories in the Opium Wars, their subsequent occupation of Hong Kong and other "treaty ports," and the Allies' later defeat of Chinese forces in the Boxer Uprising (1899–1901) were accompanied by press depictions of the Chinese as ineffectual or even comical.[1] Instead, two images dominated

Figure 2.1. Chinese workers unloading tea from the *Louden Castle* (Hankow) on the East India Docks. (*Illustrated London News*, December 8, 1877. Courtesy of the Tower Hamlets Library and Local History Archive.)

British descriptions of Chinese men in the empire. The most prevalent was the Chinese "coolie," who was depicted as an industrious, docile worker suitable for a variety of unskilled employments. Indentured Chinese men had been employed as agricultural laborers in British Guiana and British Malaysia since the mid-nineteenth century.[2] "Coolie" was a term also commonly applied by British commentators to Indian indentured laborers throughout the empire. In contrast to the pervasive assumption that Chinese laborers in North America, the Caribbean, and British-colonized Asia were all "coolies" (i.e., indentured laborers), however, indentured labor constituted only 11–12% of Chinese emigration in this period.[3] The inaccurate designation of all Chinese workers as "coolies," in addition to eliding the differences between Indian and Chinese laborers, thus effaced variations in the latter's economic and legal status and emphasized their subordination in the Western imperial labor system.

The other common image employed by British observers in their descriptions of Chinese men was the "cunning Chinaman" or "heathen Chinee," a violent, sly figure of low morality. This stereotype well predated the Boxer Uprising, although that event certainly boosted the popularity of such depictions in the Western press. The image of the Chinese as a deceitful people was so intrinsic to Western views that it even appeared prominently in the entry on China in the ninth edition of the *Encyclopedia Britannica*.[4] By the closing decades of the nineteenth century, the stereotype of "John Chinaman," a Chinese everyman that combined elements of both the "coolie" and the "cunning Chinaman," had also entered common parlance in Britain, Australia, Canada, and the United States. Politicians, journalists, travel writers, and union leaders employed the term whether they were discussing Chinese seamen in London, Chinese market gardeners in New South Wales, or Chinese shopkeepers in British Guiana.

Portrayals of Chinese men in late nineteenth-century London reflected this ambivalent view of their character. Two of these early depictions also highlighted the importance of labor issues and the prominent voice of legal officials in the portrayal of Chinese immigrants in London. The first, an illustration that appeared in an 1877 issue of the *London Illustrated News*, depicted Chinese workers unloading tea from a ship at the London docks (Fig. 2.1). The Chinese laborers, adorned with their characteristic queues, work diligently alongside Victorian gentlemen, the former unloading cargo while the latter inspect the manifest and discuss business among themselves. The second portrayal was written by a London police court magistrate, Montagu Williams. In his 1892 memoir, *Round London: Down*

East and Up West, which was published in London and New York and for which Charles Dickens Jr. wrote the preface, Williams described an incident he supposedly witnessed in the East End "Chinese Quarter," near the notorious Ratcliff Highway, in the 1870s. The scene Williams related was one of frightful horror, with "pools and trails of blood on the pavement and in the roadway; here and there the prostrate form of a human being."[5] The magistrate and his police escort, having arrived in the wake of the mayhem, were told that a number of Chinese men who had been drinking with white women had accused the latter of robbing them, and when a group of white men had tried to intervene, an affray had broken out: "The Chinamen arranged themselves in a body, drew their knives from their pockets, and, shouting 'amok! amok!' fought their way into the road and rushed upon all they met, stabbing and cutting men, women, and children indiscriminately."[6] "The knives of these people," Williams informed readers, "are particularly adapted for ripping flesh, and thus the wounds inflicted were for the most part serious." For all its macabre tones, however, Williams's account was curiously conflicted in its assessment of Chinese character. Immediately prior to their arrival on the bloody scene, Williams and his police companions had been amicably smoking opium with the Chinese proprietor of a "den," whom the magistrate described as polite, courteous, and "extremely intelligent." The opium itself, Williams wrote, "neither drugged me nor made me ill," but "had a very soothing effect" with "no unpleasant consequences."[7]

In contrast to the ambiguous views of Chinese immigrants that appeared in Britain during this period, in Australia, negative stereotypes of Chinese residents commanded a broad consensus. In the latter locale, a substantial Chinese immigrant population suffered under the burdens of popular prejudice, an exploitative labor system, poverty and its attendant social ills, and the relentless mockery of sensationalized journalism and cartoon satire. Opponents of the Chinese justified their hostility with a combination of economic, moral, and nationalist arguments. Such opposition was concentrated among working-class miners, maritime workers, and urban skilled artisans, though it also had strong representation among Liberals and radicals in the colonial legislatures and among the journalists whose primary reading audience consisted of these groups.[8]

Economic competition alone is an insufficient explanation for the virulent antipathy expressed toward Chinese immigrants in Australia. Chinese workers, despite frequent claims by politicians and journalists to the contrary, rarely competed directly with white laborers, and anti-Chinese sentiment was not confined to the working class.[9] The debate over Chinese labor in Australia, like the debate in South Africa that followed, was intimately bound up in three broader issues: the movement toward national unification and independence, the concurrent construction of a national identity based on the concept of "whiteness," and the quasi-scientific categorization of the Anglo-Saxon and Chinese races as being two fundamentally incompatible groups locked in fierce competition for regional and global dominance.

British politicians, union leaders, writers, and other public figures who took up the cause of "white Australia" in Britain itself tried to garner domestic support for laws regulating Chinese immigration and residency in Australia. They did so by arguing that the issue was one of consequence for "British" workingmen throughout the empire, and not merely a concern for Australia alone. The Australian debate penetrated British discourse on race, labor, and law at a number of levels, most notably through deliberations in Parliament and through the colonial experiences of important British writers and politicians. In the discussions about Chinese workers in Australia, we also see the first prominent public articulation of the corrosive moral effect that Chinese immigrants allegedly had on white communities. In both Australia and Britain, opponents of the Chinese argued not only that they competed unfairly with white labor in the colonies but also that they spread the vices of gambling; brought disease, squalor, and overcrowding; corrupted white womanhood; and weakened the British race through miscegenation. The accusation that British employers were demoralizing local communities by importing Chinese labor was particularly damning, since it challenged the basic moral justifications of Britain's imperial project.[10] White workers and their supporters in Australia and Britain insisted that those responsible for importing Chinese labor were undercutting the "civilizing" mission of the British empire, and the more immoral their representations of the Chinese were, the more effective such condemnation became.

Anti-Chinese labor agitation and legal restriction had been an issue in Australia ever since the first contingent of Chinese immigrants arrived in the 1850s to work in the newly discovered gold deposits of Victoria. In 1855, following violent clashes between Chinese and white miners, legislation restricting Chinese immigration was introduced.[11] Similar measures followed in New South Wales in the 1860s and in Queensland in 1877.[12] Seamen, a cohort that would later be at the center of anti-Chinese agitation in Britain, were responsible for the most serious Australian organized labor demonstration against the Chinese in this period.[13] As the first true pancolonial labor dispute, the maritime strike of 1878 was an important step in the coalescence of an Australian national labor identity around the support of "white labour" and the exclusion of Chinese workers. The strike, which began on November 17, 1878, was a coordinated effort by seamen in Victoria, New South Wales, and Queensland to prevent the Australasian Steam Navigation Company from replacing white Australian seamen with lower-paid Chinese sailors. It brought together seamen from across the colonies, as well as laborers in other industries, including miners in New South Wales and dockworkers in all three colonies.

By the time of the 1878 maritime strike, most official assessments indicated that the Chinese population of Australia, which still numbered in the tens of thousands, had fallen from its apex in the late 1850s, though reports often differed on the exact numbers.[14] But even as the number of Chinese residents overall had appeared to decline, in part due to the increasing poll taxes levied against them, their geographical and economic dissemination throughout the colonies had broadened as they moved from Victoria to Queensland, New South Wales, and New Zealand; from the rural mining towns to the major cities; and from mine work to small retailing and furniture manufacture. Despite a prominent report by the Parliament of Victoria that insisted the Chinese did not pose any direct threat to white labor, their visibility in urban communities, their industry, their willingness to work for lower rates of pay than white men were, and their adaptability to a diverse array of low-status occupations fostered a perception among white laborers that the threat was a real and imminent one.[15] Stories of Chinese debauchery, lechery, and immorality often accompanied their migration from mining areas to the towns and cities of the Australian colonies, though official investigations revealed little concrete evidence to support such accounts.[16]

"Chinese labour" and the moral impact of Chinese immigration to Australia did not become a noticeable issue in Britain itself until the late-1880s. In this period, Chinese immigration to the colony appeared repeatedly in British parliamentary debates and in press commentaries even as the broader issue of Anglo-Chinese race relations was becoming an important topic in the intellectual and political circles that connected Britain to Australia. The most prominent figures on the British side of the debate were the MPs Henniker Heaton and George Baden-Powell, and the Oxford professor Charles Pearson, author of *National Life and Character: A Forecast* (1893), arguably the most influential tract on race written by an Englishman in this period. But even William Gladstone himself stepped in on more than one occasion to state his opinions on the Chinese in Australia. Heaton, Baden-Powell, and Pearson had all spent considerable time in

Australia, as well as in other parts of the British Empire, and their observations of racial tensions and the apparent success of Chinese immigrants in adjusting to life in the empire had convinced them to oppose Chinese immigration wherever a white population held political and economic dominion. Heaton, an MP from Canterbury (Conservative) who had lived and worked in New South Wales as a journalist and politician from 1864–82, introduced Chinese immigration to Australia as a parliamentary issue in May 1888. He presented to Parliament the protest of the New South Wales government over Chinese immigration and outlined their argument for the imposition of a Chinese exclusion law similar to the one recently introduced in the United States, but he eschewed the dramatic language of racial conflict that they had adopted.[17] The Australian delegation, led by Henry Parkes, insisted that unless the British government permitted New South Wales to impose more severe legal restrictions on immigration, "there can be no sympathy, and, in future . . . there will be no peace, between the races" there.[18] Heaton, in a letter published by the *Times*, was less hyperbolic in his description of the issue than Parkes had been. But, like the representatives of the NSW government, he too raised the specter of violent racial conflict with his references to "most fearful riots" between white and Chinese gold miners.[19]

Sir George Baden-Powell, another prominent Conservative MP (Kirkdale, Liverpool), was more forceful in his public condemnation of Chinese immigration to Australia. Like Heaton, Baden-Powell had spent several years in Australian politics, subsequently traveling to administrative positions in the West Indies and South Africa. And, like Heaton, he was a committed advocate of free trade.[20] Despite this predilection, however, he expressed his staunch support for the restriction of Chinese immigration to Australia, arguing that although the Australian workingman's opposition to further European immigration was retarding the colonies' economic progress, Chinese labor was "a wholly different matter." [21] The question was "not economical, nor is it one of morality," Baden-Powell insisted in an extensive letter to the editors of the *Times*, "but essentially one of politics." But Baden-Powell's elaboration of "politics" revealed his underlying argument that at issue was a fundamental racial incompatibility between the Chinese and the white Australian population, which was "Anglo-Saxon in its traditions, habits, institutions, and aspirations." Chinese immigration threatened to transform Australia, a nation still "in its youth," from a bastion of Anglo-Saxon civilization—which Baden-Powell synonymously employed with British culture and politics—into another appendage of "Mongolian" civilization. In his analysis,

Australia was the battleground upon which the contest between the two races was being fought, and the potential victory of Chinese civilization through massive immigration was therefore "a consummation devoutly to be counteracted by all British citizens." Like Heaton, Baden-Powell's approach to the issue was built on the proposition that the restriction of Chinese immigration to Australia equated with support of both the British workingman and of the British race and British civilization in general. There were no Australian workingmen in their parliamentary constituencies, but British ones and supporters of British civilization there were aplenty, and both politicians brought imperial anxieties home by describing Chinese immigration and labor in ways that made them relevant to British voters.

Baden-Powell's justifications for his opposition to Chinese labor and immigration would find more formal expression in the theory of "Anglo-Saxonism," which rapidly gained popularity among both Australian and British politicians in the early 1890s. The architect of this theory was Charles Henry Pearson, who had studied and later lectured at Oxford and Cambridge before moving to Australia and entering politics there. His experiences in Australia had a profound effect upon his understanding of race, law, and immigration. Rather than approaching these issues from the more secure standpoint of a British resident, Pearson's time in Haiti and in Australia prompted him to view them from the white colonial perspective.[22] Pearson, and his friend and contemporary, James Bryce, another noted historian and British politician whose travels abroad had a lasting affect upon his understanding of race and history, promoted the theory that white men were suitable occupants of temperate zones only. The territory available to them was therefore, they both asserted, limited and precious.

Unlike Bryce, however, Pearson was not sanguine about the continued predominance of Anglo-Saxons in world affairs and argued instead that they were losing their vigor even as the "Black and Yellow" races were multiplying, strengthening, and expanding their territory.[23] He insisted that Africans and Asians, although far more suited than Anglo-Saxons were to the tropical zones, were by no means confined to them and that the technological improvements made by the "higher races" only facilitated the growth and progress of non-European populations there. As a consequence, legal restrictions on the immigration of Asians and Africans to areas currently occupied by Anglo-Saxons were profoundly necessary, and in Australia, the fate of the nation, its character, and its manhood—all interrelated concepts in Pearson's view—were at stake.[24] Pearson's theories were central to the "white Australia" policy, so much so that when the first prime minister of Australia addressed the first federated Australian Parliament in support of exclusionary immigration measures, is was Pearson's book, *National Life and Character*, that he held in his hand and quoted extensively.[25] But Pearson's perspective was global and his dire predictions held implications not only for Australia but for all regions currently occupied by Anglo-Saxons. Like Heaton and Baden-Powell, Pearson argued that Chinese immigration to Australia and to other areas where white men held dominion was an issue that should concern the leaders and voters of Britain. William Gladstone, although he argued against legal restrictions on Chinese labor, was so impressed by Pearson's theories that he insisted anyone who wished to be educated about world affairs should read his book.[26]

Pearson's articulation of Anglo-Saxonism and the parliamentary agitation of Heaton and Baden-Powell emphasized the incompatibility of Britons and Chinese and presented the legal restriction of the latter's immigration as a political, economic, and moral imperative. But they said little about the morality of Chinese immigrants themselves. In their arguments, it was the vast numbers of the Chinese, their industriousness, and their adaptability that made them a threat to British racial hegemony. The leaders and advocates of the Australian labor movement, on the other hand, were outspoken on the topic of Chinese immorality. In speeches and articles, labor activists, union leaders, and journalists for radical newspapers and magazines combined their economic objections to Chinese immigration with what one British commentator called "a holy horror of the dreadful immorality of the Chinese."[27] Rose Summerfield, a prominent Australian feminist and labor activist, was particularly vociferous in her condemnation of Chinese immigrants on moral grounds, dramatically emphasizing their lust and vice in her speeches to Sydney workingmen in the early 1890s. White women could not even walk the streets of the city, she told one audience, without suffering the "lewd eyes" and jeering catcalls of Chinese "beasts."[28]

The popularization of anti-Chinese discourse in Australia set a direct precedent for its later expression in both South Africa and Britain. A host of Australian labor leaders (some British-born) that had been important supporters of anti-Asian policies and were instrumental in promoting the ideology of "white Australia" would later become prominent leaders of the South African white labor movement. [29] Their ideas about race, labor, and law would find a receptive audience among white miners and skilled urban workers there. The opposition of labor interests in Australia to Chinese immigration was also directly communicated to British labor leaders via the correspondence between the Trades and Labour Council of News South Wales and the members of the Colonial Labour Committee (CLC) of one of Britain's largest labor organizations, the Trades Union Congress (TUC). In 1886, the CLC reported at the TUC's annual convention that, according to their counterparts in New South Wales, Chinese labor was becoming a serious threat to the position of white workers in the joinery and cabinet trades. In response, the CLC proposed a resolution stating that the TUC opposed any state support of immigration until the approval of the workers of the colonies that would be affected had been obtained.[30]

By 1890, the moral effect of Chinese immigrants on white communities had become a subject of debate at the highest levels of British politics as well. In May, at the Prince's Hall in Piccadilly, William Gladstone publicly criticized the widespread adoption of anti-Chinese legislation in the Australian colonies in 1888 and 1889.[31] Speaking on behalf of the supporters of free trade, he insisted that the moralization of the issue by Australian politicians was merely a ploy to disguise their true motivation of economic protectionism. "Because he does more work for the money; because he is less exacting; because he is satisfied with less; and, moreover, because he consumes a great deal less of alcoholic liquor. On these grounds the Chinaman is a formidable rival," he declared. "It is not for his vices but for his virtues that he is so treated."[32] In response, Francis Abigail, an ally of Henry Parkes and a fellow legislator in New South Wales, submitted a long letter to the *Times* enumerating the many accusations that had been leveled at Chinese immigrants by white Australian workers and their advocates in previous years. The Chinese were a cunning people of poor morals, "their sanitary arrangements [were] dreadful," and their communities were rife with vice and overcrowding.[33] Abigail used these allegations as evidence that the exclusion of Chinese immigrants was necessary to preserve "the true type of British race in our Australian homes." English, Irish, and Scots were welcome additions, as were Germans, but "Chinese never . . . their mode of life is altogether un-British." It was for these reasons, he maintained, that Australian workingmen opposed the Chinese, and their stance and that of their supporters in no way contradicted the principles of free trade championed by Gladstone—the issue was one of morals and racial incompatibility, not economics. Another correspondent argued that such distinctions were beside the point in any case. The Chinese worker was a threat to the economic position of the Australian workingman, to the political progress of white Australians, to the survival of British civilization in Australia, and to the moral climate of white communities. Without laws preventing their immigration, he asserted, "the Chinese would descend upon us, not in bands, but in hordes. We should find ourselves outnumbered in a very short time by an alien community, whose habits, morals, and way of living are entirely different from our own . . . if Mr. Gladstone had said that the Chinaman was dreaded for his virtues as well as for his vices no one would have disputed the statement."[34]

In this same period, opponents of Chinese immigration and labor in Australia also produced two iconic portrayals of the Chinese menace to white communities—portrayals whose echoes would later be heard in Britain itself. In 1887, William Lane, the radical journalist and founder of the Australian Labour Federation, published *White or Yellow? A Story of the Race-war of A.D. 1908*. *White or Yellow* depicted the disastrous consequences for Australia if Chinese immigration and race mixing were to continue unchecked.[35] The novel, which pitted the white workers and farmers of Australia against an inundation of the Chinese, the latter supported by wealthy interests in both Britain and China, appeared as a twelve-part serial in Lane's weekly paper, *Boomerang*. Lane had been born and raised in Bristol, but his attitudes

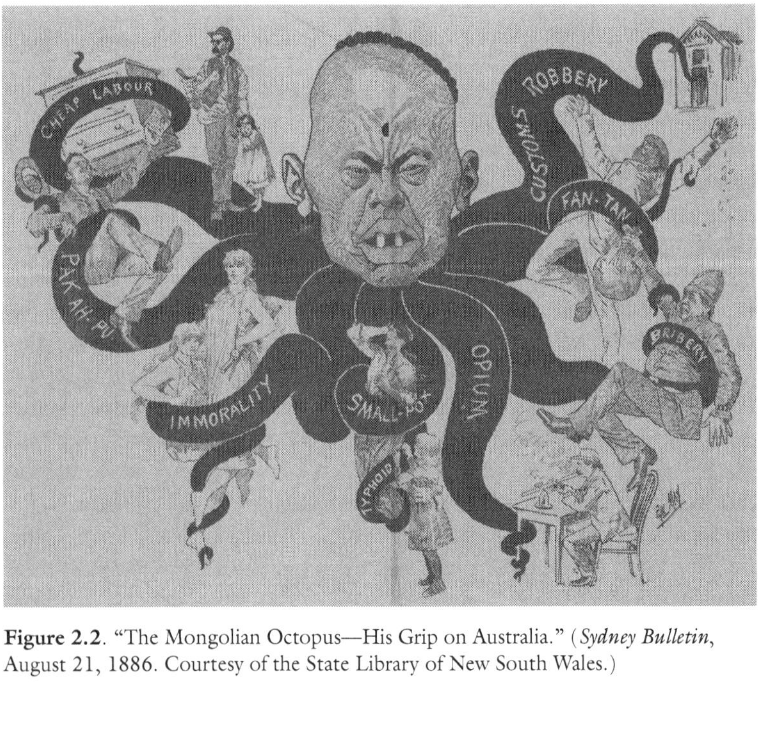

Figure 2.2. "The Mongolian Octopus—His Grip on Australia." (*Sydney Bulletin*, August 21, 1886. Courtesy of the State Library of New South Wales.)

toward race—like those of others who contributed to the anti-Chinese discourse in this period—had been shaped by his experiences abroad in Canada, the United States, and finally, in Australia. The second of these screeds, Phil May's illustration of "The Mongolian Octopus—His Grip on Australia," which was published in the radical *Sydney Bulletin*, held Chinese immigrants responsible for everything from police corruption and unemployment to the spread of prostitution, smallpox, and typhoid fever. May, who was originally from Leeds, had traveled to Australia in the 1880s to find work, and upon his return to London in the 1890s, he would become one of *Punch*'s most prominent and prolific illustrators.[36]

These images of the Chinese menace in the empire soon reappeared in a domestic context. In 1898, M. P. Shiel, a British novelist, published *The Yellow Danger*, the first true "Yellow Peril" novel produced in Britain.[37] Like Lane's *White or Yellow*, Shiel's story, echoing the anxieties raised by Charles Pearson's work, depicted a massive Chinese invasion of "white" territory—in this case, Britain and continental Europe itself. Although the Boxer Rebellion would later heighten British anxieties about anti-Western sentiment among the Chinese and lend a prophetic tinge to Shiel's depictions of Chinese savagery, the initial reaction to his work was one of amused incredulity rather than shock or anger.[38] It would take nearly two more decades for Londoners to associate all the threats that appeared in the British domestic debate over "white Australia" and that were aptly represented in these three portrayals—invasion, unemployment and the devaluation of white labor, miscegenation, gambling addiction, the corruption of white women, commercial avarice, disease, opium smoking, and the powerful figure of a Chinese corrupter overarching all—with the small Chinese population of the metropolis. Chinese wishing to immigrate to Australia, on the other hand, felt their effects almost immediately. The first major legislative act of the newly federated Commonwealth of Australia was the passage of the Federal Immigration Restriction Act of 1901, which effectively excluded Asian immigrants by requiring a "language test" for all prospective arrivals.[39] True to the pledges that pro-federation Australian politicians had made to garner labor support, the act ensconced "white Australia" as official government policy.[40]

"Chinese Outrages": The Debate over "Chinese Labour" in South Africa

In the early twentieth century, the intersection of labor interests, race, and imperial politics made "Chinese labour" a prominent issue in Britain. The next significant evolution of anti-Chinese stereotypes in British public discourse was prompted by their "importation" as indentured laborers to South Africa. After a period of considerable debate and contention, in 1904, the Transvaal legislature voted in favor of the Labour Importation Ordinance (LIO).[41] The LIO was a brainchild of Alfred Milner, the British governor of the colony, and George Farrar, president of the Transvaal Chamber of Mines. It authorized the mass importation of indentured Chinese workers in order to address a shortage of unskilled labor in the Witwatersrand ("Rand") gold mines in the wake of the Second Anglo-Boer War (1899–1902).[42] Even more so than in Australia, the rise of organized labor and domestic political conflict between the Conservative establishment and the Liberal opposition were tied to the public outcry against "Chinese labour" in South Africa. From the very beginning, Liberal and Labour interests in Britain voiced staunch opposition to the importation of Chinese workers on grounds similar to those adopted in the Australian debate. Chinese labor, according to its opponents, would debase the value of white labor, corrupt white communities, and threaten white hegemony in South Africa.

During the Boer War, both the government and the British press had mobilized public opinion in support of Britain's colonial war against a white nation.[43] With its cost in British lives and resources and the concurrent scandal over the "concentration camps" erected to house Boer civilians, however, the war had both shaken Britain's national confidence and challenged British claims to be moral colonizers. Even as the enthusiasm for imperial adventures waned in the wake of the controversial and costly conflict, the British public—and particularly the working class from whose ranks the soldiery had been drawn and in whose name, allegedly, the war had been fought—continued to pay close attention to events in South Africa. These circumstances presaged the situation in Britain after World War I, when the sacrifices of the British workingman, in the name of nation and empire, would again come to the fore in discussions of race and the role of Chinese immigrants in British society. As in the Australian debate, the issue of national unification and independence, the construction of "whiteness" and of South Africa as a "white man's country," and the assertion that Anglo-Saxons and the Chinese were two fundamentally incompatible groups locked in fierce competition were also all essential in attitudes toward "Chinese labour" in South Africa.

Both those who supported "Chinese labour" in the Transvaal and those who opposed it claimed commitment to maintaining the superior social, economic, and political position of white men in the region—they merely differed as to whether Chinese labor would encourage this or undercut it. Alfred Milner's stated goal was to make South Africa "a white man's country . . . not a country full of poor whites, but one in which a largely increased white population can live in decency and comfort."[44] He was initially reluctant to consider the wholesale importation of Chinese labor to the Transvaal, fearing a repeat of the tensions that had recently arisen between Indians and white settlers there and in Natal.[45] For Milner, one advantage of indentured workers from China over Africans imported from other parts of the continent was that the former could be easily repatriated while the latter might remain in the region and further skew racial demographics.[46] Although Milner was "dead against" Asians settling or trading in South Africa, he argued that unskilled Chinese indentured laborers would not prove "uncontrollable," provided the proper legal mechanisms were adopted and strenuously enforced.[47] As had been the case in Australia, the strict application of law along racial lines was seen as the key to insuring public order and the maintenance of white hegemony. [48]

In the months before the LIO was signed into law, the relative advantages and disadvantages of Chinese labor versus white labor, African labor, and Indian labor were debated in government circles and in the pages of the British and South African press. Such discussions typically revolved around which racial group—Chinese, Africans, or Indians—made the most obedient and law-abiding unskilled laborers, the relative moral standing of each, and their overall impact on the white community (both social and economic). One letter, penned to the *Times* by a retired member of the Indian Civil Service, anticipated many of the arguments that would later be used against the Chinese immigrants in Britain. Indian labor was far preferable to Chinese labor, the author argued, because Indians "are certainly more tractable and easily managed than the Chinese; and they do not form secret societies."[49] Unlike the Chinese, moreover, Indians were "under the control of a friendly and British Government" and "relatively civilized in their habits." The author asserted, furthermore, that there would be no concerns about Indians taking up residence and shifting the racial balance in Transvaal communities, since "the Indian coolie is always willing and anxious to return to India." According to the civil servant's letter, Indian labor was solidly within the sphere of British political, legal, and cultural authority, and therefore its importation reinforced the power and cohesion of the empire. Chinese labor, in contrast, was alien and threatened to erode them.

Within the context of this public debate over the importation of Chinese labor, it is worth noting that gambling, opium, and interracial sexuality—three issues that would later dominate public discussions concerning the legal regulation of the Chinese in Britain—were initially absent.[50] The most oft-voiced concerns were the willingness of Chinese laborers to work for less money than their white counterparts were and the possibility that such a large influx of aliens would undermine the economic and social position of white settlers and workers in the region. The alleged global competition between Anglo-Saxons and Chinese and the fear that Asian races would overwhelm the white race—two concepts that had been central to the Australian debate—became prominent issues in the South African debate as well. In 1903, however, the supposed threat of Chinese immigration arose more from their industriousness, sobriety, and docility than it did from their reputation for immorality. The experience of white workers in Australia, a cohort prominently represented among labor leaders in South Africa, was that Chinese workers were a greater threat than African workers were precisely because of the former's reputation for hard work and adaptability.[51] In labor policy decisions, however, the economic demands of employers and the focus on profits initially outweighed both the protests of labor interests and public anxiety over the influx of alien workers. The opinion of the Chinese workers themselves on their indentured labor in the Rand went all but unheard. Chinese labor would arrive, and in considerable numbers, but only under conditions tightly controlled by the terms of the LIO. The standard contract of indenture was for three years with the possibility of a single renewal.[52]

From the very beginning, the Transvaal government, in cooperation with mining interests, instituted a strict legal regimen for the monitoring and control of the importation, transportation, labor, and repatriation of Chinese workers. Some of these regulations—such as those stipulating that a careful record be kept of all workers entering the country, that importers enter into a bond to repatriate each imported laborer, and that heavy penalties would be levied against any illegal importation—applied to the employers and importers of labor.[53] But the most stringent regulations applied to the Chinese workers themselves. The LIO severely limited their freedom of movement and empowered local authorities to use whatever methods necessary to keep the population under a veritable social quarantine. Chinese workers were confined to segregated labor compounds where exit was forbidden except for brief periods under an authorized pass (maximum forty-eight hours).[54] They were also required, at all times, to carry identifying documentation (a "passport"), which had to be renewed yearly.[55] Any Chinese worker caught outside his respective compound without both pass and passport was subject to immediate arrest, without warrant, by any member of the local police or the South African Constabulary.[56] The use of such "pass laws" was an established practice in South Africa long before the first Chinese workers arrived. In the 1870s, the British had passed laws restricting the movement of Africans in diamond-mining areas, and in 1895, the then-independent Transvaal legislature had enacted a pass law that allowed employers to exert greater control over the movement of their African workers.[57]

The impetus behind the continued debate in Britain on the subject emerged from domestic political rivalries. Liberal politicians and labor leaders in Britain, in opposition to the Conservative government under Arthur Balfour, quickly seized on the "Chinese labour" issue as a lever to use against their political opponents.[58] The Chinese issue appeared as a prominent factor in a British election for the first time in mid-February 1904. The opponents of Rutherfoord Harris, a candidate in the parliamentary by-elections for Dulwich (South London), began putting up posters that read, "Vote for Harris and 'Chinese Labour.'"[59] This was followed by statements from the General Federation of Trade Unions and the Parliamentary Committee of the Trades Union Congress in opposition to "Chinese labour," a phrase that, by late February, had become synonymous with the cynical exploitation of foreign labor to the detriment of white workers.[60]

Running parallel to this argument—that employers of Chinese labor in the Rand and those who supported them in Britain were acting in an immoral fashion against the interests of British workers—was a new focus on the moral threat posed by the Chinese workers themselves, with the antipathy expressed in Australia serving as a touchstone.[61] In February 1904, the Bishop of Worcester argued that importing Chinese men without their wives might encourage the introduction and spread of prostitution among them and that, once introduced, "such demoralization would probably spread to the surrounding population."[62] A few days later, a House of Commons committee that included James Keir Hardie (Merthyr Tydfil, Labour), Herbert Samuel (Cleveland, Liberal), Sydney Buxton (Poplar, Liberal), Thomas James Macnamara (North Camberwell, Liberal), and Charles Trevelyan (Elland, Liberal) met to protest the importation of Chinese labor to the Rand. The meeting began with the reading of a strident letter written by Sir William Harcourt, the venerable statesmen and staunch critic of Britain's imperial policy in South Africa, wherein he disparaged the proposed employment of "animals in human form" in the Rand mines.[63] Herbert Samuel subsequently declared in the House of Commons that the Chinese who emigrated were "a degraded people . . . vicious, immoral, and unclean . . . in Australia, in New Zealand, in the United States, in Canada—everywhere the presence of Chinamen has been found by white men to be intolerable."[64]

This thread was picked up again by Robert Crewe, the future Colonial Secretary, in March. Crewe, speaking to a Liberal audience in London, made prominent mention of the "moral contagion" represented by the imported labor force.[65] He also argued that the issue of "Chinese labour" was of paramount importance in British domestic politics, claiming that 70 percent of his constituency's support came from their opposition to the Conservatives' endorsement of the LIO.[66] Throughout 1904 and 1905, Liberal and Labour politicians rapidly adopted opposition to "Chinese labour" as one of the key avenues of attack on their Conservative opponents. Progressive candidates' opposition to Chinese labor was also integrated into their platforms in London municipal elections, where it was linked to a broad spectrum of issues ranging from tariff reform to anti-clericalism to temperance and licensing laws. Repeating the arguments first put forth in Britain during the debate over Chinese immigration to Australia, opponents of Chinese labor in South Africa, which included Sir Henry Campbell-Bannerman and Lord Coleridge, insisted that it threatened white labor not only in the Transvaal but also throughout Britain and the British Empire. On at least one occasion, it was even suggested in the House of Commons that the importation of Chinese workers to South Africa might presage their introduction as agricultural laborers in Britain itself.[67] While economic issues remained at the center of the arguments made by the LIO's supporters, their Liberal opponents insisted that there were far greater issues at stake than profit or loss. In addition to stressing the negative moral effect of Chinese immigration on South Africa, Liberals also emphasized that it would be a serious obstacle in the Transvaal's progress toward political independence.

But the most vociferous opposition to Chinese labor in South Africa, and the most negative portrayals of Chinese immigrants themselves, came from British union leaders and the Liberal press.[68] At the heart of the arguments made by labor interests and popular journalists was the claim that the contributions of white working-class men, in blood and treasure, to British victory in the Boer War had earned them the right to exclude Chinese workers from any job that a white man was willing to do. "Chinese labour," they insisted, was not a South African issue but a British one and one against which all white men in Britain and throughout the empire must speak out. Although the Trades Union Congress's opposition to Chinese labor dated back to the 1880s and the Australian debate, by 1904, it had moved to the center of their petitions to Parliament and their campaigns for political representation. In a resolution forwarded to Parliament in February 1904, the TUC's Parliamentary Committee called on every workingman in Britain to "register his condemnation" against the importation of Chinese labor to South Africa, where British dominion had been "so dearly bought by the enormous sacrifice of the life and money of the people of this country."[69] As evidence of the desperate betrayal represented by the LIO, the committee pointed to the "many thousands of British workmen, both in this country and South Africa [who were] out of employment and thus on the verge of starvation." In March 1904, union leaders, Liberal MPs, and nonconformist leaders merged economic objections with anti-slavery rhetoric in a protest against "Chinese labour" and "slavery" in South Africa, which attracted tens of thousands to London's Hyde Park.[70] The Hyde Park protest brought together representatives from a diverse array of unions, industries, and interests. Prominent speakers included Thomas James Macnamara, James Ramsay MacDonald, and Dadabhai Naoroji. Although Joseph Havelock Wilson and other representatives of maritime labor would join with miners' union leaders in the call for British workers to "Unite Against the YELLOW PERIL," the vast majority of those who attended represented industries where Chinese workers had never been accused of competing with white labor.[71]

The Hyde Park event demonstrated the effectiveness of opposition to "Chinese labour" in rallying a broad spectrum of Liberal politicians, labor leaders, and their constituents as a political force in Britain even as, in a broader context, it had become a common rallying cry for the supporters of "white labor" throughout Britain and the empire. The central themes of the Hyde Park demonstration were also reflected in the reports of *Daily Chronicle*, a Liberal halfpenny paper that would, by the eve of World War I, become one of the most widely circulated newspapers in Britain. The paper had sent Thomas Naylor as a "special commissioner" to the Transvaal with the express purpose of reporting on the issue. Naylor wrote that the Chinese were cunning and riotous, murderous and addicted to gambling, and that their presence in the Transvaal demoralized the entire region. They also brought with them a penchant for interracial sexuality—a penchant made even more damaging by the prevalence of venereal disease in their ranks—that threatened the introduction of "a new mongrel race" to South Africa. [72] Like the arguments made previously against Chinese labor in Australia, Naylor's claims blended economic opposition and support of "white labour" with a direct condemnation of the Chinese themselves for their alleged villainy and corruption. For all the fiery rhetoric exchanged between the opponents of Chinese labor and its advocates in Britain, however, there was considerable agreement across the lines of party and class on the basic nature of race relations between Chinese immigrants and white communities. Regardless of whether they saw Chinese labor as a boon or a curse to South African mining, commentators on the issue all argued that the Chinese and Anglo-Saxon races were fundamentally incompatible; that any British-controlled territory should remain "white man's country" whenever the climate allowed it; that Chinese immigration and labor should be tightly controlled, with a particular eye toward preventing disruptive contact between races; and that laws and regulations were the most effective means by which these goals could be achieved.

As of December 1904, 21,462 Chinese men were working in the Rand mines, and mine owners would bring in over 40,000 more in the next two years.[73] By the summer of 1905, mines employing large numbers of Chinese laborers were experiencing serious work disruptions, outbreaks of rioting, and incidents of violence. An official return from the Transvaal government in July 1905 showed that, of a Chinese population that numbered roughly 45,000, there had been 1,735 convictions for desertion and that 2,342 workers had been jailed for striking, rioting, or deserting.[74] These statistics were merely the opening salvo of a letter written to the prime minister, Arthur Balfour, by members of the same committee of Liberal MPs that had opposed Chinese labor from the beginning.[75] "It is known," the letter continued, "that bands of deserters, wandering over the country . . . have invaded the houses of farmers and the stores of shopkeepers, and have committed a series of grave outrages."[76] In the process of criticizing the policies of their opponents, British politicians had tarred the Chinese with the brush of violence and immorality. The issue of "Chinese outrages" and how best to prevent or contain them would be a prevalent aspect of all future discussions and policy changes regarding the Chinese in South Africa. The reports of "Chinese outrages" received considerable coverage in the British press, appearing not only in the *Times*, which generally took a bipartisan stance on imperial issues in this period, but also in the halfpenny radical *Morning Leader*, which had steadfastly opposed the Boer War, in Liberal papers such as the *Daily Chronicle*, and in the *Daily Express*.[77] The *Leader*, *Chronicle*, and *Express*, having engaged the interest of a broad readership with their often sensationalized reporting during the war itself, were quick to take up the latest scandal emerging from South Africa.

As would later be the case in responses to Chinese immigrants in Britain, however, the press reports were exaggerated and the official policies adopted were grossly out of proportion to the actual threat. Despite the wild stories of blood and mayhem that Chinese deserters and their alleged depredations had generated, as of February 1906, only four white deaths had been attributed to Chinese suspects.[78] In response, Lord Selborne, who had succeeded Milner as the high commissioner for South Africa and the governor of the Transvaal and Orange River colonies, rearmed the same Boer population that Britain had paid such a tremendous price to suppress and disarm just four years earlier. While the distribution of free firearms to local white residents served to mollify some of their fears and to address the alarm of the British public over "Chinese outrages," the most substantial outcome of the new regulations was that they facilitated even greater supervision and control of the Chinese workforce. As of December 1905, for example, mine managers could temporarily imprison Chinese offenders without trial, pending the arrival of a "Resident Magistrate." The most extraordinary aspect of the new regulations was the legal powers it granted private white citizens of the Transvaal, who were henceforth authorized to arrest, without warrant, any Chinese laborer found outside the mining district, and to receive compensation for any expenses incurred in the process.[79] For both British colonial officials and mine owners, an increasingly strict regimen of laws governing the movement and behavior of the "coolies" seemed the best way to guarantee both an orderly labor force and the segregation of the Chinese workers from the local white population.

The end of the "Chinese experiment" in South Africa was sig naled by two elections, one in Britain and one in the Transvaal. In December 1905, the Conservatives were ousted and a Liberal government under Henry Campbell-Bannerman took office in Britain. "Chinese slavery" in the Rand was a significant issue in the general election that followed, which David Lloyd George would sum up as "the most emphatic condemnation at the hands of the people that has ever been passed upon any Prime Minister."[80] The "Chinese slavery" issue added another arrow to the quiver for Liberal and Labour political campaigners, who used it in conjunction with their arguments on the Education Act, the Licensing Act, and the tariff issue. The result was a Liberal landslide, with the party capturing not only every seat from Wales and two-fifths of those from Scotland but also a majority of English seats for the first time since 1880.[81] But the leaders of the new government had little time to celebrate their victory before a fresh wave of scandal and public outrage emerged over the Chinese in South Africa. In late 1906, portions of the Bucknill Report were leaked to the British press by a British MP.[82] The report, a confidential inquiry into the sexual practices of Chinese workers in the mining compounds, drew on the testimony of dozens of witnesses and the reports of compound medical officers. It portrayed the Chinese mineworkers in the worst possible light and was highly critical of the local administration and of white officials in the Rand. The Bucknill Report concluded that not only was the practice of homosexuality rampant among the Chinese but that this "unnatural vice," as it was commonly called, was tolerated by mine officials and, worse yet, was even spreading to the native Africans.[83] Winston Churchill, then an undersecretary at the Colonial Office, insisted on keeping the report confidential when his fellow MPs pressed him on the matter, stating only that Lord Selborne had been made aware of the report and had "replied in a manner which leaves no doubt as to the stringency of the measures to be taken."[84] Selborne would respond to the report's conclusions with alacrity, deporting 131 suspected "catamites" in 1906 alone.[85]

The scandal generated by the Bucknill Report left Britain's new Liberal leadership, which had campaigned vigorously on the issue of "Chinese labour," with only two options: either the Chinese workers in South Africa had to be employed under less degrading conditions or the practice of employing indentured labor would have to be abandoned altogether. Campbell-Bannerman's commitment to restoring South African self-rule, a goal that he felt was unachievable while indentured Chinese labor remained a disruptive and divisive presence in South African politics and society, insured that the latter option prevailed. His proposed solution, however, which was to release the Chinese from the indenture system, was unacceptable to mining interests and Boer leaders alike. Legislation, passed by the British government in December 1906, that threatened to turn the indentured Chinese workers into a "free" labor force by abrogating the terms of the LIO helped bring a *Het Volk* government into power in the February 1907 Transvaal elections.[86] The new Transvaal government was led by Louis Botha, and although it extended the indenture system, it also initiated a gradual repatriation program that would send the last Chinese worker back to his homeland by 1910. In 1911, the government of the newly formed Union of South Africa would put a final coda on the story of "Chinese Labour" there by enacting a law "preventing all further immigration of Asiatics within the Union."[87] In an apt reflection of the fierce debate that had taken place over the issue, the motion was carried by a single vote.

Although British politicians and labor advocates had often couched their opposition to the Transvaal scheme in terms of sympathy for Chinese laborers, their statements on the broader issues of race relations had replicated the negative stereotypes of the Chinese that had emerged from the Australian debate. The shared set of assumptions about the characteristics of the Chinese, their threat to white labor, and the intrinsic racial differences between Britons and Chinese that had been popularized in the course of the debate would linger in Britain long after the last Chinese miner had left South Africa. These images of the Chinese and their impact on white communities had evolved under the worst possible circumstances for the Chinese themselves. In the context of an exploitative and abusive indentured labor system, the alleged propensities of Chinese men for violence, immorality, and vice, and the justification they provided for race-specific legal regulations to control them, had been firmly established in British public discourse. The insistence by labor leaders and the Liberal press that the sacrifice of white men in wartime had entitled them to jobs that, perforce, must be denied to Chinese immigrants would be revived in Britain during World War I and in the economically tumultuous interwar period. The assertions that "Chinese labour" was a dire threat to "white labour" worldwide and that Chinese and Anglo-Saxons could not coexist peacefully would resurface in Britain much sooner than that.[88]

"A Black List of Yellow Men": Joseph Havelock Wilson and the Campaign against "Chinese Labour" in Britain

In July 1910, Joseph Havelock Wilson, the Liberal MP for Middlesbrough (Yorkshire) and the founder and president of the National Sailors' and Firemen's Union (NSFU), delivered a scathing critique of the government's policy toward Chinese labor aboard British ships. The NSFU was a large and powerful organization, and by 1913, its membership would number over 80,000.[89] Speaking to a gathering of seamen at the gates of London's West India Docks, Wilson accused the government of allying with shipping magnates to permit the Chinese to settle and work in Britain's major ports. He claimed that it was "damned hypocrisy," on the government's part, "to make such a yowl about the Chinese in South Africa, and yet to allow the Chinese to be dumped down right here in this country. Drastic action was taken in South Africa, but colonies of Chinese were being founded in all the chief ports of the British Isles."[90] Wilson declared that if the government did not respond promptly, he would initiate a strike of "200,000 seamen in British and Continental ports" that would bring the entire British shipping industry to a grinding halt. According to him, the legal mechanism was already in place to protect British seamen from an inundation of Chinese competitors. Wilson and other opponents of "Chinese labour" legitimized their opposition to Chinese seamen on British ships by insisting that, in the interests of safety and compliance with the nation's laws, the "language test" of the Merchant Shipping Act of 1906 should be strictly enforced. The test, which required a perspective seaman to demonstrate a basic competency in English before he could sign on to crew a British ship, was similar to measures adopted by Australia in 1901 and by Natal in the late 1890s in order to restrict Asian immigration (aka the "Natal test").[91] For Wilson and his allies, as for legislators in Australia before them, the regulation effectively excluded Chinese immigrants without violating British legal principles, since "language tests" did not overtly refer to race.

By 1908, the political debate over "Chinese labour" in South Africa had been resolved, with both British and South African officials enacting policies that would bring an end to the importation of indentured Chinese workers to the Transvaal. At the same time, however, Wilson and his colleagues in the NSFU were introducing rhetoric on the employment of "Chinese labour" in Britain itself as a prominent element in their public contestation with shipowners and using the failure of the South African "experiment" as a justification for excluding the Chinese from Britain as well. Wilson's comparisons ignored both the vast differences between Rand mining and British maritime labor and the considerable contrast between the Rand Chinese labor force itself, which consisted primarily of unskilled labor drawn from the northern Chinese peasantry, and the skilled, cosmopolitan Chinese maritime workforce.[92] His efforts to restrict Chinese employment reached an early apex in the summer of 1908, with newspaper polemics, mass demonstrations, and violent organized resistance to Chinese employment aboard British ships. [93] The NSFU's campaign to portray Chinese men and those who employed them as bitter enemies of white labor helped sustain "Chinese labour" and its attendant evils as prominent issues in London's East End, in Britain's maritime districts, and among British labor leaders for many years afterwards.

Wilson's opposition to Chinese labor aboard British ships arose in the context of a rapid increase in the small numbers of Chinese sailors signing on in British ports from 1905–8. According to figures from the Board of Trade, the number of Chinese signing on to British ships in London had risen from 448 in 1905 to 1,211 in 1907, and was estimated to increase to over 1,700 by the end of 1908.[94] Other ports in Britain where Chinese sailors sought employment—Liverpool, Glasgow, Cardiff, Barry, and Newport—had witnessed similar surges, with the overall number of Chinese sailors signing articles in these ports rising from 1,424 in 1905 to 3,173 in 1907, and to an estimated 5,600 in 1908.[95] Although these numbers represented only a small proportion of the foreign sailors in domestic British shipping, what alarmed Wilson and others in the NSFU was the rate of increase in Chinese seamen.[96] The number of Chinese sailors employed between 1905 and 1907 had trebled, while the number of foreign and "Lascar" sailors had not even doubled in the previous fifteen years.[97]

Wilson insisted that the growing Chinese presence on British ships was a threat not only to white sailors but also to the entire shipping industry upon which the empire depended, and to British society as a whole.[98] If current trends continued, he argued in 1908, "the great traditions of the British sea dog should be taken over and upheld in all their grandeur by an imported horde of underpaid Chinese starvelings."[99] Wilson, like so many others who had addressed the issue before him, framed his objections to Chinese labor in British shipping within the context of a looming global conflict between Anglo-Saxons and Asians. "The trouble is not local, it is universal," he wrote in January 1908, "and that, of course, only increases the peril."[100] As evidence of this, he pointed to the "universal white upheaval of 'white' sentiment against the brown or yellow races" in the Transvaal, Canada, and the United States, and paid particular heed to Australia, where the population was "passionately determined that there shall be nothing but 'a White Australia.'" Several incidents involving foreign seamen aboard British ships in 1908, and the subsequent trials and official inquiries, gave Wilson ample ammunition for his arguments. The loss of the steamship *Huddersfield* off the northern coast of Devon on January 27, 1908, became a centerpiece of Wilson's campaign.[101] A Board of Trade inquiry blamed the loss of the ship, in part, on the two lookouts' lack of fluency in English. According to the presiding magistrate, T. W. Lewis, the foreign seamen aboard had been not merely incompetent but cowardly and mutinous as well. He closed the case by declaring that the *Huddersfield* incident proved the need for the strict legal regulation of foreign seamen. [102]

The magistrate's statements in the *Huddersfield* inquiry could have been drawn from a script written by Wilson and his allies in the NSFU, were they not lacking one important element. Neither of the seamen blamed for the loss of the ship were Chinese. One of the men accused of incompetent seamanship was Brazilian and the other was Greek. In the course of the inquiry, there was no mention of any Chinese seamen aboard the *Huddersfield* at all. This posed a problem for Wilson and his allies, whose campaign against Chinese maritime labor built on the sentiment stirred up in the debates over "Chinese labour" in South Africa. But the *Huddersfield* inquiry proved easy enough for Wilson and his allies to adapt to their purposes in their parliamentary speeches of March 3, 1908—they simply invented a Chinese culprit. When Charles Fenwick MP (Wansbeck, Liberal), an ally of Wilson's, brought up the *Huddersfield* incident as an argument for enforcing the language test of the 1906 Merchant Shipping Act, he was asked by another MP if any of the foreign seamen questioned by the board of inquiry had been Chinese. Although there was no evidence to indicate that was the case, Fenwick replied that "one was a Greek, and he believed the other was a Chinaman," and then continued his speech.[103] With "Chinese labour" gaining popularity among NSFU officials and their parliamentary allies as bywords for incompetent foreign seamanship, no one saw the need to confirm the involvement of Chinese seamen. When the loss of the *Huddersfield* was referred to subsequently in public discussions, it was always with the implication that a Chinese sailor was somehow to blame.

The language test championed by Wilson and his allies in the NSFU had gone into effect January 1, 1908, but Chinese seamen in Britain adapted very quickly to its provisions by exploiting a loophole that exempted "British" seamen. By February 1908, Chinese seamen had begun to avoid the strictures of the language test by declaring that they were from the crown colonies of Hong Kong or Singapore or by means of other false assertions.[104] These practices quickly became commonplace. In the spring of 1908, Hudson Kearley, the Parliamentary Secretary to the Board of Trade, announced to Parliament that over 80 percent of the Chinese seamen signing on to British ships in the East End were declaring one of the two crown colonies as their birthplace, as compared to a little over 30 percent the previous year.[105] Kearley, propagating the stereotype of Chinese cunning, told the House of Commons that "the wily Chinaman has detected the weak spot in our armour and is utilizing it to his own special advantage."[106] The Chinese, he continued, apparently had little trouble obtaining the documentary evidence to back up their claims. When the marine superintendent at Cardiff had refused the claims of one group, Kearley explained, "they immediately trooped into the town and came back armed with statutory declarations [of their claims]."[107] The *Shipping Gazette* reported that the Chinese had another tactic for avoiding rejection—disguise. "The Chinese sailor well knows the difficulty which the average European has in distinguishing, say, Ah-Sin, from Wun-Lung. Therefore being rejected on one occasion, he finds that he has only to come forward on another."[108] Through such means, the *Gazette* declared, the Chinese had succeeded in "getting their pigtail through the new regulation."[109]

Wilson and his allies in the NSFU were infuriated by the Chinese employment of "the Hong-Kong dodge," as they labeled it. Kearley's attempts to defend the shipowners by deflecting blame onto the Chinese themselves only worsened the prejudice against the latter. Wilson and his allies responded with a fierce attack on the morality of the Chinese in Britain. What had begun as a campaign against shipowners and their employment tactics now changed direction to focus squarely on the Chinese themselves. They were, according to Kearley, not mere tools of the shipping interests but conniving and subversive in their own right. The successful adaptation of Chinese workers to a law intended to exclude them only increased the danger they posed in the eyes of Wilson and the other putative defenders of "British" maritime labor. Proponents of Chinese labor in British ships, on the other hand, such as the Scottish shipping magnate William Hannay Raeburn, continued to justify their hiring practices by arguing that Chinese sailors were more hardworking and dependable than their British counterparts were.[110] According to Wilson and other opponents, however, the threat of Chinese labor lay less in their industriousness and more in their capacity for amoral intelligence and callous manipulation of the law. The discourse of "Chinese labour" was increasingly superseded in public debate and the pages of *The Seaman* by images of the "bland celestial," who, "with inscrutable countenances, swear that every one came from Hong Kong."[111] It was thus through the conflict between British maritime labor interests and British shipowners over the enforcement of the laws restricting "Chinese labour" that the stereotype of the "the cunning Chinamen" was portrayed as a direct threat to working-class interests in Britain itself.

Wilson's attacks on "Chinese labour" adhered to the same pattern that had characterized the Australian and South African debates, with moral objections following quickly on the heels of economic arguments. "Another evil" of Chinese maritime labor, he asserted, was that, in a reversal of British colonial dynamics, "actual colonies of Chinamen" were establishing themselves in British ports, "springing up, with mushroom growth."[112] Not only were Chinese residents proliferating and displacing British residents, he declared, they were further lowering the moral atmosphere of London's Docklands, an area which already had a reputation for vice. "During the past eighteen months," Wilson told Parliament in March 1908, "there had been an increase of no less than ten Chinese boarding-houses in the East End of London . . . if any [MP] visited the West India Dock-road tomorrow he would wonder where all the British inhabitants had gone to, because the Chinaman monopolized every public-house and every den of infamy in that particular locality."[113] This tendency to occupy Britain's ports, Wilson argued, made Chinese seamen a far greater threat to British labor and society than Lascars were, even though the latter represented a much larger contingent in British shipping.[114] Whereas the Chinese were settling in British ports and using their wages to encourage vice, he explained, Lascars were "engaged in India, commenced their voyage there, and went back to India and were paid off there."

For Wilson, Fenwick, and their allies in the anti-Chinese campaign, the alleged immorality, cunning intelligence, disregard for British law, and looming threat of Chinese residency in Britain were all epitomized in the sinister figure of the Chinese boardinghouse keeper. These men, who were mostly long-term residents of Britain, were acting as employment brokers by recruiting Chinese seamen, advertising their availability and affordability to British shipowners, and even serving as interpreters when Chinese crews signed on to British ships at mercantile marine offices.[115] Fenwick, in a speech before Parliament in March 1908, argued that these practices, known as "crimping," were in contravention of Section III of the Merchant Shipping Act of 1894. Section III stipulated that the only individuals authorized to supply or engage seamen for British ships were official license holders from the Board of Trade, shipowners and their staff, and ship's officers.[116] This illegal system of labor supply and distribution, Fenwick argued, was rapidly driving British seamen out of work, and, worse yet, "opening the ports of the United Kingdom and making them practically collecting grounds for men of foreign nationality."[117] Wilson, in his follow-up speech, insisted that Chinese "crimps" were colluding with the Chinese seamen in their efforts to evade the language test by encouraging them to falsely claim Hong Kong as their place of birth. [118] Although Chinese men were signing on to British ships in increasing numbers, the dire picture that had been drawn by Fenwick and Wilson of Chinese crimps flooding the London labor market with cheap Chinese sailors was not borne out by more objective assessments.[119] The first official survey of seamen's lodging houses in the East End, conducted in 1910, revealed only 13 Chinese-owned establishments, which could altogether house a legal maximum of 157 occupants.[120]

Wilson's assertions that the Chinese were intentionally evading the law and threatening the employment of white British sailors initially failed to move Parliament to adopt a stricter stance. His statements did, however, provoke a counterargument from the supporters of Chinese maritime labor. British captains, ships' officers, and shipowners answered the anti-Chinese rhetoric with a steady stream of letters praising the positive qualities of their Chinese employees. Their compliments mirrored the statements that Rand mine owners and British colonial officials had made in support of Chinese labor during the debate over the LIO. Chinese seamen, British captains wrote, were hardworking, orderly, sober, and obedient.[121] Wilson and his allies, responding to this chorus of praise, disseminated an even more fiercely negative image of Chinese seamen. Moving well beyond their initial arguments that the Chinese were merely cunning and manipulative, Wilson and his allies now began to portray them as violent, mutinous, and even murderous. Citing a series of court cases as evidence, the May 1908 issue of *The Seaman* listed an extensive catalog of the crimes allegedly committed by Chinese crewmen across the course of the previous five years. Headlining the list was a recent case prosecuted in the Dartmouth Police Court against seventeen Chinese crewmen of the London steamer *Clam*. A report of the case that had originally appeared in the *Western Morning News* recounted how the Chinese crew had mutinied against their English officers. The representative of the owners, Mr. Hutchings, emphasized in court "the necessity of dealing severely with the men, for the lives of the English officers aboard were really not safe in their hands."[122] According to his account, seventeen of the forty-two Chinese crewmembers had "rushed the chief officer with knives, etc. They pushed him aside, cut the ropes which held one of the boats, took possession of the craft, and pulled ashore." Although *The Seaman* subtitled the article on the *Clam* incident "Knives and Mutiny," the trial itself revealed an episode more reminiscent of a labor dispute gone awry than of a life-threatening disaster. The Chinese crewmembers' desertion had taken place only after several rounds of negotiation, and their final, desperate escape had been provoked by the officers' attempts to starve them into submission. The majority of the Chinese crewmen, moreover, had remained obedient to orders, and the "mutiny" of the seventeen defendants had not been accompanied by any violence.

To bolster the evidence of Chinese seamen's villainy offered by the *Clam* incident and subsequent trial, which alone were hardly convincing to any reader not predisposed against the Chinese already, *The Seaman* provided a roll of sixty-seven separate incidents of violence and mutiny allegedly committed by Chinese seamen on British ships in the previous six years.[123] A third of the incidents had taken place in London, with the remainder occurring in Liverpool, Cardiff, Glasgow, Shields, and Barry, and a few listed in foreign ports such as New York, Singapore, and Hong Kong. The implicit argument in this list was that Chinese maritime criminality was an issue throughout Britain and its commercial empire, but that London was the epicenter of the problem. *The Seaman* provided no details of the cases, giving only a one-line, and in some cases, a one-word, summary of each. Entries such as "Chinese crew paralyzed with fear," "Chinese mutiny; leave whites to their fate," "Murder in caste war," or simply, as was the case in several instances, "murder," sufficed to tell the whole story of a particular incident. The editors of *The Seaman* thus transformed the trials from events where multiple interpretations were possible—as was the case in the *Clam* trial—into a mere catalog of Chinese atrocities. Divorced of all context, the trial summaries aptly fulfilled the promise of the column's title by providing readers with "A Black List of Yellow Men."

In May 1908, NSFU leadership translated their anti-Chinese rhetoric into popular, violent agitation against Chinese seamen in London. By then, the public campaign waged by Wilson and his allies had succeeded in polarizing the maritime labor community of London's East End into two groups, with the British and European seamen united in their opposition against Chinese seamen. In the ensuing conflict, both sides tried to deploy the force of law and the authority of the state to their own advantage. In the local press reports that followed the episode, moreover, although the British and European workers were the aggressors and the violent offenders, the Chinese would receive the blame. The trouble began on May 9, when a crew of Chinese seamen appeared at the Poplar Board of Trade offices on the East India Dock Road.[124] Their intention was to sign on to the British steamship *Zambezi*, which was currently at the Surrey Commercial Docks (southeast London). What happened next was a matter of some debate. *The Seaman* reported that NSFU officers redirected the train carrying the Chinese, thus delaying their arrival long enough for the white seamen to gather their forces in Surrey. Another account, printed in the *East End News*, claimed that the Chinese failed the language test, but were sent to the docks anyway to sign "coasting articles" for Cardiff.[125] Regardless, both accounts were in agreement that when the Chinese finally arrived at Surrey Docks, they found an angry crowd of several hundred British and European seamen and laborers opposing them. *The Seaman*'s account claimed that European seamen took control of the ship and threatened to deny the Chinese access by overturning the gangway. The *News*, in contrast, reported that the ship's officers, wary of the angry crowd and eager to sail with the tide, signed on a "white crew" instead of the new Chinese arrivals. Either way, the *Zambezi* eventually sailed with a European crew and the Chinese returned to their lodgings.

The *Zambezi* incident, however, was only the prelude to a much more violent clash that took place two days later. Whether it constituted "The Revolt of the White Seamen," as *The Seaman* titled it, or merely a "Seamen's Conflict at Pennyfields," as the *News* reported, May 11 witnessed the most serious incident of anti-Chinese violence in London to date. The scene was again the Board of Trade offices in the East India Dock Road. There, according to *The Seaman*, a crew of Chinese sailors appeared to apply for berths on the British ship *Strathness*.[126] NSFU officers, anticipating the arrival of the Chinese seamen, had recruited large numbers of unemployed European sailors to form picket lines and to occupy the Board of Trade building. As in their organization of the *Zambezi* demonstration, the union officers again made no distinction between British and non-British white seamen. The tactics adopted by NSFU officers were putting Wilson's discourse of January 1908, which pitted white men against Asians in a global conflict, into practical effect. But the elision of national differences also belied the claims by NSFU leadership that their policies were not racially constructed and that their only goal was to protect "British" labor. A campaign that had maintained a pro-British façade initially was now clearly anti-Chinese. It is also telling that NSFU officers made no attempt to incorporate Lascars into their demonstrations even though many of them, like the Chinese sailors from Hong Kong and Singapore, were subjects of the crown. For the NSFU, and for the white seamen of London, race superseded both national identity and imperial status as continental European sailors joined "British" sailors to defend white maritime workers against the influx of "Chinese labour."

The organizers of Chinese labor in London, however, had learned the lessons of the *Zambezi* incident and had taken steps to prevent a recurrence. These new measures were likely orchestrated by Chang Ahon, the proprietor of several local Chinese boardinghouses.[127] Not only were the police forewarned of possible opposition by white sailors, but the Chinese sailors were themselves disguised as European seamen. "As each had his pigtail rolled under his hat," *The Seaman* recounted, "and was dressed in European clothes, while the leader was a smart young yellow gentleman in a clean straw hat and navy blue lounge suit, they had almost escaped notice."[128] Arriving at the proper entrance, the police and the Chinese seamen once again found their way obstructed by unemployed European sailors who had been organized by the NSFU officers. The police intervened directly, clearing out the white sailors and escorting the Chinese seamen into the offices. Accounts of the event in both the *News* and *The Seaman* contrasted the fear and circumspection of the Chinese with the determined resolve of the police leadership, *The Seaman* going so far as to admire the manly physique of Mr. Walmsley, the presiding police officer, and to describe him as a "stalwart chief inspector, six feet high, and broad shouldered." In these press descriptions of the *Strathness* incident, the Chinese resorted to cunning disguises and deception to achieve their goals, while the British inspector spurned such tactics in favor direct, muscular action.[129]

Walmsley's efforts were in vain, since the Chinese seamen promptly failed the language test and were therefore unable to sign on as crew. When the Chinese emerged unsuccessful from the Board's offices, a large mob of infuriated white seamen chased them several blocks from the East India Dock Road into Pennyfields, where they took shelter in Chang Ahon's boardinghouse. According to *The Seaman*'s coverage of the *Zambezi* and *Strathness* incidents, however, the blame for any excesses lay firmly with the Chinese sailors and the British shipowners who had tried to hire them. "The records of white labour teem with illustrations and instances of how white men can act when the hunger line is being reached," their coverage ran. The authors also explicitly compared white seamen's campaign against "Chinese labour" with the London Dockers' Strike of 1889, one of the great turning points in the nineteenth-century struggle for unionization and workers' rights.[130] *The Seaman* predicted far worse events in the future, should the practice of hiring Chinese sailors continue. "Breadwinners are not apt to remain quite model members of society when they see the food being taken out of the mouths of their wives and children through the agency of a disgraceful competition . . . the European seamen is not going to succumb to his Chinese rival without making a fight of it. That is human nature." The paper asserted that the recent conflicts in London were best understood in relation to the violent racial clashes that had taken place in the United States. "Although bowie knives, revolvers, and noosed ropes were missing," the story ran, "East London had some experience yesterday of the anti-Asiatic troubles of America." But if white seamen could be violent, it was violence in defense of their birthrights, homes, and families, *The Seaman* explained, while the Chinese were mere mercenaries, devoid of such loyalties or connections.

The district's local paper, however, in a less polemical account, painted a very different picture of the conflict. According to the *East End News*, the final confrontation in the *Strathness* episode had taken place not between European and Chinese seamen but between police and British seamen, much to the latter's dismay. "The whites were very indignant," the *News* reported, "about the action of the police and maintained that they exceeded their duty . . . the seamen, many of who are ratepayers in the district, maintain that the police had no right to be used for the purpose of assisting the captain of a ship to get a crew of Chinese in preference to Europeans."[131] Inspector Walmsley defended his actions by referring to his official role and to the strictures of the law. But despite Walmsley's claims to neutrality, the Metropolitan Police were willing to go only so far in protecting the Chinese sailors—not a single charge was made against the riotous and violent crowd of white seamen that had chased them half way across Poplar.

The *Strathness* and *Zambezi* disturbances triggered another round of public acrimony in Parliament between the opponents of Chinese maritime labor and representatives of the Board of Trade. Joseph Havelock Wilson challenged Winston Churchill, then president of the board, to take action against the Chinese "crimps" of London and their alleged illegal involvement in the recruitment, coaching, and provision of Chinese crews.[132] Wilson's demands were followed up in June by a deputation of thirty seamen, led by Wilson himself, who approached Churchill in his offices to protest the lax enforcement of the language test against Chinese seamen. Churchill commiserated with the deputation, expressed his "anxiety" that a "regular system" was springing up by which Chinese seamen were being brought to Britain in order to replace British seamen on British ships working in local trade, and vowed to do his utmost to stop this "invasion of Chinese." [133] "I have not the slightest intention," he told the deputation, "of ever allowing the British mercantile marine in home waters and in home ports to be invaded by these strangers from the other end of the world, who, whatever their virtues or vices, cannot be brought into close contact with European civilization and European labor without producing the greatest hardship and injustice, and even great social and political danger." Churchill translated this promise into policy by distributing a circular to marine superintendents and mercantile marine officers that encouraged them to apply the language test with the strictest possible standards. But the opportunity for evasion remained, since the circular also reminded officials that British subjects and inhabitants of British colonies were exempt.

The dogged determination of Wilson and the NSFU to exclude the Chinese from British ships through the strict application of the language test, granted urgency by organized mass demonstration and violent opposition in the *Zambezi* and *Strathness* incidents, finally seemed to be producing tangible results. Wilson's insistence on Chinese racial difference, from both white seamen and from other "Asiatics," and the consequent necessity for the legal, economic, and social segregation of the Chinese from Europeans and Lascars was now being reproduced, in discourse and policy, at the highest levels of the British government. Such measures as Churchill now encouraged were targeted specifically at the Chinese, since the stipulations of the Merchant Shipping Act exempted the largest group of "Asiatic" seamen—Lascars—from the language test. Chinese attempts to avoid discrimination by claiming birth in Hong Kong or Singapore, furthermore, had been seized on by Wilson and his allies as proof positive of their deviousness and immorality and therefore ample justification for stricter measures against them. Churchill's statements, which mirrored Wilson's claims about the grave perils posed by the influx of the Chinese into Britain's ports, gave considerable encouragement to the opponents of "Chinese labour" in British shipping. In mid-June, British seamen, heartened by Churchill's actions, took to the streets of London by the thousands to demonstrate their approval of the new policies. Marching from Tower-Hill, Canning Town, and Poplar, three different processions, with bands and banners, converged on Victoria Park to hear Wilson speak. "This was a red-letter day in their history," he told the crowd of 3,000 seamen.[134] "They had gained a great victory in the declaration of Mr. Churchill. What was bad for South Africa was equally bad for England."

In the long run, however, Wilson's victory would prove to be illusory. A year later, the *East London Observer* reported that there were now twenty Chinese boarding houses in Limehouse alone.[135] "The trade of the Chinese boarding master," the *Observer* explained, "in Limehouse and elsewhere, is too profitable to go under to a mere [language] 'test' . . . it was confidently expected that the imposition of the test would close many of these houses. It did nothing of the kind. They are as numerous and as prosperous as ever." Chinese seamen and their organizers continued to adapt to attempts at legal regulation, practicing "other little dodges," the paper reported. One such method was to arrange for a proxy with a better grasp of English to take the language test, and then to substitute the original crewman afterwards. Here, the *Observer* reported, the Chinese were taking advantage of Westerners' inability to distinguish between them. Such substitutions were difficult to detect, "for all Chinaman, to English eyes, look very much alike."[136] In addition, the paper reported that an Englishman now came daily from the West End "and goes from boarding-house to boarding-house, giving lessons in English to Chinese seamen at 2 shillings a lesson." As a result "the Chinese colony has improved wonderfully in its knowledge of English since the beginning of the year." "The guileless John [Chinaman]," the paper concluded, "was not going under for want of a struggle."

In April 1910, the NSFU sent a second deputation to Sydney Buxton, the new president of the Board of Trade, and received the same promises of stricter enforcement of the language test. Buxton also reassured the British seamen that he would request that all British ports post notices informing Chinese and Lascar seamen of their right to claim compensation for injury incurred during service, under the terms of the Worker Compensation Act of 1906.[137] But Buxton, who had been an outspoken critic of "Chinese labour" in South Africa six years previously, sounded a conciliatory note that was a far cry from the urgency of Churchill's announcements in 1908. "He thought perhaps there was an undue alarm regarding the increase of the Chinese," he told the deputation, and argued that the issue was metropolitan rather than national.[138]

Wilson may not have succeeded as far as he had hoped in restricting Chinese employment on British ships, but he had helped bring the issue of "Chinese labour" to the attention of both policymakers and the British public to a degree not witnessed since the South African debates of 1903–6. By the end of 1908, the typical residents of London, Liverpool, Cardiff, and Glasgow may or may not have met a Chinese person in the flesh, but it is likely that they would have read or heard about them, most commonly in association with their increasing presence in British ports, their threat to white labor, or their alleged propensity for violence, cunning, disguise, and evasion of the law. The anti-Chinese campaign of Wilson and the NSFU could also claim one other tangible, if indirect, result. By the end of 1909, the Chinese boardinghouse keepers that Wilson and his allies had vilified were coming under increasingly strict scrutiny by metropolitan authorities. On January 1, 1910, the London County Council, drawing on the authority of the Merchant Shipping Act of 1894 and the LCC bylaws of 1901, issued an order requiring the licensing of all lodging-house keepers and providing for regular inspections of their premises.[139] The

LCC inspection of Chinese boardinghouses was a harbinger of things to come, signaling the beginning of a new campaign of legal regulation against Chinese residents in Britain that would continue almost unabated for more than a decade.

By the end of the first decade of the twentieth century, the opponents of "Chinese labour" in South Africa and British shipping, drawing on the precedents of the Australian debate, had popularized the image of Chinese immigrants as immoral, violent, intrinsically incompatible with white communities, and a direct threat to the British working class. Serious concern about the Chinese in Britain and the empire had been expressed across a broad spectrum of British society, from parliamentarians and journalists to union officials and police in London's East End. Opinions on the role and character of Chinese men in Britain's cities and its labor force, however, remained divided. A uniformly negative image of Chinese immigrants in Britain had yet to be broadly accepted, and neither the average London resident nor the average British newspaper reader had serious cause to fear them. The popular imagination also lacked a compelling Chinese villain, an individual who could give the abstraction of the Chinese threat in London a cohesive form. In 1912, British popular literature would witness the arrival of that villain, "the yellow peril incarnate in one man," who possessed "all the cruel cunning of an entire Eastern race, accumulated in one giant intellect, with all the resources . . . of a wealthy government."[140] Its creator was a London journalist turned popular fiction author whose stories would assert that the greatest racial threat to Britain and its empire lurked within the imperial metropolis itself.

Chapter 3

The Dragon and Saint George, 1910–14

From 1910 to 1914, the Chinese population of Britain became an increasingly prominent concern in law and culture. Following the strikes of 1911, in which anti-Chinese sentiment and anti-Chinese violence played a significant role, magistrates and police began to speak openly of the threat posed to white communities by the Chinese men in Britain's maritime cities. Negative depictions of Chinese immigrants also began to proliferate in newspapers, plays, and popular fiction. Portrayals of the Chinese threat in these media, reflecting the broad social spectrum of their audience, focused not on "Chinese labour" but on a global racial conflict, Chinese immorality, and interracial sexuality.

Although British anti-Chinese sentiment in this period centered on the domestic Chinese population, it remained strongly informed by the imperial context. The images of the Chinese in Britain continued to draw upon the precedents set in the South African and Australian debates, as well as on anti-Chinese discourse emerging from Canada and the United States. Chinese residents in London were rarely granted the status of an independent community by their detractors, and those who publicly discussed race relations did so on the basis of imperial experience or in reference to a looming, worldwide racial conflict. The cultural, social, and economic heterogeneity of Britain's urban communities, and of the Chinese communities overseas, were ignored in favor of stark divisions between "yellow" and "white." The growing public concern over the Chinese in London also coincided with increasing anxiety in government circles and the British press about the political situation in China itself and its potentially destabilizing effects on Britain's position in Asia.

In practice, however, the Chinese residents of London had much more to fear from British officials and public prejudice than white Britons had to fear from the Chinese, nor did the latter group need to look to events as far afield as South Africa, Australia, or China to confirm their mistrust. Incidents in which the behavior of Chinese men in London seemed to contradict negative assumptions about them were often downplayed, ignored, or recast to offer confirmation of anti-Chinese stereotypes. In the public debate over whether Chinese men were orderly and industrious or violent and sinister, it was the latter image that increasingly guided their treatment by London officials and their portrayal in newspapers and popular literature. The actions of Chinese residents received a disproportionately harsh official response, and Chinese confrontations with, police, judicial officials, and the white working-class residents of Britain's maritime cities set the precedents for far more serious clashes in the years that followed.

"The Trouble in Limehouse Chinatown": Strikes, Violence, and Legal Intervention in London's Chinese Community

By 1911, according to official estimates, there were fewer than 300 permanent Chinese residents in London, roughly half of whom lived in the Limehouse "Chinatown" district.[1] The addition of short-term residents and itinerant seamen could, at times, increase the total Chinese population of the neighborhood to over 600.[2] Nationwide, the Chinese population was a little over 1,100, with the largest community residing in Liverpool (403), though there, as in London, temporary residents and itinerant seamen could make this number fluctuate significantly.[3] In the prewar period, union opposition insured that this small Chinese population continued to attract attention out of all proportion to their numbers or their impact on the domestic labor market. As had been the case in 1908, when Joseph Havelock Wilson mobilized the NSFU against the threat of "Chinese labour," Chinese workers in British shipping (4,595) remained only a very small proportion of the overall workforce.[4] Even after wartime demand tripled this number, they would make up only 5 percent of the workforce, which would rise to 250,000 by 1915.[5] In prewar numbers, Chinese seamen were exceeded by Scandinavian seamen (5,948), far exceeded by Lascar seamen, and dwarfed by British seamen, who remained the vast majority overall.[6] Yet, when Wilson and other union officials helped organize a national seamen's strike in 1911, they once again vilified Chinese labor as the cause of the British workingman's troubles, and Chinese residents in Britain bore the brunt of popular hostility.[7]

Economic self-interest remained the ostensible justification for speeches and actions taken against them during the 1911 strike. Lascar seamen, for example, were not targeted by NSFU officials because they demonstrated solidarity with the wage demands of white British seamen.[8] British shipowners, moreover, had indeed threatened to bring Chinese seamen in from Hong Kong as strikebreakers. But the threat was translated into action only on very few occasions.[9] The British Home Office and the Board of Trade, the latter under the leadership of Winston Churchill, were also quick to respond, in the name of preserving public order, with further legal restrictions on the importation of Chinese workers.[10] Nonetheless, the fear of white Britons in the maritime industry and port districts that legions of Chinese would soon occupy their streets and their jobs was a potent weapon that both shipowners and union officials did not hesitate to employ.[11]

The strike initiated by the NSFU in the summer of 1911 soon expanded into a series of broader strikes across the nation. In August, after months of violent confrontations between police and demonstrators, the Liberal government brokered a resolution. But the threat of "Chinese labour," which had been popularized in Britain during the South African debate and the 1906 general election, was lent renewed vigor by the events of 1911. In the years that followed, the insistence that Chinese workers were immoral and would overwhelm white labor if given half the chance remained an important part of Wilson's attacks on shipping interests and their allies in Parliament. In June of 1913, as part of his political campaign to secure the parliamentary seat for Wandsworth (south-west London), he and his supporters covered the town with posters "depicting a laughing horde of Chinamen being engaged to go on board a ship, while a crowd of dejected Englishmen are going off in the direction of the workhouse."[12] The poster resurrected the cover image of the June 1908 issue of the *The Seaman* (see Fig. 3.2), but its ultimate origins lay in the protests of the radical press in Britain against indentured Chinese mine labor in South Africa.[13] The original drawing had appeared in the *Morning Leader* in 1904, and in that instance, it had depicted Chinese "coolies" disembarking in South Africa as dejected white miners boarded ship for London (see Fig. 3.1).[14] Wilson's easy adaptation of the image to a domestic context stood as stark evidence of the legacy left by the South African debate and of how much nearer to home the threat of "Chinese labour" had come in the intervening years.

Several incidents during the summer 1911 also suggested that opposition to the Chinese presence in Britain was becoming both more widespread and more overtly racial, expanding beyond the conflict between British maritime workers, shipowners, and Chinese seamen and into a broader opposition of working-class white Britons against Chinese residents in general. In London, for example, an attempt to sign on eight Chinese seamen for a ship docked at Barry prompted a small but violent demonstration by a group of local residents with no apparent involvement in maritime industry. Those participating in the attack on the Chinese crewmen were not British seamen but rather "a small crowd of casual loafers" and a woman, the latter who was subsequently arrested for attempted assault.[15] Just as the participants in such attacks were not confined to white seamen, the victims were

Figure 3.1. "Chinese labour" replacing British miners. (*Morning Leader*, January 25, 1904. Courtesy of the British Library.)

Figure 3.2. "Chinese labour" replacing British seamen. (*The Seaman* 8, June 1908. Courtesy of the British Library)

not limited to Chinese seamen either. In Cardiff, which witnessed the most serious and widespread racial conflicts during the 1911 strikes, there were several assaults on Chinese crewmen. The leader of the strikers there, "Captain Tupper," was quick to point out the hypocrisy of a government that protected "Chinese Blacklegs" after it had been elected on the promise to abolish "Chinese labour" in South Africa.[16] Tupper led several violent demonstrations against Chinese seamen in Cardiff, and his supporters—which included English, Scottish, Welsh, and, on at least one occasion, black maritime workers—were eventually joined by several other unions in the region.[17] The most serious attack, however, was made against the property of permanent Chinese residents with no ostensible connection to British shipping. On the night of July 20, a crowd of angry white residents threatened Chinese boardinghouses in Cardiff, but met a strong police force assigned to guard the establishments. Prevented from reaching their original goal, the crowd instead destroyed all but one of the twenty-two Chinese laundries in the adjoining district.[18] Even though the owners were permanent residents and the laundries served a white and Chinese clientele alike, their identification as "Chinese" was enough to make them the targets of popular wrath.[19]

The events of 1911 proved that despite the negligible economic impact of Chinese workers in Britain, their alleged threat to white labor could serve as a powerful rhetorical tool in the hands of those willing to employ it. But what of the dangers that Chinese violence and immorality posed to white communities, dangers that had also been prominent aspects in the anti-Chinese rhetoric of the Australian and South African debates? In South Africa, the public alarm and official concern over "Chinese outrages" on the Rand had been severe enough to justify a constellation of stern legal controls and even the wholesale rearming of Boer farmers at public expense. In the first major twentieth-century trial involving Chinese residents of London, the stereotyping of Chinese immigrants as violent and immoral once again became a significant factor in their experiences at the hands of magistrates and police. But, ironically, the trial was prompted by a violent attack *on* them rather than *by* them. In May 1911, shortly before the initiation of the seamen's strike, the tensions between European seamen and London's Chinese population boiled over into fatal violence when a Scandinavian sailor stabbed two Chinese men in Pennyfields, killing one of them.[20] The course of the inquest that followed highlighted both the racial tensions among the British, foreign European, and Chinese residents of the East End and the intersections of race, gender, and sexuality in metropolitan social relations. It also demonstrated how, even when Chinese residents were the victims of brutality rather than its perpetrators, popular images of them as violent, deceptive, and sexually immoral could influence their treatment in London courts.

The immediate trigger of the events that led up to the murder was clear. Three Scandinavian sailors—August "Ang" Sepp, Karl Horden, and Washi Wali—had begun to harass several Chinese men who were talking to two young white women outside of an East End public house. Witnesses reported that the assailants had called out "rotten Chinese" and shouted curses.[21] When one of the Chinese group told them to "be quiet," the Scandinavian sailors attacked. The Chinese men retreated toward a nearby lodging house from which several more Chinese men emerged to aid their compatriots. In the course of the melee that ensued, witnesses reported that August Sepp stabbed Lee Fong in the chest and Ah Ling (aka Sea Heng) in the throat. Ah Ling, who had been part of the contingent of Chinese men who had rushed out of the lodging house, had died of his wounds almost immediately. The coroner's inquest called more than a half dozen different individuals, European and Chinese, to the stand to recount what they had seen. But despite the plethora of eyewitnesses, the details of the incident proved exceedingly difficult to determine. Not only did the witnesses give conflicting and contradictory accounts, sometimes denying statements that they had made earlier to the police or even refusing to speak altogether, but the coroner and the jury foreman both insisted that the Chinese witnesses were either concealing information or lying outright. The jury foreman also expressed his opinion that the Chinese predilection for being armed and violent had been a greater factor in the incident than witnesses were letting on. When one witness, a Pennyfields cellarman, testified that Ah Ling had struck one of the European seamen with his fist, the jury foremen replied, dubiously, that "this is the first time I have heard a Chinaman fights with his fist." [22]

Although it was a Scandinavian sailor who was being accused of assault and murder, the coroner's inquest was as much an indictment of the Chinese involved in the incident as it was of August Sepp and his companions. The *Times*'s coverage had highlighted the role of interracial social contact in the affray, describing the circumstances that triggered the violence as "two Chinamen . . . in the company of three young girls."[23] Even the nicknames of the two Chinese victims, "Katie, buy me chocolates" and "Kiss me on my birthmark," which were revealed in the inquest, seemed to attest to their questionable sexual mores. The refusal of the Chinese witnesses to cooperate fully with the investigation, their conflicting accounts, and their refutation of their initial statements did little to raise their esteem in the eyes of judicial authorities. In the Central Criminal Court trial that followed the coroner's inquest, despite Lee Fong's positive identification of Sepp as the man who had stabbed him, the jury acquitted the defendant of both that crime and of the murder of Ah Ling.[24]

Chinese witnesses, as is clear from August Sepp's trials, could face considerable prejudice from both judges and juries in London courts. The likelihood of misinterpretation and miscommunication between judicial authorities and Chinese immigrants was further exacerbated by differences of culture, custom, and language. Familiarity with the British legal system was a highly prized asset in Britain's Chinese communities, and some Chinese residents, particularly long-term ones or those who had assimilated into the community through intermarriage, demonstrated considerable acumen this regard. [25] But, like a workable command of English itself, such knowledge was far from universal. The dominant image of magistrates and law courts held by Lee Fong and the other Chinese witnesses, as itinerant seamen, would likely have been based more on Chinese models than on British ones.[26] The time that the Chinese witnesses had spent in the East End, where working-class residents often demonstrated a distinct mistrust of police and judicial officials, would have also done little to encourage their cooperation. According to the Poplar coroner, fear of punishment by the community for being too closely associated with the police was also a factor in the reticence of witnesses to cooperate fully with the investigation.[27] The challenges of applying British law to Chinese defendants had become apparent decades earlier in British attempts to administer criminal justice in Hong Kong. There, the obstacles posed by cultural and linguistic differences had often prompted British officials to forgo formal British judicial procedures in favor of summary justice.[28] This tendency was exacerbated by the evolving goals of British officials in Hong Kong. Although they had initially hoped for the fair and full application of British law, by the latter decades of the nineteenth century, their overriding concern had become the maintenance of public order and the suppression of an unruly colonized population—a situation similar to that described by opponents of "Chinese labour" in South Africa and, in the decades that followed the 1906 election, by East End magistrates in their references to Chinatown.[29]

Considering the suspicions of Chinese morality and character evinced by local officials, it is perhaps understandable why the Chinese in the East End, even more so than the white working-class residents of the district, often demonstrated a strong preference for settling private disputes without recourse to the police or to local courts. [30] This practice had been commented upon by critics of "Chinese labour" in South Africa and was also popular in China itself, although, in the latter locale, the use of magistrates' courts in serious disagreements over property was not uncommon among those who could afford the price of official influence.[31] Journalistic accounts sometimes highlighted the role of organized Chinese community organizations in Britain—such as the Chung Yee Tong and Chee Kong Tong benevolent societies—and of propertied, well-respected community members in the provision of advice, charity, or conflict mediation to other Chinese residents.[32] The tendency of East End Chinese residents to avoid officialdom and to resolve (or continue) disputes privately further damaged their reputation in the eyes of local magistrates, who disparaged this practice in working-class neighborhoods and had, over the preceding decades, strongly encouraged local residents to employ the courts for the resolution of interpersonal conflicts.[33]

In the Ah Ling murder case, the stereotypes of Chinese men as violent and deceptive, which had gained noteriety during the earlier debates over Chinese labor and immigration in the empire, had strongly informed the attitudes of both the adjudicating magistrate and the jury members. In the next serious outbreaks of violence in Chinatown, which took place in April and May 1912, the significance of the imperial context was far more direct and apparent. Not only did police officials and press accounts portray the incidents as threatening largely because of nefarious connections between local residents and clandestine Chinese organizations worldwide, but the decision to punish harshly those involved was made by an official who had built his career on developing effective methods to classify and control Asians and Africans in the British Empire. On April 15, 1912, the *Times* reported that there had been a disturbance between two groups of Chinese men in Chinatown. Although there were no serious injuries, the combatants had employed a number of weapons, including axes and "choppers." Even more alarmingly, "revolvers were fired from neighboring windows."[34] The cause of the "affray" appeared to be Chinese politics—"a discussion between a number of Chinese on the state of affairs in their country," the story ran, "led to an exchange of blows, some of the men being in favour of a Republic and the others of the old *regime*."[35]

Subsequent reports in both the *Times* and local East End papers attributed the continuing outbreaks to more sinister causes. According to an extensive report in the *East End News*, the Chinese had been fighting not over politics but over the control of gambling in Chinatown by a secret society called the "White Lily." [36] White Lily members, the report claimed, had suspected that another prominent Chinese resident had been working as an informant for the local police. The alleged informant had been under particular scrutiny by his rivals because his wife's sister was the husband of a well-known police officer. It was only timely intervention by the police, who had been forewarned, that had prevented even more serious violence. A second, graver incident occurred on April 18, when two large groups of opposing Chinese men, armed with hammers and iron bars, came to blows in the West India Dock Road. Mass arrests followed, likely exacerbated by the inability of police to distinguish between individual Chinese men.[37] Thirty constables were required to restore order and the case was serious enough to attract the personal attention of the Commissioner of the Metropolitan Police, Sir Edward Henry.

Not satisfied with charges of assault against the combatants, Henry had the suspects committed for trial on charges of being engaged in a common affray. When the initial case was heard in court, Detective-Inspector Saunders, the prosecuting officer, justified the escalation of the charges by referring to the supposed involvement of the White Lily.[38] Chinese combatants' use of "traditional" weapons such as battle axes and iron bars swathed in red cloth, along with past connections between the White Lily, the "Triads," and the Boxer Rebellion, provided further reason for judicial authorities, newspaper reporters, and readers alike to view the events of May as having arisen out of something more menacing than mere local rivalries.[39] Newspaper coverage drew on the threat of Chinese internationalism to emphasize the ominous implications of the violence. Like Joseph Havelock Wilson in his speeches of 1908–10, local press reports portrayed the White Lily incidents in the context of the broader threat represented by Chinese emigration around the globe. The communities of Chinese in Britain, the *East End News* asserted, maintained strong ties to the home country, and this coherent network of communication and coordinated action left little hope for their enemies. According to their coverage, the secret society "extends over the whole of China, and wherever Chinamen may settle there will be found members of the same, and one of the roles of 'The White Lily' is that whenever a certain course of action is decided upon against an individual or individuals, there is no rest or peace for those upon whom has devolved the order to carry into effect the edict issued. In strength the 'White Lily' Society is said to far exceed that of the Masonic Order the world over."[40] Whatever truth may or may not have lain behind the tales of the White Lily, its relation to the Boxer Rebellion, and its other sinister activities, the prominent discussions of it in relation to outbreaks of violence in Chinatown provided judicial officials with strong justification for the harsh treatment of Chinese defendants and London newspaper readers with a sinister frame of reference.[41]

The primary concern of East End judicial authorities was to restore public order and to prevent white residents from coming to any harm. Thames Police Court magistrate John Dickinson made it clear at the conclusion of one trial of eleven Chinese defendants that "he was not so much concerned for the antagonists' welfare as for the public, who went about risking a crack on the head with a hatchet."[42] Despite Dickinson's expressions of concern, however, not a single white bystander had been injured in the April incidents, nor had any of the police who intervened been hurt. The other residents of Poplar and Stepney seemed to view the conflict in Chinatown more as entertainment than as hazard. Following the April 13 violence, hundreds of curious onlookers ventured to Pennyfields and Limehouse Causeway, "anticipating further street scenes."[43] If they were hoping for a glimpse of "East End Warfare," as the *East London Advertiser* dubbed the events of April, they were disappointed, since "the Chinamen remained peaceful, having apparently a very wholesome respect for the strong body of police present, ready to deal with them should they run riot again."[44]

It was the Chinese residents themselves who took the first steps toward a permanent resolution of the conflict. On May 4, the *Advertiser* reported that "the leaders of each party had met and agreed that no further attacks should be made."[45] Although judicial and police authorities were cautiously optimistic about this reconciliation, which accompanied the cessation of violence on the Limehouse streets, this alone was not enough. For police and magistrates, the only sure solution to the problems posed by "the turbulent Chinese" was their expulsion.[46] With dozens of Chinese men in jail and many more awaiting trial, Commissioner Henry declared he would forego any further incarcerations if those charged would agree to leave the country immediately, and he encouraged Dickinson to adopt a similar stance.[47] The magistrate obligingly bound over the remaining defendants to keep the peace on the promise that they would soon follow their fellow countrymen to sea. Dickinson's sentences, handed down at the encouragement of the police commissioner, amounted to de facto deportation orders. Unlike a formal recommendation for deportation, which had to receive approval from the Home Office and was only permissible in cases where an "undesirable alien" had been sentenced to imprisonment with no option of a fine, such measures could be taken quickly and without further appeal to higher authority.[48]

Formal deportation was an uncommon practice in prewar Britain, and in 1912, it was employed only a handful of times.[49] Such incidents often evoked considerable commentary in the national press, but barely a murmur was raised when Dickinson and Henry, with little fanfare, forced more than two dozen Chinese residents to leave the country.[50] The practice of summarily expelling Chinese seamen from Britain dated back to 1878, when Montagu Williams (who later became a London police court magistrate), in his capacity as defense counsel for thirteen Chinese defendants being tried for assault in the Old Bailey, recommended it as an alternative to imprisonment. [51] If the 1912 expulsions had been included among the official figures of formal deportations of "criminal aliens" calculated earlier in April, the Chinese would have represented roughly 10 percent of all such deportations executed in the metropolis (254) and roughly 6 percent of those in England, Wales, and Scotland overall (380).[52] Considering the miniscule proportion of the metropolitan and national populations that the Chinese comprised, this made them, per capita, the single most deported cohort in Britain that year. The high proportion of itinerant seamen among the Chinese population, however, makes it probable that at least some of those forced to depart were temporary residents who would likely have shipped out voluntarily in the future.[53]

In the decisions of Sir Edward Henry, the police administrator who urged Dickinson to deport the Chinese defendants, we once again see the impact of the imperial context on the dynamics of race and law in the metropolis. Henry was a vector not only for racial attitudes from the empire but also of concrete methods of identification and classification inspired by racial difference and employed as a form of racial control abroad. He had formed his conceptions of the relationship between Britons, Asians, and Africans not in Britain itself but in imperial posts in Bengal and the Transvaal, where a small number of white officials held authority over vast colonial populations. The underlying colonial ideology in both locales held that British legal authority was a boon to colonized peoples and that Chinese, Indians, and Africans were prone to deception and disorder. In such circumstances, controlling the mobility of the native population and the migration of "habitual criminals" in particular were essential considerations.[54]

In response to these issues in India, South Africa, and, later, in Britain, Henry pioneered the introduction of fingerprinting as a means of identifying and regulating colonial laborers, immigrants, and criminals. Henry had first been introduced to the practical application of fingerprinting during his service in India. Sir William Herschel, a prominent British magistrate in Bengal, employed a primitive version of it to prevent wage fraud among Indian laborers, whom British officials had trouble distinguishing from one another.[55] Following the adoption of fingerprinting as a system of identification throughout India in 1897, Henry introduced it to the Transvaal when he was posted there to reorganize the civil police force in the wake of the Boer War.[56] According to his biographer, Henry found that fingerprinting enhanced the effectiveness of the "pass" system then in use to monitor and regulate the movement of African laborers.[57] Subsequently, fingerprinting was adopted in Natal and the Cape Colony as a method for tracking and restricting Chinese immigration, and in the Transvaal itself to identify Chinese indentured laborers and to prevent wage fraud, much as it had been used in Bengal by Herschel.[58] By the end of the decade, a similar system was also in use to monitor and restrict Chinese immigration to Australia.[59]

Although fingerprinting was rapidly adopted for use in the empire as a method of labor control, immigration restriction, and criminal identification, when Henry returned to take a post at Scotland Yard in 1901, he encountered much greater resistance to its adoption in Britain itself—what was appropriate for use in the regulation and identification of Asians and Africans was deemed unfit, by some, for employment in a domestic context.[60] Eventually, these objections were overcome, and Scotland Yard adopted fingerprinting as the standard method of criminal identification. The negative connotations of using the same method to identify and regulate both Chinese immigrants and criminals, however, were not lost on Chinese residents themselves in South Africa. Many objected strongly to the Asiatic Law Amendment Act (1907) and to the Immigrants Restriction Act (1907), which required them to submit to identification and registration protocols that white residents were spared. When Chinese protesters, along with Mohandas K. Gandhi and other members of the South African Indian community, mounted a campaign of passive resistance from 1907–11, hundreds of them were arrested and imprisoned and scores were deported.[61]

The Chinese residents of London in 1912, however, were a much smaller community and had neither the means nor the support to mount organized resistance against the sentences handed down by Dickinson and Henry. With Henry's unofficial expulsion of many of those involved, "the Trouble in Limehouse Chinatown," as the *East End News* later dubbed it, had been resolved to the relative satisfaction of the London police and judiciary.[62] But this calm was merely a façade, the paper's report continued, and grave doubts still lingered as to whether the Chinese could peacefully reside cheek-to-jowl with white residents in the metropolis. The police must remain ever vigilant, because the White Lilies were only in abeyance, and there were ominous signs that they would soon return, more deadly than ever. "Recently, quite a number of Chinamen have been purchasing firearms," the *News* reported, "and they have been heard inquiring in local Post Offices if they can be supplied with a license 'for pistol.' The 'Lilies,' apparently, even though at peace, are not quite so white as they are being painted."[63]

The Chinese perspective on the White Lily affair is exceedingly difficult to establish, but the behavior of the Chinese men involved provides some insight into their relationships with one another and with the East End police and judicial authorities. It is clear that the

Chinese community preferred to solve their conflicts privately and did not voluntarily seek the interference of East End officials. The Chinese aversion to official intervention and the highly specific nature of their violence was further demonstrated by their conduct during the event itself. Despite the reported presence of battle-axes, knives, iron bars, and revolvers, there was only one injury inflicted upon another Chinese man that was serious enough to require hospitalization, and no police or bystanders were injured at all. The London magistrate H. L. Cancellor would later describe the restraint of Chinese men in this regard as the "most striking" feature of violence among them. "Although the Metropolitan Police interfered with a crowd of infuriated Asiatics at the risk of their lives," he wrote in his memoirs, "members of the force hardly got a scratch or slight wound in the execution of their duty."[64] For Cancellor, however, such moderation by the Chinese was simply further evidence of their cunning nature and served as apt proof of the widely held opinion that "the Heathen Chinee knows a thing or two."

If the Chinese wished to avoid entanglements with the police or local magistrates, why had they attacked one another in the first place? One clue lies in the *News*'s report that one of those involved in the affair, probably the lodging-house keeper that was the victim of the initial assault, had married into the family of a prominent local police officer. That relationship, in conjunction with the earlier raid and subsequent arrests of Chinese men running a local gambling parlor, served as the initial catalyst of the April violence. Another possible cause of the conflict lies in the diversity of London's Chinese population itself. Contrary to popular belief at the time, London's Chinatown was not a single, culturally unified community but one characterized by "marked sectarian dividing lines" between the residents living west of the West India Dock Road and those living east of it.[65] Oral history sources have confirmed that Limehouse Causeway was settled mostly by Cantonese immigrants (especially those of Hong Kong origin), while in Pennyfields, Chinese residents were predominantly from Shanghai.[66] The Liverpool Chinese community, which newspaper reports claimed had also contributed to the disorder, similarly included members from both Hong Kong and Shanghai.[67] This division provides another potential explanation for the competition and occasional incidents of public disorder, but it was not one entertained by police or judicial authorities at the time. For them, as we have seen, a Chinaman was a Chinaman, and whether he lived in the East End or the Far East, he represented a menace to white communities, a menace that had to be addressed with the sternest possible measures. The tendency of journalists and other commentators to conflate the

Chee Kong Tong (Chinese Freemasons) benevolent society with the violent criminal "Tong" gangs reported to be active in New York and San Francisco only blurred the issue further.[68] Despite the absence of any fatalities, the relative ease with which the violence had been contained, and the lack of any tangible connection between the disruptions in London and the internecine Chinese violence in U.S. cities, the "trouble in Limehouse Chinatown" would be remembered for decades afterwards as London's "Tong" feuds.[69]

"The Awakening of the Vast Mongolian Empire": Interracial Contact and International Conspiracies in London and the Empire

The White Lily incidents had brought the threat of Chinese residents to the attention of the metropolitan police and magistrates, provoking a swift and severe response. The 1911 strike and accompanying demonstrations and riots had similarly heightened public awareness of the small Chinese population that had resided in Britain, mostly unmolested, for decades. The Chinese Revolution of 1911 had also drawn the notice of the British press and reading public to events in China itself. In particular, the modernization of the Chinese Army (symbolized by the cutting off of soldiers' queues) and the growing popularity of Western political ideas fostered fears that China, like Japan, might soon challenge European hegemony in Asia.[70] The constant reiteration by journalists, politicians, police officials, and union leaders that the British Chinese community was firmly connected to Chinese residents worldwide made Anglo-Chinese tensions abroad more relevant than ever to the domestic context and lent sinister overtones to the stories of violence and immorality emerging from London's Chinatown. As a result, London newspapers began to devote more time to reporting on the district and their articles disseminated negative Chinese stereotypes to an ever wider readership.

In the summer of 1911, the *London Magazine*, a popular publication whose focus was on arts, culture, and general interest stories, printed the first major exposé on the Chinese community in Britain. The paper was owned by the British newspaper moguls Alfred C. W. Harmsworth and Harold Harmsworth, whose launching of the *Daily Mail* in 1896, a pro-empire daily aimed at a lower-middle-class and suburban readership, had helped introduce the "New Journalism" to Britain.[71] To an audience whose interest in Britain's Chinese residents had been galvanized in part by the recent riots and in part by the tumultuous political events in China, the *London Magazine* articles replicated all the stereotypes that the Australian and South African debates had propagated, but transplanted their significance onto the Chinese population of Britain itself. The author, Herman Scheffauer, had formed his own opinions of the Chinese in his hometown of San Francisco, where, according to the editorial introduction, he had "studied the yellow problem for years."[72]

Scheffauer, who tailored his articles for a readership that would have included few working-class members, downplayed the labor issue in favor of warnings about Chinese immorality and race mixing, and of dire premonitions of "a vast and convulsive Armageddon to determine who is to be the master of the world, the white or yellow man."[73] The greatest immediate hazard, he insisted, was the intermarriage between English and "Mongolians," which posed "a danger to the purity of the Anglo-Saxon blood."[74] Chinese men held an "inscrutable, irresistible lure" for white women, and the "exotic charm" of the Chinese overcame white women's "instinctive repugnance to a race of alien blood and colour" (Figure 3.3).[75] "The awakening of the vast Mongolian Empire" and the looming worldwide conflict between races posed an even greater threat. If drastic steps were not taken, Scheffauer warned, East End scenes of "slant-eyed cabin-boys, triumphantly smiling, [having] their boots blackened by white men" foreshadowed the future domination of "white" by "yellow."[76] China was "a nation teeming with vitality . . . slowly modernized, then suddenly eager for expansion, perhaps for conquest, for world-power, if not for revenge for wrongs inflicted upon it by nearly every European power."[77]

The Chinese community of London was allegedly at the center of these momentous developments. "In this room off of the dark little courts among the London Docks," Scheffauer wrote, "the future of the colossal Mongolian Empire is discussed, measures and resolutions adopted, and conspiracies arranged by these humble Chinese democrats in touch with the exiled brethren in Singapore, Australia, America and Japan."[78] Building upon his portrayal of Chinese homes and businesses as places where dark plots were hatched, the author directed his harshest opprobrium not at itinerant seamen but instead at the owners of Chinese laundries and at other permanent, property-holding Chinese residents. According to him, Chinese laundries were the most common locales for unsavory assignations between Chinese men and young English girls, Chinese men used their wealth to tempt young working-class girls into such unions, and the shops and homes

Figure 3.3. *In the Lamplight.* "In the street, a strange pair of lovers halt and whisper beside a lamppost. The man is a bland, furtive-eyed young Chinese, his companion, a pretty, well-dressed English girl who lifts a pair of large and insolent blue eyes as I pass. A Constable approaches and the couple vanish into a house that is as dark and silent as a tomb." (Herman Scheffauer, "The Chinese in England: A Growing National Problem," *London Magazine*, June 1911.)

owned by Chinese men hosted all manner of immoral activities, from international conspiracies to gambling and opium smoking.

Scheffauer also expressed undiluted scorn for Chinese men who tried to assimilate by adopting Western customs and clothing or by making false conversions to Christianity. Such efforts were, at best, a vain attempt to resolve irreconcilable differences between two utterly incompatible races and, at worst, a cunning plot to learn the ways and weaknesses of the West for use in the looming global conflict between "white" and "yellow." [79] Ultimately, according to the author, "Saint George" had to be prepared to defend himself against "the tenacious Chinese dragon" that had made for itself "three comfortable lairs" in London, Liverpool, and Cardiff.[80] A peaceful coexistence between the two races was impossible, but given the inevitability of racial conflict, white Britons had two powerful weapons available to confront the growing Yellow Peril in Britain. The first was their imperial experience and the "vast knowledge" that they had acquired of "other tribes, peoples, and races" during the process of colonization, and the second was the law.[81] Imperial race relations were the best guide to understanding domestic race issues, Scheffauer argued, and law was the most potent tool available to address them. In particular, he advocated a law "forbidding the intermarriage of whites and Asiatics" in order to deal with the "abominations" of mixed-race unions and proposed stern application of the Aliens Act of 1905 to prevent Chinese immigration to Britain.[82] He also spoke supportively of a Liverpool MP's stated intention to introduce a bill "for the deportation of all Chinese in England."

Home Office officials thought Scheffauer's articles significant enough to distribute them among various parties interested in the issue and to file them with other official reports relating to Chinese residents in Britain. But there was still no consensus in British government circles or among officials in London that Chinese immigrants posed any measurable threat to white Britons. In early 1911, the headmistress of one London County Council school filed a report attesting to "the deplorable state of things between Chinamen and young girls who had just left school."[83] According to the correspondent, Miss Robinson, affluent Chinese men were corrupting former students from her school, using wealth and opium to seduce them. A report from an inspector of the Public Control Department, however, contradicted Robinson's report on almost every count. According to Inspector McIntyre, intimate relationships between Chinese men and white women generally led to marriage, not prostitution, and currently there were only fifteen interracial married couples in

Limehouse. White women had no contact with opium, Macintyre further argued, and he sharply dismissed Robinson's assertions that parents accepted remuneration from wealthy Chinese men in return for allowing their daughters to frequent opium dens. On the contrary, he insisted, "there are no opium dens in London." Both Macintyre and Sir John Pedder, the senior Home Office official who reviewed both reports, were distressed by the mixed-race unions taking place in the East End. But they concluded that although it was certainly "undesirable" that white women consorted with or married Chinese men, the men in question generally treated them well and no laws were being broken.

In the empire, on the other hand, tensions between Chinese and white residents, particularly over labor competition and the supposed hazards of association between Chinese men and white women, continued to mount. With the issue of Chinese immigration temporarily resolved in Australia and South Africa through increased legal restrictions, Canada became the focal point of anti-Chinese agitation in the empire. There, the demand for cheap labor had fostered substantial Chinese immigration and a subsequent rise in tensions between them and white residents. The Chinese had initially come to the province of British Columbia in the late 1850s when the discovery of gold there, and the growing anti-Chinese sentiment in California, had made immigration to Canadian territory an appealing prospect. Thousands more had begun arriving there in the early 1880s in order to work on the Canadian Pacific Railway. By the mid-1880s, the Chinese population of British Columbia had grown to over 4,000 and comprised nearly 10 percent of the overall population of the province.[84]

With the completion of the Canadian Pacific Railway and the subsequent decline in the demand for Chinese labor, public pressure mounted against further immigration. In response, the Canadian government enacted the Chinese Immigration Act of 1885, which imposed, along with other restrictions, a head tax of $50 on any Chinese person wishing to enter the country. Although this measure initially slowed immigration, the respite was temporary, and by 1901, the Chinese population of Canada had grown to nearly 16,000. The vast majority lived in British Columbia, which was estimated to have a Chinese population of 14,376, with particular concentrations in the cities of Victoria (2,715), Vancouver (2,011), and New Westminster (738).[85] Canada also had a significant population of Japanese residents, and estimates numbered this latter group at around 6,000 individuals. The social and cultural incompatibility of white and Asian residents was a perennial issue in both the Canadian press and official government reports on immigration. In the Report of the Royal Commission on Chinese and Japanese Immigration, first published in 1901, the Chinese and Japanese were sharply criticized for their failure to assimilate with the white population, but the report's authors indicated that this was a more serious problem with the former than it was with the latter.[86] As had been the case in Australia and South Africa, hostility against the Chinese in British Columbia was strongest among labor interests, who argued both that Chinese workers would undercut wages and that they would threaten the racial hegemony of whites in the territory. Opposition voiced by prominent politicians and labor leaders prompted a series of head taxes to restrict Chinese immigration. In the years that followed, however, the demand for labor in the mining and lumber industries drove wages so high that immigration remained an attractive option for Chinese men. They were also much in demand as domestic servants in the cities of western Canada, where, according to a *Times* correspondent, "the Chinaman is declared to be industrious, sober, peaceable, law-abiding, and strictly honest. He will take over the conduct of the house and fulfil [*sic*] his duties to the complete satisfaction of his employer."[87]

The combination of legal restriction, racial prejudice, and labor opposition made it all but impossible for Chinese residents of Canada to assimilate with the white population or to establish family households of their own. On the one hand, the head tax discouraged them from bringing their wives and children with them as they sought to make their fortunes in "Gaan Sam" ("Gold Mountain"), the name Chinese immigrant workers, or "sojourners," commonly used to refer to the western United States and Canada.[88] Once resident in Canada, however, Chinese men were subjected to suspicion and criticism for their lack of the quotidian domestic ties that were so central to Victorian male identity. Sensationalized newspaper reports and popular pamphlets worsened public hostility toward the Chinese by emphasizing their corrupting influence on young white girls, whom they supposedly led into prostitution, and by claiming that the Chinese spread disease through the unsanitary conditions of their laundries and restaurants. The author of one particularly vituperative tract, *The Oriental Canker in Canada* (1912), demanded not only the prohibition of all further Chinese immigration but also the immediate adoption of laws that forbade interracial marriage, banned Chinese employment of white women, and segregated the Chinese population into designated districts in the towns and cities where they resided.[89]

Responding to popular hostility toward interracial sexuality and the employment of white women by Chinese business owners, Canadian provincial legislatures began to take matters into their own hands. In 1912, the Saskatchewan legislature passed a law that expressly forbid white women or girls from working in any "business or amusement, owned, kept, or managed by any Japanese, Chinaman, or other Oriental person."[90] In Vancouver, which had been the center of anti-Chinese sentiment in Canada since the early 1870s, when motions for restrictions against Chinese immigration had first been proposed in the province's legislative assembly, incidents of racial violence were not uncommon.[91] Serious anti-Asian rioting had broken out in the city in 1907, with a mob of several thousand whites attacking Chinese and Japanese businesses. Anti-Chinese sentiment there in the prewar period reached a crescendo in April 1914, when the disappearance of the wife of a prominent railway official prompted a grisly discovery. Police bloodhounds, searching the house of Charles Millard, the chief ticket agent of the Canadian Pacific Railway, had led officers to the basement of the home. There, they found the remains of a body that had been "hacked to pieces and burned in a furnace."[92] The jewelry found amid the "charred bones" in the ashes allowed police to identify the victim as Millard's wife. The police subsequently detained Jack Kong, the household's seventeen-year-old Chinese domestic, who soon confessed to the murder, claiming that it had been the unpremeditated result of an argument between him and his employer over breakfast.[93]

The Chinese community in Vancouver responded swiftly to Kong's confession, "expressing sympathy with Mr. Millard and asserting their earnest desire that the murderer may be punished," but this did little to quell popular fury. The reports of Millard's murder and Kong's confession again sparked serious anti-Chinese disturbances in the city, disturbances that rapidly spread from Vancouver to other cities and towns in British Columbia. Chinese people were assaulted and hotels and restaurant managers were warned (reports did not specify by whom) to fire their Chinese waiters or risk losing customers.[94] Not surprisingly, many private households that employed Chinese men as servants released them from service. Newspapers in Canada, the United States, and Britain reported on the Millard murder and the subsequent rioting. It was the only murder in Canada covered that year by the *Times*, which labeled the crime "the most revolting in the history of the province."[95] The paper followed its coverage of Kong's confession in court with several long articles on the general hostility of "Europeans" against "Asiatics" in Canada, focusing on labor opposition, racial violence, and the attempts to limit Chinese immigration through law.[96]

But the most shocking revelation came on April 13, three days after the *Times* reported that forces led by "White Wolf" had sacked several Chinese cities, killing hundreds in the process. White Wolf was a former Chinese military commander turned bandit that the *Times* had labeled the worst "scourge . . . let loose on China since the days of the Taipings."[97] By March 1914, his exploits in the Chinese provinces of Henan and Anhui had attracted international attention and had caused a minor sensation in the British press, but there had been little to connect his campaign of pillage and destruction with the Chinese communities in the British Empire.[98] On April 13, however, the official investigation of the Millard murder revealed "the existence of an active revolutionary society among the Chinese in Vancouver and B.C."[99] The Vancouver police suspected that Kong was a member of this secret society and that he "had been stealing regularly to get money to send to the Chinese brigand White Wolf." As the police inquiry broadened to include the activities of this secret society, they claimed to have uncovered a conspiracy linking the Chinese population of Vancouver to White Wolf via the shipping lines that ran between British Columbia and Hong Kong. Along this route, the police asserted, "the Chinese of Vancouver and Victoria dispatched . . . a shipment of rifles and revolvers valued at £800." The Chinese authorities had learned of the shipment, but were too late to stop it from continuing toward its destination "in the interior." Millard's murder and Kong's arrest had in no way deterred the Chinese from their activities, the police claimed, as "the society of which the confessed murdered is a member are [*sic*] arranging to send another shipment of arms to White Wolf."

The decision by the editors of the *Times* to cover the Millard murder, alone among all murders in Canada that year (in 1914, there were sixty-one other murder trials and thirty convictions), attested to the story's interest for a domestic audience.[100] The vilification of Jack Kong was not an isolated incident but part of a broader culture of sexualized Chinese villainy that was growing in popularity among British readers, as I discuss later in the chapter.[101] The concerns raised by the Millard murder and the alleged White Wolf connection also foreshadowed what would become central issues for London judicial authorities and national policymakers in their dealings with Britain's Chinese residents in the years that followed. If violence could travel from China into a Vancouver home, where could it appear next? If the disparate communities of Chinese living among white Britons were still bound to one another and to China through nefarious ties, could any Chinese person anywhere ever be trusted? And finally, could Chinese men ever coexist safely and peacefully with white Britons, and with white women in particular? The members of British Columbia's provincial legislature did not think so—using the Millard murder as a justification, they outlawed the employment of white women by "Oriental" businessmen.[102] The legal and discursive bind faced by Chinese men in Canada, where they were prevented from importing their families, faced hostility from legal authorities over any close associations with white women, and were then criticized for their failure to establish a moral domestic environment, would also be reflected in the circumstances confronting the London Chinese community in the interwar period. By then, popular prejudice and judicial opposition to interracial sexuality would make romantic unions with the local white populace—a key avenue to social and cultural assimilation—highly problematic.

"The Yellow Peril Incarnate in One Man": Chinese Villains in London Literature and Theater

The 1911 seamen's strike, the "White Lily" violence, political disorder in China, and racial tension and violence in Canada all contributed to the growing concern that the Chinese in Britain were a threat to their white neighbors. Negative stereotypes that had previously been popularized in Australia, South Africa, and Canada, all of which held exponentially larger numbers of Chinese residents than Britain did, held increasing resonance in Britain itself. This was in part because public discourse almost invariably linked the British Chinese community, through clandestine channels, to an alleged global Chinese conspiracy. A sense of mutual suspicion was also growing between Chinese residents and the Metropolitan Police, the latter under the command of a commissioner who had pioneered methods of racial identification and monitoring in the empire. Although no consensus on the matter had yet been reached among Home Office officials, London magistrates, at least, had demonstrated their willingness to deport Chinese seamen for internecine violence and disruptions of public order.

It was in theater and popular fiction, however, that the most negative depictions of the Chinese and the most frightening portrayals of the threat they posed to white Britons were to be found. The growing public concern over the Chinese, events in China, and the affairs of Limehouse Chinatown created a receptive audience for the introduction of the cunning Chinese master-villain into British literature and drama. This figure of racial menace had already been an important aspect of fiction, cartoons, and sensationalized journalism in Australia, Canada, and the United States, but it was not until the events of the prewar years drew public attention to the Chinese community in Britain itself that the image became popular in the domestic context.

First introduced to Britain at the end of the nineteenth century in M. P. Shiel's novel *The Yellow Danger* (1898), the next popular iteration of the Chinese master-villain was in *Mr. Wu*, an "Anglo-Chinese Play" by Maurice Vernon and Harold Owen. *Mr. Wu* opened on the Strand in November 1913, with the well-known stage actress Lillian Braithwaite in the leading female role of Mrs. Gregory, and the Canadian-born Shakespearean actor Matheson Lang playing the title character. The figure of Mr. Wu blended elements of West and East into a potent and dangerous mix, creating "an uncanny blend of Oriental ferocity and Western culture."[103] The writers demonstrated an awareness of political events in China by presenting modernized Chinese characters without their traditional queues, "a first for Chinese plays in London," the *Times* reported. The play revolved around the relationship between two families in Hong Kong, one Chinese and one English, and the dangers of sexual contact between races. The blossoming affair between Nan Ping, daughter of the powerful mandarin Wu Li Chang, and Basil Gregory, the son of a British steamship company owner, formed the central plot of the play. Wu learns of the affair, has his own daughter put to death for her dishonor, and holds her erstwhile lover captive. He then cunningly foils an attempt by Basil's father to coerce him into releasing his son and demands an audience with the boy's mother instead. When Mrs. Gregory visits his home, the truly diabolical nature of Wu's plot is revealed as he promises the mother her son's freedom only if she will consent to have sexual relations with him. Just as Basil dishonored Wu's daughter, so must Mrs. Gregory dishonor herself to save him. For all Wu's culture and intelligence—the play reveals that he studied at Oxford before returning to China to take up a prestigious official appointment—the character is defined primarily by his calm, amoral cunning and by his lust for Mrs. Gregory. The writers and actors were highly successful in portraying this latter inclination as loathsome and repellant. The "amorous" encounter at the play's climax, which lasts a quarter of an hour, was so well executed, according to one reviewer, that watching it "makes your gorge rise—which is of course just the effect desired."[104] Ultimately, Wu's own romantic gestures are his undoing. When he insists on sharing a cup with Mrs. Gregory, he unwittingly drinks the poison she had intended for herself, and after "horrible contortions," he falls dead. The message of the play was clear—Chinese men may have learned the English language and, in some cases, adopted Western ways, but such contact had not moderated their character one whit. Beneath the guise of culture and civility, they remained both brutal and amoral. In such circumstances, sexual contact between Britons and Chinese could only lead to tragedy for all involved. For a white woman facing such a terrible fate, death was preferable to defilement.

Mr. Wu was set in China, not Chinatown, and its portrayal of interracial sexuality as an urgent issue outside of England (rather than within it) was replicated in the attitudes of most British officials at the time, as was clear in the tepid Home Office response to Miss Robinson's accusations against the Chinese residents of Limehouse. But the same year that *Mr. Wu* opened also witnessed the first publication of a best-selling novel that, like Scheffauer's articles, located the center of the Yellow Peril in Limehouse itself. In the summer of 1913, the first of Sax Rohmer's "Fu Manchu" novels, *The Mystery of Dr. Fu Manchu*, was published in Britain, the United States, and Canada (in the latter two markets as *The Insidious Dr. Fu Manchu*).[105] The novel had already been serialized in *Collier's Weekly* magazine beginning in 1912, and the popularity of the stories had prompted their reissue as a novel. Rohmer's novels built on preexisting trends of racial anxiety about the Chinese in London, but also helped to strengthen and refine them in British culture. Fu Manchu, the primary villain, embodied all the negative stereotypes that had already appeared in parliamentary debates, statements by British officials, newspaper reports, and popular culture dealing with Chinese communities in Australia, South Africa, Canada, and the United States. The Chinese villain's most deadly characteristics were, on the one hand, his cunning, and, on the other, his international connections, particularly with China itself. It was these two features, the "cruel cunning of an entire Eastern Race" combined with "all the resources . . . of a wealthy government," that made Fu Manchu such a dire threat to the West.[106]

Fu Manchu represented the global racial threat of a resurgent China—references to Fu Manchu's "web" and the evocation of an octopus whose "tentacles" extended across the globe highlighted the internationalism that was often emphasized by observers in Britain and the empire as the most frightening aspect of the Chinese menace (see Fig. 3.4).[107] But reflecting the increasing focus of press, law, and official attention on the Chinese population of Britain itself, Fu Manchu masterminded his sinister plots from London's Chinatown. From within the very heart of the East End, he orchestrated a secret plot to overthrow the British government. Rohmer's villain, who would be endlessly reproduced in books, on radio shows, and in the newest medium of popular entertainment—the cinema—was truly "the yellow peril incarnate in one man."[108] Fu Manchu was also, quite explicitly, a product of political turmoil and modernization that China was experiencing. His powers were both mystical and scientific, and his merging of the methods of "modernity"—science, technology, and rationalism—with "Oriental cunning" in his project to dominate the West seemed to herald the decline of British power in Asia and to reveal the failures of modernism itself.[109] In Rohmer's writing, a healthy assimilation of the two cultures is impossible. Britons seeking knowledge of the of the Chinese find only death, while Chinese men who acquire knowledge of the West use it only as a weapon in their ongoing racial struggle against Europeans.[110]

The assessments of the Chinese threat in Rohmer's work were, like the portrayals of the Chinese immigrants found in the British press, more revealing about the character of white Britons' racial anxieties than they were about the Chinese, their culture, or their intentions toward Britain and its residents. In contrast to the multiple murders attributed to Fu Manchu in the first novel, for example, the only actual "Chinese" murder in London up until 1913 had been *of* a Chinese man by European sailors, and the only other violence had been *between* Chinese men and had been nonfatal. Rohmer himself admitted that it was his ability to tap into the popular apprehension over the Chinese in Britain, the timing of his novel's release to coincide with violent racial disturbances involving Chinese residents in London and in the United States, and the recent political upheaval in China that had made "conditions for launching a Chinese villain on the market . . . ideal."[111] His knowledge of China and the Chinese themselves, he readily confessed, was minimal.[112] Rohmer's lack of knowledge on these subjects, which was mirrored in the ignorance of his readership, made the Chinese a perfect canvas onto which the racial anxieties of prewar Britons could be painted.

The correlation between Rohmer's depictions of Chinese villainy and the progress of anti-Chinese discourse in press and law was hardly coincidental, since Rohmer began his writing career as a journalist and maintained strong ties with the Metropolitan Police and with the British government—he would work for British military intelligence during World War I—throughout his career as a novelist. His repeated assertions that the threat of the Chinese to British society was genuine, whether they were heartfelt beliefs or merely shrewd marketing tactics, further enhanced his fiction's capacity to frighten and shock readers.[113] His villains, though sensationalized, were sometimes drawn directly from police reports on the Chinese residents of Limehouse, and Rohmer used his background in journalism to intentionally blur the boundary between "nightmare and news story."[114] His journalistic explorations of Chinatown and his relationship with the police, which developed during the period of sporadic racial violence in the prewar period, provided the source material from which the plots and characters of his novels later emerged. The origins of Fu Manchu lay in a newspaper editor's assignment to Rohmer to seek out the elusive figure of "Mr. King—vaguely referred to as 'a Chinese master criminal' backed by 'a syndicate.'"[115] As Rohmer explained in an interview with Cay Van Ash, who would later write the author's biography: "The idea [of Fu Manchu] took shape gradually, as I realized that what was happening in Limehouse was happening likewise in the Chinese communities of foreign cities throughout the world. To the Asiatic mind, our conception of humanity in terms of individuals is an absurdity. We were fighting against crime organized not even into gangs but into guilds—guilds which were international! Mr. King ran *pakapu* [i.e., gambling] in Limehouse on a financial backing in Canton."[116] These purported connections, via a worldwide criminal network, between the relatively small Chinese community in London and China itself further invested London's Chinatown and its residents with a terrible menace. "Falling afoul of these people," Rohmer explained, "a man could be murdered in London on a directive issued in New York! And his murder would be the more difficulty to solve, since nobody in the vicinity would have had any ostensible motive for killing him."[117] This electric combination of journalistic style, real-world locations, and global racial terror would fascinate legions of devoted readers, including U.S. President Calvin Coolidge, who was reportedly so engrossed by the Fu Manchu stories appearing in *Collier's* that he would regularly send a White House messenger to get advance copies from a newsstand on Pennsylvania Avenue.[118]

Rohmer also found another way to make the small number of Chinese residents in Britain, a group that had committed very few violent acts against white Britons, disproportionately terrifying to readers. Their relative peacefulness and negligible size supposedly masked a terrifying omnipresence and a murderous intent, as Nayland Smith, the former Burmese colonial official who was the hero of the first novel, explained to Dr. Petrie, the narrator: "We mark such and such a man as one alive to the Yellow Peril and we warn him—if we have time. Perhaps he escapes; perhaps he does not. But what do we know, Petrie, of those others who may die every week by his murderous agency? We cannot know *every one* who had read the riddle of China. I never see a report of someone found drowned, of an apparent suicide, of a sudden, though seemingly natural, death, without wondering. I tell you, Fu Manchu is omnipresent; his tentacles embrace everything."[119] The agents of the Yellow Peril in Britain were invisible because they wished to be, the narrator asserted, and it was this false sense of security that made the West so terribly vulnerable to the designs of "Secret China." In such circumstances, racial paranoia was entirely justified. Even in the idyllic English countryside, to Dr. Petrie, "every shadow [held] fantastic horrors . . . every sound [was] a signal of dread."[120] This sense of menace was amplified in London, a city that was characterized in Rohmer's writing by its dark spaces and hidden cellars and made exotic by the presence of many races and many cultures. It was a place that, like the Chinese themselves, was both unknown and unknowable.[121] With its reputation for crime and violence, London's East End hardly needed to be transformed into a place of dread for many readers, but Rohmer was the first to suggest that its tiny Chinese population was its most frightening aspect. The background of Anglo-Saxonism, Chinese membership in "secret societies" like the White Lily or Tongs, and the debates over Chinese communities in the empire were all essential in this regard, since they supported the assertion that Chinese immigrants were dangerous for the vast racial menace that they *represented*, regardless of their actual numbers in any given locale. Although the Fu Manchu mythos built on Victorian portrayals of both the "alien enchanter" and the sexual villainy and moral menace of the East End, its unique power lay in this relation of an imaginary villain to the tangible threat of the "Asian horde."[122]

Fu Manchu was violent and cunning, unreadable and unknowable, and effeminate, but surrounded by beautiful women.[123] He was, in short, the polar opposite of the masculine, forthright, virtuous ideal of the Victorian imperial men arrayed against him. Each of these protagonists mirrored the attitudes taken by the London press, judicial officials, and labor leaders in this period, all of whom had portrayed the battle against Chinese villainy as part of a global racial conflict between Europeans and Asians. For Rohmer's heroes, the fight against Fu Manchu was a "struggle with the titanic genius whose victory meant the victory of the yellow races over the white."[124] Another clear example of how Anglo-Saxonism permeated his vision of Chinese racial menace was Fu Manchu's ability to unify the colonial other into a powerful counterforce against British imperialism.[125] Like the heroes he opposed and like the victims of his plots, Fu Manchu was very much a *Homo imperealis.* As the vanguard of an imperialist China that sought to dominate the West, he employed a vast array of other colonized subjects in his plots. From across the length and breadth of Asia, Fu Manchu recruited Indians, Malaysians, Lascars, and a host of others, all of whom brought their specialized talents to bear against the very colonial officials, explorers, business entrepreneurs, Orientalists, scientific and medical professionals, and missionaries who had furthered the Western imperial project in Asia.

Figure 3.4. Movie promotional poster, London, 1923. (Courtesy of John Soister.) "England at present is the web. The spider will be waiting" (*The Mystery of Dr. Fu Manchu*, 1913).

In one particular instance of this, Fu Manchu imported *thuggee* assassins to carry out his designs in Britain. After the same "uncanny wailing" that heralded the deaths of Western businessmen and doctors in Burma was heard in London, Nayland Smith surmised that Fu Manchu had imported this "mysterious epidemic" to dispose of his enemies in the metropolis. With these descriptions, Rohmer meshed Fu Manchu's threat as a counter-imperial force of unified Asian opposition with another perennial anxiety of European colonizers, the threat of physical infection and deterioration through disease.[126] "My God!" Smith exclaimed to his companions, "to think that fiend Fu-Manchu has brought *that* to England . . . a new agent of death, Petrie! Something born in a plague-spot of Burma—the home of much that is unclean and much that is inexplicable."[127] Fu Manchu and his allies thus threatened to destroy the British Empire through the very elements of its foundation. The same avenues of finance, trade, migration, and cultural exchange that linked Britain to Asia became conduits down which those who sought to dominate Britain traveled to the imperial metropolis. The web of empire, co-opted by the Chinese mastermind Fu Manchu, became his web of destruction, and in the metropolis itself, those who represented the West in its racial struggle against Chinese domination "die like flies."[128]

"In the Hands of Far Easterns": Opium in Law and Literature

Rohmer's novels and short stories are, for several reasons, a useful lens for examining the progression of anti-Chinese discourse in Britain. They were immensely popular and widely read—it is no exaggeration to suggest that the images of the Chinese circulated through his stories, books, and magazine articles were central to the popular imagining of them in British society. Beginning in the 1920s, the portrayal of Fu Manchu in films disseminated negative Chinese stereotypes to an even broader segment of the British populace. Rohmer's work was also significant because it highlighted the reciprocal relationship between depictions of Chinese villains in fiction and the legal regulation of the Chinese residents of Britain. Rohmer drew upon the police observation and prosecution of Chinese men in Limehouse for his inspiration, and the popular racial anxieties and hostility against the Chinese that his books exacerbated, in turn, justified further legal regulation of Chinese residents. There was just enough fact in his fiction to make his stories plausible and just enough fiction in his facts to make them terrifying. By the interwar period, the existence of a Chinese master-villain at large in Limehouse, a villain who was plotting the corruption of white Britons, had become a standard device in popular London journalism, and the pursuit of this elusive figure had even infiltrated the anti-vice campaigns of Scotland Yard and the Home Office.[129]

Regardless of the popularity of Rohmer's work, concrete evidence of the threat posed by London's Chinese residents in the prewar period remained scant. In Australia, South Africa, the United States, and Canada, government officials, facing a combination of much larger Chinese populations, determined labor opposition, and, in the case of Australia, close proximity to China itself, had imposed legal restrictions on immigration and interracial sexuality. The danger of the Yellow Peril in prewar London, however, whether one looked to the press, to official reports, or to popular literature, remained most frightening in its potential rather than in its actuality, just as the immigrant Chinese population loomed much larger in its public portrayals than it did in its physical presence. Although the most ardent opponents of the Chinese in Britain had called for regulations similar to those proposed in the empire, the only measurable increase had been the strengthening of the Merchant Shipping Acts to restrict the permissible numbers of Chinese passengers on merchant ships and a broader employment of deportation, the latter only in cases where magistrates and police had claimed that Chinese offenders were a direct threat to public order and to the physical safety of white Londoners.

The same contrast existed between the empire and the metropole on the issue of opium and opium use. Like interracial sexuality and Chinese immigration in general, opium was a much greater concern abroad than it was in Britain itself in the prewar period. Opium smoking, although recognized as a Chinese "vice" and certainly looked upon by magistrates, police, journalists, and the reading public as an unsavory habit, seemed to pose no particular hazard to prewar Britain, nor was it commonly connected, in official opinion or the British press, to the broader perception of the Chinese in Britain as a threat to white labor, to white women, or to the rise of Chinese power on the international stage. It was only later, when opium smoking was publicly linked to the Chinese seduction of white women in Britain, to the moral and physical degradation of white communities in London and Liverpool, and to a global apparatus of smuggling and violence operating out of Chinese neighborhoods in British cities, that the use and trade of it became a public issue and a focus of legal regulation.

Even in the empire, attempts to legislate against opium were late in coming, lagging decades behind the United States, which had been passing laws limiting the use and importation of opium since the

1870s.[130] The contrast between British and American attitudes was particularly apparent when the United States and China signed a new treaty in 1880 that, along with excluding the entry of Chinese laborers, prohibited the Chinese from bringing opium to America. James Russell, the Colonial Treasurer of Hong Kong, far from endorsing the treaty, asked the British Colonial Office if it could intervene in order to protect a trade worth hundreds of thousands of pounds annually.[131] The Canadian government, spurred on by official reports that the habit was spreading to white women and by the hope that sterner legal regulation of Chinese immigrants might reduce civil unrest among white workers, took its first substantial steps against the opium trade in 1908 and 1911.[132] This campaign was spearheaded by William Lyon Mackenzie King, a Liberal MP and labor relations expert who became Canada's first Minister of Labour in 1909 and would eventually, as the longest serving prime minister in the history of the British Commonwealth, play a seminal role in shaping the country's political destiny.[133] The Australian government also passed laws to limit the use, manufacture, and importation of opium, and was particularly keen to see that the habit did not spread to the aboriginal peoples.[134] The Australian anti-opium campaign owed much to the Chinese immigrant community, which, under the leadership of the Sydney merchant Me Quong Tart, had begun the effort in earnest in 1884 when they petitioned the Colonial Secretary to ban all importation of opium.[135]

In contrast to the anti-opium legislation passed by the American, Canadian, and Australian governments, opium use in London's Chinatown in the prewar period failed to prompt significant official action from metropolitan police and judicial authorities.[136] The 1908 Poisons and Pharmacy Act (an extension of an 1868 law) had outlawed the preparation and distribution of opium by anyone except licensed pharmacists, but there is no evidence that this law was strictly enforced in London.[137] And why should it have been, when the Chinese population of London remained small, official opinion on the opium trade in India and China was split, and opium smoking in Britain itself was not widespread?[138] When, in 1909, an expansion of the 1894 Merchant Shipping Act made it illegal to run a seamen's lodging house without a license, evidence of opium smoking was included as one of the conditions that could lead to the revocation of such licenses. Considering the determined campaign waged by maritime union leaders against Chinese "crimps," however, it is debatable whether these regulations were really intended to punish opium smokers or were rather part of the broader effort to restrict Chinese maritime labor in Britain. This latter interpretation is leant support by the public credit later given to

NSFU officials for the passage of these regulations.[139] London County Council inspectors, in a reflection of the strong differences of opinion between British shipowners and British maritime labor leaders on the desirability of "Chinese labour" aboard British ships, enforced this law only sporadically.

Although the British government, responding to both international and domestic pressure, agreed in 1907 to reduce the amount of opium imported from India to China, in the prewar period, it was the Chinese government that seemed more adamant about halting the trade and use of opium.[140] In Britain, the opposition to opium was often loudest among those who had formed their opinions of the drug while in China, and former missionaries such as Hugh Stowell Phillips were particularly voluble in their objections to Britain's continued involvement in the trade. After the general election of 1906, which brought several supporters of the anti-opium movement to Parliament, the tide of official opinion began to turn. By 1911, with the Chinese government expressing its strong commitment to stamping out the opium trade in China, the British government was coming under increasing pressure from public opinion, anti-opium campaigners in Britain, and the growing international anti-opium movement to halt the importation of Indian opium to China altogether. That year, the British and Chinese governments signed an agreement that scaled back the importation of opium from India to China, with the goal of completely eliminating the trade by 1917.[141] But even among the most prominent of Britain's anti-opium campaigners, the international opium trade and the small-scale opium use by Chinese residents of London were two very different affairs. Sir William Collins, for example, one of the staunchest proponents of the anti-opium movement and a member of Britain's delegations to the three Hague anti-opium conferences, did not see opium smoking in Limehouse as a serious issue.[142] Like the Chinese residents of Sydney, Chinese residents in Britain also voiced strong objections to the use of the drug through petitions and letters to newspaper editors.[143]

Opium and opium use in Britain were more concertedly and effectively vilified in British literature than they were in British domestic law or public policy.[144] Opium had first become a notable subject in literature through the poetry of Samuel Taylor Coleridge and through Thomas De Quincey's 1821 story, *Confessions of an English Opium-Eater*. Charles Dickens's *The Mystery of Edwin Drood* (1870) further sensationalized the locale of the opium den and fixed it as a site of immorality, as did Arthur Conan Doyle's *The Man with the Twisted Lip* (1887) and Oscar Wilde's *The Picture of Dorian Gray* (1891).

These latter works firmly located opium and the "dens" where it was consumed in London's Chinese communities, portrayed such locales as decadent and vice-ridden, and highlighted the pernicious effects of the drug on its white users. Particularly notable in Dickens's work is his depiction of the opium den as a degraded space where different races mix indiscriminately in drugged abandon. In the opening scene of *The Mystery of Edwin Drood*, a lascar, a Chinese man, and a white woman all lie together (albeit clothed) with the narrator in a disheveled, dirty bed.[145] The supplier of opium in *Drood*, however, is not a Chinese man but a slatternly woman who has forgone alcohol in favor of the pipe. Dickens makes it obvious that opium is a Chinese vice, however, when he describes how the woman who runs the den "has opium-smoked herself into a strange likeness of the Chinaman. His form of cheek, eye, and temple, and his colour, are repeated in her."[146] What she has consumed within has been manifested without, as her "Chinese" habit has literally transformed her into a Chinese person. When the opium threat finally did move beyond literary depictions to become a prominent public issue during World War I, its most sinister aspect was this power to break down racial boundaries and to reverse imperial racial dynamics in Britain by putting white women in the power of Chinese men, by placing wealth and property in Chinese hands, or by affecting the slow moral and psychological transformation of white Britons into Chinese.

Opium's potential to reverse the racial balance of power was also central to its depiction in the first Fu Manchu novel, though opium played a very minor role in Rohmer's initial portrayal of Chinese villainy. Fu Manchu occasionally smoked opium and, at one point, he was confronted by the book's heroes in an opium den. The narrator, Dr. Petrie, expressed disgust at the habit and its adherents but little alarm. The most sinister aspect of the den, to him, was neither the drug nor its effects but the manner in which the locale, under Chinese ownership and in Chinese control, reversed colonial dynamics for white Britons who entered it.[147] Such was the power of the Chinese, the scene suggested, that they could assert their control over white Britons in London itself, even if only within a limited area.[148] "I experienced a curious sense of isolation from my fellows—from the whole of the Western World," Petrie mused.[149] Even the protection of the police who had surrounded the "dope shop" known as "Singapore Charlie's" did little to alleviate Petrie's sense of unease at his perceived relocation to a foreign realm.[150] "I realized fully how, with the place watched front and back, we yet were cut off, were in the hands of Far Easterns, to some extent in the power of members of that most inscrutably mysterious race of the Chinese." Opium itself was not a threat, but the racial ascendancy of the Chinese over white Britons, expressed *through* the organization of the den and the power that the drug gave the supplier over its users, was. The alleged capacity of the drug to aid one race in enslaving another other would have been all too familiar to some British readers.

In contrast to their long—if hardly extensive—history in literature, opium dens appeared only sporadically as topics in London newspapers in the prewar period.[151] Journalists who tried to confirm the scandalous literary portrayals of opium dens were usually disappointed by the placid scenes of opium smoking that they encountered in Chinatown.[152] In late 1907, even as Chinese and British government officials were working to close down the opium dens of Shanghai and to stop opium smoking aboard merchant ships operating in the Far East, the *East London Advertiser* ran one of the only stories on the opium dens of London's East End that would appear in the prewar London press.[153] The story warned readers that "in their very midst" there were some half-dozen "resorts existing solely for the purposes of meeting the requirements of slaves of this insidious drug."[154] As with literary depictions of opium dens, the key issue for the reporter in this case was the power that opium gave Chinese proprietors over white users in London, particularly those of means.[155] "The patrons of these places are by no means only Orientals," the story ran, "for there are many Europeans residing in London who are as greatly addicted to opium as the Chinese themselves. Two of the most prosperous opium establishments in the East End are patronized extensively by Englishmen, who include men with names well-known in various walks of life."

In the *Advertiser*'s story, the den was a place of vice, and a locale where Chinese power and Chinese culture commanded the patronage and obedience of a white clientele, but opium posed little threat to the general population, and the Chinese men who ran the dens were not eager to advertise their presence or to recruit new smokers. On the contrary, the article asserted that "averseness to the fierce liyht [*sic*] of publicity" was a universal predilection of the Chinese, and that the proprietors of the majority of East End opium dens, which catered primarily to other Chinese men, were "very chary of admitting strangers."[156] "Unless a visitor is in the company of a regular patron," the reporter wrote, "he stands little chance of being allowed to enter." The story portrayed opium smoking as a habit confined largely to Chinese immigrants and well-to-do London men with a taste for the "exotic." In these circumstances, it is hardly surprising that the "opium dens" in London, if they existed at all, had failed thus far to attract more attention in the British press. The violence, immorality, and sexual depravity attributed by reporters to the Chinese in China, Australia, Canada, and South Africa provided far richer press copy than the relatively limited and orderly consumption of opium in the East End did.

Six years after the publication of the *Advertiser*'s report, a correspondent for the *Times* ventured into the East End to research a story on "Chinatown in London." In the intervening period, Chinatown had been subjected to fierce official scrutiny for its internecine violence and dozens of its residents had been coerced into leaving Britain altogether. The *Times*'s story, which was the lead article on page six of the November 25, 1913, issue, portrayed London's Chinatown as "orderly, clean-living, after its national ways, and very gentle-mannered."[157] The author discussed the opium habit, which he said was openly practiced in the neighborhood, but argued that calling the locales of consumption "dens" was a gross misnomer. "For all that," he wrote, "they are so clean and orderly and so little withdrawn from public gaze." The *Times*'s portrayal of opium dens had more in common with the London missionary Joseph Salter's relatively innocuous depiction of them in 1895 as a place of leisure where the seamen of many nationalities could mingle and relax unmolested than it did with the images of degradation and corruption that had been propagated by Dickens, Doyle, and Wilde. [158]

In short, the reporter concluded, there was little to be gained from the legal prosecution of London's Chinese residents for smoking opium or for gambling. To do so, he argued, would only drive the practices underground and foster vice and disorder rather than discouraging it. Had anything changed in the community as a result of the intense judicial intervention to which London Chinese residents had been subjected during "the trouble in Limehouse Chinatown"? Yes, it had—the residents were more watchful and suspicious of outsiders than they had been before, "so news that strangers are about soon spreads, and as they emerge from one door or another [visitors] will be conscious of being watched by little knots of idlers in the road." "But on the surface," the reporter concluded, "the visitor will be met with nothing but smiles and courtesy."

It may seem odd that that the same police who once imposed something approaching martial law in Chinatown in should now, according this report, "give the Chinese in Limehouse an excellent character," and that the neighborhood once plagued by "East End Warfare" was now portrayed as a place where children played in the streets.[159] Had the negative image of Chinatown been a fabrication of the press all along? The correspondent for the *Times* suggested as much, arguing that it was perhaps the prying eyes and wagging tongues of reporters that had brought such swift official intervention to Chinatown in the previous year.[160] In a response letter, Hugh Stowell Phillips begged to differ. He argued that the Chinese residents of London could only be understood in relation to the Chinese population worldwide, and that firsthand experience with the Chinese in their homeland was the only reliable avenue for understanding the significance of their immigration to Britain. "Few who have actually lived among the Chinese," Phillips, the former missionary, insisted, "would . . . share your Correspondent's views as to the effect opium upon the Chinese. I have seen a wife sold before my eyes that the poor besotted husband might buy opium."[161] Living among white Britons in London, he wrote, had not transformed the Chinese into an orderly and respectable people. Instead, they had simply supplemented their own immoral habits with those popular among the white residents of the East End.

Phillips's view of the moral threat posed by Chinese men and their opium habits was supported by an article that appeared in the *Daily Graphic*, one of London's most prominent morning dailies, the same year.[162] But there, too, the hazard was rooted in the imperial context and in the issues of interracial sexuality and Chinese racial dominance over white Britons. The first sentence of this article, "The Oriental Opium Invasion," described the ominous "awakening of China from her long opium sleep," and asserted that the greatest danger lay in the transmission of the opium habit to young white girls and wealthy white men, who could become helplessly addicted with "a single smoke."[163] The author demanded that the British government follow the precedent set in the empire and make the sale of opium entirely illegal, lest the habit that they themselves had fostered in China return to Britain as "the greatest retribution." The *Daily Graphic*'s presentation of the opium habit also justified the broadest possible application of such laws, for the article made no distinction between locales devoted solely to opium use and seamen's lodging houses where opium was consumed. Any place where the habit was practiced was, by their definition, a "den," and thus a site of depravity, debauchery, and demoralization that demanded a harsh legal response.

Conclusion

Regardless of whether British observers viewed the Chinese population of London and the empire more broadly as a source of labor, as a source of immorality, or as a dire threat to white communities, few could deny that the years from 1904–14 had been troubling ones for relations between white Britons and Chinese men. The controversy and contest over Chinese indentured servitude in South Africa, labor demonstrations against Chinese maritime labor in Britain, anti-Chinese violence in London, the Chinese Revolution, the popular imagery of a looming worldwide racial conflict between Europeans and Asians, and inter-Chinese violence in Limehouse had fostered one crisis after another. The negative depictions of Chinese men in popular culture had heightened anxieties over the Chinese presence throughout the empire. But 1913, the year that the *Times*'s feature article on the Chinese residents of London was published, seemed to provide a respite, however brief. Chinatown was quiet, Yuan Shikai had temporarily restored order in China, and the crimes of White Wolf and Jack Kong were still in the future. The character of Chinatown's residents itself seemed to be changing, as the sometimes unruly population of seamen, whose presence had provoked a strong reaction from British union leaders, was increasingly leavened by shop owners and tradesmen who brought a measure of respectability to the district in the eyes of at least some observers.[164]

Although the dragon and Saint George had briefly lain down together in the metropolis, each had kept a wary eye open. And to some London officials, the Chinese and their habits remained an undesirable presence. Late summer 1914 witnessed the first attempt to enforce the Pharmacy Act of 1908 in Limehouse. Using undercover agents and careful observation, representatives of the Pharmaceutical Society of England cajoled two Chinese merchants into selling them opium illegally. One merchant, Kwong Tai, had demonstrated no fear of prosecution whatsoever and had reclined on a bed, smoking opium himself, as his young assistant conducted the transaction.[165] The merchants were promptly arrested, tried in the Thames Police Court, and fined—Kwong Tai for 20 shillings and Wong Ku Chong for £5. The cases were not a legal watershed, or even a particularly significant moment in the history of Anglo-Chinese relations in the metropolis. But they did foreshadow a much more serious campaign to enforce a British vision of law and order in Chinatown, a campaign that would send many of its residents back across the oceans as a great tide of fear and destruction rose to engulf the world.

Chapter 4

"Most Insidious Is the Oriental in the West"

Chinese and Britons in Wartime London

The World War I period witnessed several important shifts in the legal treatment of Chinese residents and in their portrayals in British culture. Reflecting anxieties prompted by the war, negative Chinese stereotypes in newspapers and popular fiction focused on Chinese gambling and opium smoking, on the supposed threat of long-term Chinese residents and their control of wealth and property, and on the hazards that their alleged immorality posed to white men rather than to white women. The Chinese population of the East End also became, for the first time, a subject of serious concern at the highest levels of the government and the judicial system.

But the same increase in the small Chinese population of Britain that had fostered greater fears of their impact on white residents was itself a response to the wartime demand for labor in British shipping and other war-essential industries. Even as Chinese "vice" seemed, to some, to pose an ever greater threat to the morality, masculinity, and national security of Britain, the value of Chinese men as inexpensive maritime laborers and their direct contribution to the war effort itself prevented their wholesale persecution. The divided views on the Chinese in Britain were reflected in both official reports and the press, which depicted London's Chinatown and its residents as vice-ridden and immoral one day and as orderly and respectable the next.

The increasing legal persecution and public vilification of London's Chinese residents during World War I was presaged by a sharp shift in both official views and popular attitudes toward aliens in Britain. The first day of the war saw the swift passage through Parliament of the 1914 Aliens Restriction Act, which significantly expanded the British government's authority over immigration and resident aliens.[1] Although the intended targets of the new regulations were aliens from enemy nations, London judicial authorities would employ their new powers broadly, particularly toward the end of the war. Meanwhile, the war was also punctuated by several incidents of anti-alien violence in British cities.[2] China was not an enemy power during World War I, and the Chinese in Britain were therefore not enemy aliens, but the diplomatic relationship between the two nations grew increasingly strained as the war progressed and Britain solidified its alliance with Japan.[3] All three of these developments, the vastly increased power of the state over resident aliens, the growing public sentiment against aliens, and the deterioration of Anglo-Chinese diplomatic relations, left the Chinese residents of London more vulnerable than ever before to both popular hostility and legal prosecution.

"Woman and a Chinaman's Money": Chinese Men and White Women in the Courts of Wartime London

The second year of the war witnessed a legal milestone for the Chinese residents of Britain. For years, Chinese men had been portrayed in popular fiction and theater as being violent and murderous, but it was not until 1915 that a Chinese man was first convicted of murdering a white woman. This trial, the first major prosecution of a Chinese resident of London to take place since the war had begun, highlighted the significance of race in the execution of law in the metropolis. The persistent anxiety over interracial sexuality, which had been expressed previously in both literature and imperial law, and the growing official concern over the consequences of casual contact between white and Chinese residents in the East End were also important factors. On October 21, 1915, Lee Kun, a Chinese seaman and resident of Limehouse, was convicted of the "wilful murder" of Clara Thomas (aka "Elsie Goddard").[4] The press reports of the case provided readers with a tidy narrative—a Chinese villain, with money foremost on his mind, had used an associate to try to intimidate his white ex-girlfriend into repaying a debt. When she had refused these initial demands, Lee attempted to extort the money from her in person and, failing in that task, he had stabbed her to death, a crime for which he would now justly hang. The conviction of "wilful murder" in *Rex v. Lee Kun* indicated that the jury and sentencing justice in the Central Criminal Court judged that the killing was premeditated, rather than an act of passion, and that the accused had been fully in control of his actions at the time. Lee's statement following his arrest, that Thomas had stolen money from him and had refused to repay it, was interpreted by the jury and the bench as evidence that his was a calculated crime motivated by greed. Coverage of the trial in the *Times* supported this conclusion and highlighted the importance of race in the incident. Whereas other London murder cases that the paper covered in 1915 were commonly identified by the area of the city in which they had occurred (e.g., "The Islington Murder," "The Clapham Murder," "The Hyde Park Murder," "The Station Murder," etc.) the coverage of the Lee case appeared under the heading "Woman And A Chinaman's Money."

The story, however, was more complex than the newspaper reports of the case suggested, and there were strong indicators that race was a significant issue in the trial and sentencing of Lee Kun, who was one of only nine men executed for murder in Britain that year.[5] A fuller account of the incident suggests that strong emotion had indeed been a factor in Lee's actions, that the relationship between Thomas and Lee had been an intimate one that had lasted many months, and that the accused had tried to enlist the aid of the police on several occasions, but to no avail—all circumstances that, had the defendant not been Chinese, might have mitigated the course of the trial or its outcome, as they had in similar cases where white men had killed their lovers or wives.[6] Lee and Thomas had once lived together (it is unclear for how long), according to the testimony of William Fossard, a local landlord. But at the time of the murder, Thomas was living with a white man named "Swanny."[7] Lee claimed that Thomas had continued to draw money from his savings even while she was living with Swanny, and that when Lee had sent a Chinese intermediary to demand the return of these funds, Swanny had thrown him out. [8] When the intermediary summoned the police by blowing on a police whistle, they had arrested him rather than hearing his complaint. [9] A week later, Goddard's neighbor testified, Thomas had appeared in person and, after quarreling briefly with the victim, had stabbed her to death. Lee was promptly arrested and brought to the local police station, where he made a statement that Thomas had refused to repay him the money that she had stolen from him. At the Central Criminal Court on November 18, 1915, the jury found Lee guilty of "wilful murder" and the presiding justice, Charles Darling, sentenced him to hang.[10]

The details of the events surrounding the murder did not contradict the jury's assessment that Lee Kun had indeed killed Clara Thomas, but they did highlight how the retelling of events in the court and in the press brought Lee closer in line with popular stereotypes of Chinese men as being violent, greedy, and calculating, while downplaying any considerations that would have mitigated the verdict of dispassionate, premeditated murder. Although the general trend in British justice during this period was toward harsher punishment of male violence against women, the moral reputation and sexual behavior of both the victim and the accused remained important considerations in court cases.[11] On other occasions, London magistrates had shown sympathy for working-class men who claimed that the alleged infidelity of their female partners had driven them to abuse or violence, but such considerations went unacknowledged in Lee Kun's case. Considering the pervasive prejudice against interracial sexuality, neither the justice nor the jury was likely to have viewed Lee as possessing any claims to the sexual fidelity of Goddard.[12] Lastly, unlike other perpetrators of "wilful murder" convicted in 1915–16, Lee had not threatened Thomas or declared an intent to do her harm. In the week preceding the murder, Thomas and Lee never even met in person; Lee had preferred to communicate through his intermediary, whose only threat was to summon the police, and Lee's possession of a knife, which was a common practice among seamen, did not necessarily indicate premeditation.

The general attitude of the presiding justice, Charles Darling, toward the Chinese in Britain is unclear. His father-in-law, as a veteran of the Sepoy Mutiny and the Second Opium War, had been an eyewitness to interracial violence and the forcible suppression of colonized populations on a grand scale, but Darling himself was never vocal on the issues of race or interracial sexuality.[13] There are some indicators, however, that his views of the Chinese and of Chinese immigration were less than favorable. In 1921, adjudicating a property case from the King's Bench, Darling helped further the stereotype that Chinese men were indistinguishable, as individuals, to Britons. "Can anyone tell one Chinaman from another?" he asked rhetorically, eliciting laughter from those assembled in the court.[14] In 1902, Darling had also expressed his strong support for Chris Watson, the Australian Labour Party leader who was one of the chief advocates of the "white Australia " policy.[15] He went on to voice his general admiration for the party itself, whose relentless campaigning had prompted the policy's adoption by Australia's first Federal Parliament in 1901. This, combined with Darling's ardent enthusiasm for universal military service by all citizens of the Dominions, suggests that he was no stranger to the idea of unified racial interest that underpinned Anglo-Saxonism, even if he never formally articulated this perspective.

The direct impact of race on Lee's murder trial is, like Darling's own attitudes toward the Chinese, hard to assess. But the dynamics of his appeal highlighted both the obstacles encountered by Chinese defendants and, more generally—as Albert Lieck, the former chief clerk of the Bow Street Police Court would later comment in his description of Lee Kun's trial—"the very great handicap" that foreign prisoners faced in the British judicial system.[16] The details of the case that were revealed in the appeals process also help to explain why the judge and jury had been so quick to discount the role of emotion in Lee's actions. In making his case before the Court of Criminal Appeal, Tristram Beresford, Lee's counsel, argued that the conviction should be quashed because his client had not received the same rights and opportunities to defend himself that the British judicial system normally afforded the accused.[17] In the absence of an interpreter, Lee had not properly heard the charges against him, nor had he been able to make statements to the jury, to give evidence on his own behalf, nor to assist his counsel in cross-examinations. In short, Lee had been physically present in the courtroom during the trial, but not "present" by the legal definition of the term. The court should assume, Beresford insisted, that even foreign defendants could still be "educated and intelligent" and therefore capable of contributing significantly to their own defense.[18]

Beresford also argued that the absence of an interpreter at the Central Criminal Court had prejudiced the jury against the defendant. Unless the defendant understood what was being said, the jury could not accurately "observe the demeanour of a prisoner when he heard the evidence, and his demeanour would often tell in his favour." Lee's absence of expression, Beresford suggested, would have supported any assessment on the part of judge and jury that emotion was not a strong factor in the case. Beresford also argued that Lee, because of the language barrier, had been further denied two key entitlements of the accused, the right to challenge the jury and the opportunity to offer "a reason why sentence should not be passed upon him."[19] The justices of the Court of Criminal Appeal refused Lee's appeal. Ten days later, they justified their decision by arguing that all the evidence had been translated at the initial police court hearing and that the evidence cited in the Central Criminal Court trial had not varied substantially from it. Therefore, in their opinion, there had been no miscarriage of justice in *Rex v. Lee Kun*.[20]

But the legacy of the case lasted well beyond this final verdict. In a lengthy discussion that followed their initial judgment, the Lord Chief Justice and his colleagues examined the difficulties involved in trying foreign suspects in Britain over the last fifty years and found significant variance in the ways that different magistrates had acted.[21] Some judges, they determined, had always insisted that evidence was translated unless the defendant or his counsel stated their express wishes to the contrary, and other judges had required translation regardless. Even though the specifics of *Rex v. Lee Kun* did not merit granting an appeal, the justices wholeheartedly agreed with Beresford's argument that "the presence of the accused means not merely that he must be physically in attendance, but also that he must be capable of understanding the nature of the proceedings."[22]

Rex v. Lee Kun brought the Chinese residents of London to the center of legal controversy in Britain. A case that had begun with the unsuccessful attempt of a Chinese man to enlist the aid of the police at the local level had ended with the successful affirmation, at the highest levels of the British judiciary, of the legal rights and privileges of all foreigners tried in Britain. It was vital to the national interest, the justices emphasized, that *all* defendants, regardless of their nation or culture of origin, received a fair trial, were fully cognizant of the proceedings, and did not "forfeit life or liberty except when tried under the safeguards so carefully provided by the law."[23] The conclusions that were articulated during Lee's appeal remain as precedent in British law to this day.[24] Lee himself, however, did not benefit from them. He was hanged on the first day of the new year.[25]

Contrary to the dire consequences of interracial contact portrayed in the newspaper coverage of *Rex v. Lee Kun*, there was ample evidence that the small Chinese population of the East End was coming into increasingly regular contact, both social and commercial, with the white residents of the district. One correspondent for the *East London Observer* reported that although Chinatown was "often the scene of disorder . . . it is surprising to what extent the Chinamen enter into the lives of the ordinary East End residents around them. Laundries, general stores, tea-rooms, tobacconists' shops, seamen's lodging-houses, and many other establishments are run by them."[26] But contact and integration are two very different things. As the *Observer*'s report indicated, Chinese men might frequently encounter "ordinary East End residents," but they were still widely recognized by most commentators as being distinct from them. London court cases from this period highlighted not only the increasing social and commercial contact between Chinese residents and their white neighbors but also the tensions, exacerbated by differences of language and culture, that impeded integration between the two groups. Such trials also offered Chinese defendants the opportunity to publicly contest racial stereotypes and to declare or demonstrate their desire to be viewed as "ordinary East End residents" rather than as "Chinamen."

One illustrative case appeared before Justice Robert Younger of the Chancery Division of the High Court on May 26, 1916, when Kai Chong, a Chinese resident of Limehouse, appeared to defend himself against a suit brought by a white landlord, Mrs. Musgrave. Musgrave, represented by her agent, P. W. Cleave, had sued Kai for failing to fulfill the terms of a fifty-year lease on a house in Limehouse Causeway. Kai claimed, though an interpreter, that he did not understand English well and that he thought he had purchased the house outright rather than merely leasing it.[27] What began as a property dispute quickly evolved into a discussion of the prevalence of gambling among Chinese men in Limehouse. During Cleave's cross-examination, Mr. Matthew, King's Counsel, asked the agent for the plaintiff if "a great deal of gambling goes on in Chinatown?" When Cleave replied that he knew this was so from "police-court reports," Matthew pressed him further. "Don't you know very well that gambling goes on in seventy-five per cent. of the houses, which makes them valuable, and that a sign of a cross is exhibited to indicate that you can gamble there?"

When Kai himself came up for cross-examination by Mr. Disturnal, K.C., gambling was again at the center of the discussion. Under pointed questioning by Disturnal, Kai admitted that he had been before the Central Criminal Court three months ago on charges relating to gambling among his shop assistants and that he had been found guilty and fined £150.[28] Both Matthew and Distrunal gave the impression that the whole point of Kai's purchase of the house was to set up an illegal gambling parlor, although there was no specific evidence that this had been the case. Kai, for his part, tried to emphasize his respectability and to demonstrate his earnest desire to assimilate into his adopted community. The defendant, who "wore his hair cut short, and was in ordinary European clothes," told the court that he had come to England twenty years ago as a seaman and had been settled permanently for nine years already. He had married an Englishwoman, who spoke to him "very simple English words," and his business in the city was "that of general shopkeeper and dealer." [29] Cleave contested Kai's assertions that he could not read English or understand more than a few simple words, claiming that Kai had understood the lease perfectly. The plaintiff also emphasized the commercial and clannish character of the Chinese of Limehouse by comparing them to

London's Jews, another cohort that enjoyed the same dubious reputation. When the court once again convened on May 30, Kai's wife, "a stylishly-dressed, attractive young Englishwoman," testified that her husband's grasp of English was poor and that she had to write correspondence on his behalf. [30]

The Kai Chong case not only highlighted the impact of race on London court proceedings but also demonstrated how racial stereotypes could be contested in these forums. Kai Chong contradicted the common portrayals of Chinese men in press and literature in some ways, while confirming them in others. The defendant dressed like an Englishman for his court appearance, he was a longtime resident of England, and he claimed to conduct a respectable business. Kai's manner and attitude distanced him from the rowdy, knife-wielding seamen or languorous opium smokers that appeared as common characters in literary and journalistic portrayals of Chinatown. On the other hand, his previous conviction for gambling fit well with such depictions.

Robert Younger, the presiding justice, was no stranger to dealing with difficult cases involving immigrants. In May 1915, he had served on a government committee that had evaluated exemption claims from enemy aliens contesting their internment or deportation orders.[31] Justice Younger denied Kai's assertion that he did not fully comprehend English or the specifics of his negotiation with Cleave. He emphasized, as Kai himself had, the defendant's cultural and social assimilation. As evidence of this, Younger pointed to Kai's considerable experience with English business practices, his marriage to an English woman, and his ownership of property in London.[32] But at the same time that he offered evidence of Kai's respectability and his cultural assimilation, Younger also emphasized Kai's possession of a stereotypically "Chinese" attribute. Kai, according to Justice Younger, "was remarkably shrewd and intelligent." In other circumstances, this might have been a compliment, but in Kai's case, Justice Younger was implying that Kai had used his intelligence immorally and had tried to deceive the court. However respectable Kai seemed, Younger's comments suggested he was just another cunning Chinaman. Cleave's testimony that Kai had conducted complex negotiations without an interpreter, the suggestions made by Matthew and Disturnal that Kai intended to run a gambling den and his history of this activity, and the testimony of other witnesses that the defendant spoke English offered the court ample confirmation of Younger's suspicions. Property ownership and the possession of financial resources, far from granting Kai the benefits of respectability, had increased his vulnerability to suspicion and racial stereotyping in the courtroom. In his final judgment, Younger ordered

Kai to pay Musgrave, in lieu of fulfilling the lease, an additional £40 to compensate her for her financial loss. On top of the £24 deposit made already, this amounted to a quarter of the full cost for the fifty-year lease (£245).[33]

"A Crying Scandal": The Wartime Campaigns against Gambling and Narcotics

Even in the prewar period, Chinese ownership of property and businesses, and intermarriage between Chinese men and white women, although not common, were part of Limehouse life. White patronage of Chinese businesses was also an everyday occurrence. But wartime conditions made Chinese acquisition of property and casual interracial contact highly pertinent issues to those with legal authority, as the Kai Chong case demonstrated. The outcome of the war was thought to depend upon the preservation of British manpower and masculine strength.[34] In these circumstances, the fear that interracial contact, either through illicit commerce or through sexuality and marriage, might have a harmful effect on the moral and physical health of white residents became a central concern at both the local and national levels.[35] The wartime campaigns against gambling and opium use in Chinese communities demonstrated how these anxieties could prompt significant changes in the legal and moral landscapes of the metropolis. In the previous decade, gambling and opium had both appeared in journalistic portrayals of Chinatown. Before the war, such activities, in the absence of violence or disruptions to public disorder to exacerbate them, rarely resulted in legal prosecution or harsh punishment. They were considered nuisances, but hardly a danger to the nation, particularly since there was no evidence that they were spreading to white residents. The war changed this equation dramatically, elevating "vice" in Chinatown to a serious threat against the well-being of the nation and the military effectiveness of its soldiery. The war also expanded the authority of government officials to arrest and deport those held responsible for the spread of gambling and for the illicit smuggling, sale, and use of narcotics.

At the March 1915 trial of a gaming-house proprietor in the Westminster Police Court, Herbert Muskett, representing the Metropolitan Police, drew a sinister picture of illegal gambling in London and its deleterious effects on the military. "At a number of these fashionable gaming resorts," Muskett declared in court, "young officers lured there had lost large sums which they cannot afford . . . the evil had become so grave that it was something like a crying scandal."[36] The presiding magistrate, Charles Francis, after fining the principal defendants £250 each, warned them that "had there been any evidence put before him that young officers in the Army had been lured and impoverished at this house he would have unquestionably sent them to prison." Another police official, speaking to the press on behalf of Police Commissioner Sir Edward Henry, emphasized the threat of nightclubs to both the morality and the health of young army officers. Not only were such locales frequented by prostitutes, he asserted, but "dancing until 4 or 5 in the morning is hardly conducive to the fitness or progress of an officer in training."[37] In the succeeding months, London magistrates would try several more major cases involving military officers and gambling in the West End.

The association of Chinatown and its residents with gambling had been well established before the outbreak of war, and it did not take long for metropolitan authorities to turn their attention there. The first major raid took place in October 1915, when Superintendent Boxall, the commander of the Metropolitan Police's K Division, arrested three Chinese men for playing "fan-tan," a simplified version of roulette, in the back of a small shop.[38] As evidence, Boxall seized £300 in English money, £30 in U.S. dollars, and records showing that Wong Sing, the chief defendant, had deposited £2,800 into a local bank account in the last year. Wong denied any knowledge of the offense. "I am only a cook," he told the court, and claimed that he did not know how to gamble. The prosecutor, Comyn Carr, argued that the shop itself was merely a façade for what was, in truth, a gambling den. The court subsequently imposed heavy fines on the defendants. June 1916 witnessed a further series of police raids conducted against Chinese gambling, and the results received prominent coverage in the East End press. Boxall's public statements on these occasions replicated many of the stereotypes of Chinese residents commonly found in previous newspaper reports and literary depictions of the neighborhood. In justifying the raids, he exaggerated the number of Chinese living in London, highlighted their propensity for serious violence, argued that their presence posed a threat to public order in the district, and emphasized the prevalence of interracial sexuality.[39] Boxall's efforts to expand the anti-gambling campaign in Limehouse also triggered a violent demonstration that quickly escalated into general mêlée. Despite the superintendent's emphasis on the vicious tendencies of Chinese men, no one was seriously injured during the incident. There were also conflicting reports on the identity of both the instigators and the primary victims. The *East London Advertiser*'s account blamed the violence on Chinese and white seamen, while the *East End News* held local white hooligans responsible for the disturbance and exonerated British and Chinese seamen alike.[40] The *News*'s correspondent further claimed that the Chinese involved had been victims, not villains, and that "the chief sufferers" had been Chinese street merchants.

The police intervention in Limehouse differed in one very important respect from the initial gaming-house raids conducted in 1915—there were no military officers, indeed no white people at all, to be found there. Since the protection of young army and navy officers had been the ostensible justification for the anti-gambling campaign in London, their absence from Limehouse gambling dens encourages us to seek another explanation for Boxall's raids. The superintendent was hardly reticent to declare his misgivings about the Chinese residents of his precinct, and they were a cohort that had long been identified as a source of vice and disorder by both police and local magistrates. Had he or his superior, Police Commissioner Henry, used the prevailing sentiment against gambling among military officers as a justification to crack down on the practice among Chinese residents? Subsequent events certainly support this conclusion and suggest that local officials were more than willing to use the atmosphere of anxiety over the moral and physical state of soldiers as a rationale for the harassment of Chinese residents. Hard on the heels of Boxall's raids, a new evolution in the legal apparatus of the British state set the stage for a far more dramatic and persistent conflict. Just as wartime brought an unprecedented escalation of contact between the average resident of Britain and the mechanisms of the state, it also heralded a new phase in the relationship between the latter and the Chinese population of Britain.

In January 1916, the passage of the Military Services Act introduced military conscription to Britain for the first time in its history. That year also witnessed the introduction of limited narcotics prohibition to Britain. In the summer of 1916, the Home Office, in cooperation with local police and judicial officials in London, Liverpool, Glasgow, and Cardiff, initiated a nationwide campaign to completely eradicate illicit opium importation, exportation, and use among the Chinese residents of Britain. The campaign was leant strong impetus and was provided with more potent judicial weaponry by the passage of regulation 40b under the Defence of the Realm Act. DORA 40b, as it came to be known, criminalized the possession or sale of cocaine and opium by anyone besides licensed professionals.[41] During the course of the anti-opium campaign, which would far outlast the war itself, the Chinese residents of Britain would be investigated, prosecuted, jailed, and deported more vigorously than almost any other non-enemy foreign residents in the nation.[42]

DORA 40b was a response to the concern of the public and of military officials over cocaine use among British soldiers, concern that had been whipped to frenzy by a series of lurid *Times* editorials describing madness, physical degeneration, and painful death as the fate of any who sampled the drug. Following the unsuccessful prosecution of a cocaine possession case in the Bow Street Police Court, Herbert Muskett and the presiding magistrate, Graham Campbell, had publicly demanded the expansion of wartime emergency powers in order to deal with the spread of the cocaine habit in London.[43] Like the concerns that had helped sustain the anti-gambling campaign, the anti-cocaine hysteria that prompted the passage of DORA 40b portrayed the habit as one that did serious harm to both military efficiency and masculine morality at a time when the security of the nation and the effectiveness of its soldiery were paramount concerns.

Chinese men in London were not directly implicated in the initial discussions of the narcotics trade—the original focus of the campaign was on white men and women and cocaine, not on Chinese men and opium.[44] Nonetheless, the passage of DORA 40b had dire implications for Britain's Chinese population. By outlawing the possession of prepared opium, the new regulation criminalized a practice that had been commonplace among a significant minority of the Chinese residents in Britain for decades and that was even more popular among the transient population of Chinese seamen.[45] DORA 40b made nonlicensed possession of opium or cocaine a criminal offense punishable by two months hard labor without option of a fine. Since the terms of the 1905 Aliens Act—which had been further strengthened by the 1914 Aliens Restriction Act—allowed for the presiding magistrate to recommend deportation of any foreign resident convicted of a crime carrying a sentence of imprisonment, the regulation significantly increased the power of local judicial authorities in their dealings with Chinese residents. [46] DORA 40b gave them the opportunity to recommend for deportation, on the legal basis of the possession of even small amounts of prepared opium for personal use, almost any Chinese resident that they viewed as undesirable. It also provided police with the justification and authority to observe and investigate a much wider portion of the Chinese population than they had ever been able to before.[47]

The legal powers granted to local officials by DORA 40b were considerable, but the growing hostility in the Home Office toward the opium trade was an even greater threat to Britain's Chinese residents. Although opium use among soldiers was not initially a major concern to Home Office officials, the use of Britain's ports and shipping lines as channels for the importation of raw opium and the exportation of the refined product *from* Britain was.[48] Fears that the opium "traffic" was a threat to Britain's national integrity and to its international maritime trade network helped prompt the inclusion of opium in the DORA regulations.[49] In this context, the anti-opium campaign was more a response to the alleged threat of Chinese-controlled commerce to the strength and integrity of British urban communities in wartime than it was a reaction to opium smoking—the latter was still a practice largely confined to Chinese men and posed no apparent threat to white Britons.

The relative unconcern about opium smoking in London, opium's longer history in the metropolis, and the limited scope of its use helps explain why the Chinese residents of London were spared, initially, from the strict enforcement of Britain's wartime drug prohibition laws. But the same cannot be said of the Chinese residents of other British port cities. The Home Office campaign against the opium trade was initiated by Sir Malcolm Delevingne, an undersecretary of state who was deeply committed to halting the drug trade and who showed, throughout his career, a particular opposition toward the traffic in opium.[50] Some local police and judiciary officials shared Delevingne's antipathy toward the international narcotics trade, but most were more concerned with general Chinese vice and immorality, particularly gambling and interracial sexuality. This pervasive suspicion toward Chinese men was the initial catalyst of the most aggressive of all the wartime anti-narcotics campaigns, which took place in Liverpool. By July 1917, the Criminal Investigation Department of the Liverpool Police, working in close communication with the Home Office, had arrested 133 individuals, almost all Chinese, on suspicion of their involvement in the opium traffic.[51] In one raid alone, conducted on June 9, 1917, Liverpool detectives arrested seventy-three Chinese men. By then, twenty-four suspects, all Chinese, had been identified by Inspector Burgess of the Liverpool CID as "principle opium traffickers" and deported. In addition to the arrests and deportations, Liverpool magistrates inflicted £1,584 in fines for opium-related offenses.

Many of the Liverpool arrests, however, had been made with little evidence and on questionable legal grounds. In several cases, men were arrested who had committed no crime at all. Some had merely been under suspicion; others were simply caught up in the wide net that Burgess and his officers had cast over the Liverpool Chinese population. Here, the wartime emergency powers that allowed the Home Office to summarily deport "undesirable" aliens proved to be essential. In order to compensate for the shaky legal foundations of his arrests, Burgess, with encouragement from his superiors, often avoided trials altogether by applying directly to the Home Office for deportation orders. [52] The Aliens Restriction Act of 1914, in conjunction with the Aliens Restriction (Consolidation) Order of 1916, authorized the Home Office to deport, *without trial*, any alien whose presence was considered deleterious to the good of the nation. Delevingne and Burgess also employed threats and intimidation to coerce other Chinese residents into leaving the country. The illegal opium trade, once considered merely a nuisance, was now being treated in Liverpool as a threat to the safety and security of the nation.

The effects of the campaign and the passage of DORA 40b had also been felt, albeit less intensely, by the Chinese populations of Cardiff and Glasgow. But the results of opium prosecutions there suggest that, had Burgess been required to take his cases to the local courts rather than resorting to wartime emergency powers, the results in Liverpool would have been quite different. In Glasgow, the sheriff who presided over opium charges against three Chinese men in August 1916 fined them each a mere £1, insisting that DORA 40b had not been in effect long enough to merit strict enforcement.[53] In Cardiff, a police court magistrate fined seventeen Chinese men arrested in an opium raid between £50 and 10s. each (£245 in all).[54] Citing the same mitigating circumstances, however, he refused to deport any of them, despite the requests of the prosecution.[55]

In the midst of the Liverpool anti-opium campaign, Delevingne had expressed his hope that the Metropolitan Police would "act as vigorously as the Liverpool Police [had]" in their suppression of the opium trade.[56] But despite some journalistic accounts of the disappearance of opium smoking from public view in Chinatown, there is no indication that the police in wartime London investigated and prosecuted opium-related crimes at anywhere near the level that their colleagues in Liverpool did.[57] Although the Metropolitan Police continued their campaign against gambling in Chinatown, London magistrates did not make their first recommendation for deportation on the grounds of an opium conviction until August 1918, more than two years after the passage of DORA 40b and the mass arrests and deportations in Liverpool.[58] Judging by the failure of police and judicial officials in London and elsewhere to pick up the gauntlet thrown by Delevingne, it is clear that, regardless of their overall opinions on the Chinese and their predilections, the majority of London officials were nowhere near as committed as he was to suppressing the illegal trade and use of opium.

"The Chinaman Has His Merits": Chinese Labor during the First World War

Chinese labor, like gambling and opium, remained a prominent issue in both law and public discourse in wartime London. But on this issue as well, there was no consensus. Even as union leaders protested against the increased employment of Chinese men, British shipowners continued to make good use of their availability, Chinese spokesmen defended their work ethic and contributions to British industry, and the British military incorporated them as a vital element in the war effort. This lack of consensus forestalled any wholesale vilification or legal persecution of the Chinese on labor issues during the war. But their widespread employment by British shipowners did provide further ammunition to union leaders, and once the war ended, opposition from them and from working-class residents in Britain's port cities would have a major impact.

During the war, the availability of affordable Chinese labor remained a boon to British shipowners, and the wartime demand for maritime labor brought increasing numbers of Chinese seamen to British ports. By 1915, according to figures from the Board of Trade, there were 14,000 Chinese seamen working on British ships, but this is an aggregate number and many such seamen would not have been residing even temporarily in Britain between voyages.[59] From that point on, their numbers decreased steadily, although they did not drop below the 10,000 mark until 1919. In 1916, as the war entered its third year, British union leaders once again began agitating for legal restrictions against the employment of Chinese seamen on British ships. The tendency of maritime union leaders to exaggerate these numbers only heightened the tensions between Chinese and British seamen.[60] In a June 1916 London police court case, for example, a National Sailors' and Firemen's Union (NSFU) representative claimed that the Chinese population of London "had grown from 1,000 to 8,000," a highly implausible estimate.[61]

One prominent opponent of Chinese labor, the union official Donald Rose, evoked the patriotic sacrifice of British sailors and the insult paid to that sacrifice by the hiring practices of British shipowners: "There have been cases of seamen who have lost their all whilst on torpedoed or mined boats seeking other berths, only to find the jobs that were going were being given to Asians."[62] In his calls for the hiring of "British" maritime labor over Chinese seamen, Rose also advocated for the use of "British coloured" seamen, but not those of "other nationalities." In the midst of a bloody conflict between

European nations, it is not surprising that NSFU leaders abandoned their earlier calls for solidarity among European sailors against Chinese seamen in favor of rhetoric that included only "British" labor, whether white or "coloured." By such tactics, Rose and other maritime labor union leaders were able to link economic interest with the rhetoric of nationalism.[63]

By the fall of 1916, protests against Chinese labor in London had become serious enough to merit coverage in national newspapers. The *Daily Telegraph* reported that British labor leaders' public agitation against the increasing numbers of Chinese seamen was exacerbating racial tensions in the East End. The opponents of Chinese labor once again revived the specter of the LIO experiment in South Africa as a reference point for the current state of affairs. "When Chinese labour was imported to South Africa," the general secretary of the NSFU told a reporter for the *Telegraph*, "there was a tremendous outcry in this country. Yet to-day numbers of shipowners are engaging Chinese solely because they are prepared to work for lower wages than the Britisher or friendly alien, and cost nothing like as much to feed." Other European mariners in London, the paper reported, were also hostile toward Chinese seamen, and one result was that the Chinese were denied "the freedom of the Sailor's Home so admirably conducted by the British and Foreign Sailors' Society . . . in view of the prejudice against him, his presence there, it is said, would almost certainly breed trouble."[64] Joseph Havelock Wilson, with his usual penchant for dramatic rhetoric, warned of more trouble ahead for the Chinese residents of the metropolis if shipowners continued to favor them over white seamen. "It will be a deplorable state of affairs," he declared, "if British seamen who are now serving their King and country afloat should find when they have to return to the merchant service after the war that they are crowded out of jobs by cheap Asiatic labour."[65]

The most vitriolic attacks on the Chinese were made at the annual meeting of the Trades Union Congress that took place in September 1916 in Birmingham. There, prominent union leaders combined economic arguments with moral objections and appeals to patriotism, much like the opponents of "Chinese labour" in South Africa had. It was imperative, they insisted, that the government halt the immigration of Chinese men, outlaw their labor on British ships, shut down Chinese-owned businesses, and expel current residents from Britain. The attack was led by maritime union officials, but anti-Chinese proposals received broad support from many of the assembled union representatives. Despite the growing rift between the NSFU leadership, the TUC, and the Labour Party over the former's refusal to support more militant tactics, opposition to "Chinese labour" remained a unifying issue. Joseph Havelock Wilson called for the government to pass a law that would repatriate "all Chinese who cannot produce satisfactory evidence . . . that they are of British nationality."[66] Joe Cotter, the founder of the Ship's Stewards Union and a former Cunard Line steward himself, painted a frightening portrait of Chinese immorality in Liverpool and London.[67] Claiming that there were 4,000 Chinese living in Liverpool, he declared that "in the first house he entered he found 40 Chinamen gathered around fan-tan tables on which lay between £300 and £400, while in the bedrooms were others in a comatose state as the result of opium smoking . . . [Opium] was manufactured wholesale in these places." "In Pennyfields, London," he continued, "young girls from the ages of 14 upwards could be seen going into the Chinese lodging-house up to 2 and 3 o'clock in the morning."[68] Cotter also asserted that every one of the Chinese laundries in Britain was both an opium den and a brothel, and that he and another union representative had personally observed 1,200 pounds of opium being prepared in East End boardinghouses for smuggling abroad.

Cotter and Wilson also openly compared the Chinese to the Germans and depicted their intrusion into British cities and British ships as an invasion that threatened Britain almost as much as the Germans did.[69] J. R. Bell, another NSFU official, asserted that the Chinese seamen hired by "so-called patriotic shipowners" were the very same men that had been crewing captured German vessels, furthering the impression that the Chinese were unprincipled mercenaries and that hiring them was an act of disloyalty to the nation.[70] The willingness of Chinese seamen to work for the enemy, Bell claimed, made them "the most dangerous of all the aliens" in Britain.[71] The NSFU representatives were joined in their attacks by James Sexton, the spokesman for the Liverpool dockworkers and a future MP, who accused Chinese seamen of selling their wives and their daughters in order to obtain passage to Britain.[72]

Although Sexton called the Aliens Act (presumably that of 1914) "a fraud," all those who spoke out against the Chinese at the TUC meeting agreed that stern legal regulation was the most effective course of action.[73] Not only should new laws repatriating undocumented Chinese seamen be introduced, they insisted, but the current laws governing Chinese seamen's lodging houses and opium required stricter enforcement. Cotter gave Wilson the credit for convincing the London County Council to pass the regulations that required the licensing of seamen's lodging houses, and the NSFU credit for the passage of the laws governing opium in Britain. In a closing speech that roused cheers from the assembled audience, he urged all of those present to demand that the government expel the Chinese from Britain altogether, for if not, Cotter warned, "the evil will spread beyond our ships, and every other trade will be affected." The proposed resolution calling for the introduction of a Chinese repatriation bill in Parliament passed unanimously.[74]

Beyond the TUC, the lack of consensus on Chinese labor was apparent in the responses that these tirades prompted from the editors of national newspapers such as the *Times* and the *Daily Telegraph*. The former was sensitive to shipping interests during the war, while the latter had already attributed rising tensions in the East End to union agitation against Chinese seamen. Gauging the Limehouse reaction to the TUC speeches and the proposed law, the *Times* confirmed that the Chinese population had indeed increased and that this increase was a cause of considerable concern among the local population: "Their lodging-houses have spread from Limehouse-causeway and Pennyfields into other streets, and those who see most of the comings and goings of the men who stay at these places say that the invasion is becoming serious." Their report was more ambivalent about the negative implications of the Chinese presence in the capital, however, particularly in relation to other, less desirable minorities (who remained unnamed). "Compared with some aliens who drift in and out of the East-end," the story ran, "the Chinaman has his merits." The *Times* dismissed Cotter's assertions about Chinese sexual depravity out of hand. The report did not deny that interracial social contact and sexuality took place in Chinatown, but it put it in a very different light. Although admitting that "a certain amount of association between Chinamen and English girls does exist," the *Times* story emphasized that "the blame for this is attributed by some observers more to the girls than to the men."[75]

The *Times* editorial also highlighted the social variations within the Chinese population itself, cautioning readers against assuming "that the whole of the Chinese population in the neighborhood is undesirable. Many Chinamen are thoroughly respectable and a number of them are both smart and intelligent." Although it contradicted the worst allegations made at the TUC meeting, the *Times* report did emphasize the gulf between Chinese and British culture, identifying such differences as the chief source of tension between Chinese residents and British officials. "His ways are not our ways," the story ran, "and his recreations do not fit in with British law. He is unhappy if he cannot gamble, and in spite of raised and heavy fines gambling still goes on every day of the week in the neighbourhood of the West

India Dock-road." Opium smoking as well, although made illegal by DORA 40b, was still practiced "in a surreptitious way."[76]

A similarly ambivalent response to Wilson's and Cotter's allegations appeared the following month in the *Daily Telegraph*, which cautioned "more sober-minded people" against taking the union leaders' statements at face value.[77] Chinese men in London, according to this extensive report, engaged in vice, but that alone did not make them a danger to the surrounding community. The author acknowledged that gambling and opium smoking were "indulged in to an extent which can only be guessed at" in unlicensed Chinese seamen's lodging-houses. Gambling was much more common than opium, however, since "the drug is not easy to obtain now owing to recent restrictions." But he also derided the alarmist claims made by Wilson and Cotter at the TUC meeting. When interviewed by the paper, those most knowledgeable about London's Chinatown—police, LCC inspectors, and social welfare agents—had expressed little anxiety over the recent increases in its population. [78] Like the *Times* report, the *Telegraph*'s story emphasized the presence of respectable elements in the Chinese population and the orderly nature of Chinese men overall, pointing to their intermarriage with English women and their purchase of shops and other properties as evidence of their propriety.

The opinions of the "respectable" Chinese men alluded to in the *Times* and *Telegraph* articles were very much evident in a strident letter written by a dozen members of the Liverpool Chinese Republic Progressive Club, the Tung Yee Tong, to the *Liverpool Courier*. In the letter, which was published in September 1916, the authors strongly protested the allegations made at the TUC meeting and accused Wilson and Cotter of "setting Class against Class and Nation against Nation in order to reap for themselves notoriety." [79] They responded fiercely to Cotter's tirade against gambling and opium, accusing him of gross hypocrisy. "Who began the opium traffic we ask?" they wrote, "who first forced Opium into our Country against our will and made us poor as a nation?" According to the Tung Yee Tong members, the unavailability of opium had forced the Chinese residents of Britain to give up the habit in any case. The authors similarly decried Cotter's double standard on the issue of gambling, a practice they argued was openly engaged in by white residents. They asserted that the real threat of the Chinese came—as Gladstone had famously argued in 1890—from their virtues, not from their vices. Their industriousness, their reliability, and their willingness to work for "a trifle less money" than British seamen were made Chinese men an attractive option for maritime employers. If evidence was needed of their merits as laborers, they insisted, one need only look to the reports of shipowners themselves. Lastly, the authors labeled Cotter's accusations that Chinese men had sold their wives and children to obtain passage to Britain as "the most flagrant lie ever invented."

The usefulness of Chinese laborers was certainly not lost on the British Army. The recruitment and employment of the Chinese Labour Corps (CLC), organized by the War Committee in London in 1916, was intended to free up valuable military manpower for the Western Front. The Chinese, at the time members of a nonbelligerent nation, were forbidden to serve in combat. Over 90,000 CLC recruits were brought to France to work with hundreds of thousands of other laborers from India, South Africa, Egypt, and elsewhere in the British Empire. They dug trenches, worked the docks, built railroads, and buried the dead.[80] The pervasive fear of Chinese immorality, however, was evident in the British preparation of Chinese laborers for work in Flanders and in the treatment they received during their service. British authorities introduced Chinese laborers to continental Europe in mass numbers only after a process of forced assimilation that both reorganized them socially and transformed them physically in a manner that made them manageable and distinguishable to white British officers.[81] The fingerprinting techniques employed by Sir Edward Henry in India and South Africa were essential to British military authorities in their efforts to thwart the "little tricks and dodges" practiced by Chinese workers.[82] To insure that they did not take advantage of white officers' inability to distinguish between different individuals, "every coolie has his finger-prints taken and registered under the supervision of a Scotland Yard expert."[83] They were also given a brass bracelet, to be worn at all times, with their contract number affixed to it. In the daily musters, all CLC members would henceforth be identified by their numbers, not by their names.[84] The publicized accounts of military officials and journalists describing the CLC emphasized the gulfs of culture, character, and even personal hygiene that separated Chinese laborers from white Britons.[85] As had been the case in South Africa and was still the case on British ships, Chinese men in France were considered useful as workers only so long as they were carefully controlled and disciplined by white officers, but otherwise kept strictly segregated from Europeans.[86]

"Most Insidious Is the Oriental in the West": Wartime Race Relations in Popular Fiction

The moral consequences of interracial contact, the effects of Chinese-controlled "vices" on British masculinity, and the threats posed by Chinese wealth, business, and property ownership all figured prominently in wartime courtroom trials, campaigns against gambling and narcotics, union officials' rhetoric, and even in the military recruitment and employment of Chinese labor. They were also central themes in the wartime literary portrayals of Chinatown and race relations in London, though the same lack of consensus that was apparent in law and labor issues was likewise evident there. In popular fiction, there was general agreement about Chinese habits and Chinese character, but differing views on what impact they had on white communities. Sax Rohmer produced his most terrifying incarnation of the Chinese menace yet. *The Yellow Claw*, first published in 1915, depicted London under assault from a brutal and sinister Chinese criminal syndicate, against which only the stern and merciless carriage of masculine justice was effective. In contrast, the stories of Thomas Burke, which were far more popular, portrayed Chinatown and the character of its residents in a more morally-ambiguous light. Both Rohmer and Burke agreed, however, that British masculinity was in dire need of resuscitation and that Chinese men and the resources they controlled were contributing visibly to its decline.

In *The Yellow Claw*, Sax Rohmer discarded the grandiose machinations of his earlier works for more prosaic examples of human vice and villainy. It was Rohmer's most determined effort yet to portray racial villainy in a realistic style and to thus blend "nightmare and the news story."[87] According to his biographer, it was the author's alarm at the reported expansion of the drug trade in Limehouse that prompted him to write "a revealing study of that traffic . . . in the guise of a popular novel."[88] For Rohmer, the book was exactly that—part fiction, part journalistic exposé. The target of his earliest investigations as a journalist in Limehouse, and the later inspiration for "Mr. King," the villain of *The Yellow Claw*, was almost certainly Charles King, a British subject of Chinese origin who owned several lodging houses in Chinatown. King, arguably the most prominent Anglo-Chinese property owner in the East End during this period, was a perennial subject of police suspicion and newspaper inquiry. At the time of Rohmer's writing, however, he had never been convicted of anything more serious than violating London County Council regulations for the management of seamen's lodging houses.[89]

In *The Yellow Claw*, Rohmer transformed Mr. King and his Limehouse businesses into instruments for the corruption, enslavement, and murder of prominent white Londoners. The growing public concern over narcotics use by white Londoners and the threat of vice to Britain's masculine military strength, the supposedly demoralizing effects of interracial contact, and the well-established stereotypes of Chinese commercialism and membership in secret international societies provided readers with a compelling context for King and his sinister global drug syndicate.[90] It was in this less sensationalized incarnation that Rohmer's portrayal of the Yellow Peril would first make the transition from print to cinema. Although Fu Manchu would garner more long-lasting fame than his less fanciful counterpart, Mr. King would precede him onto the silver screen by two years, appearing in a 1921 silent film eponymous with the novel.

The Yellow Claw begins with the brutal murder, by strangulation, of a wealthy bohemian Londoner in Westminster. Although the killer was revealed only by his hands, the reader soon learns that he is Mr. King, a Chinese criminal mastermind who runs a global opium smuggling ring from his Limehouse lair.[91] The book was rife with Orientalist imagery, but the languorous sensuality of the Orient was not the chief concern of the book's hero, the French detective Gaston Max.[92] Rather, Max, with the aid of Scotland Yard and his own array of disguises and stratagems, sought to tear out the "yellow peril" from "the heart of society."[93] The "yellow peril," in this instance, referred to Mr. King and his crime syndicate, which had insinuated itself into the highest levels of British society largely by preying on the pleasure-seeking wives of prominent businessmen and politicians. "Women who acquire a drug habit become more rapidly and more entirely enslaved by it than does a man," one character, a doctor, explained. "It becomes the center of the woman's existence; it becomes her god: all other claims, social and domestic, are disregarded."[94] Neither were men immune from the seductions of the poppy. Some of the most wealthy and powerful members of London society were regular patrons at King's opium den, which counted at least one prominent Member of Parliament among its steady customers.[95] The inclusion of an MP among Rohmer's cast of opium addicts, and the suggestion that other highly-placed members of the government were also under the sway of the drug, made the King syndicate a threat to national security as well as to the moral integrity of the nation.[96]

It was the weak moral fiber of the British elite, Rohmer suggested in his story, that had allowed the "numerous and exotic vices . . . sprung from the soil of the Orient" to penetrate British society and establish a beachhead in the heart of the empire.[97] In *The Yellow Claw*, Rohmer created not just a new villain but also a secret, subterranean realm that lured English men and women into a "shadow world" of drugs and carnal fantasy.[98] King's opium den—the "Cave of the Golden Dragon"—lay in Limehouse. In the Cave, as in similar "branches in Europe, Asia, Africa, and America," white Londoners languished under the commercial, cultural, and sexual dominance of the Chinese.[99] There, in lavishly decorated smoking apartments, men and women addicted to opium willingly gave themselves over, body and soul, "to lie beneath a spell, beneath the spell of an invisible, immeasurably wicked intelligence."[100] The sexual allure of a "magnificently evil" female protagonist of mixed-race origin was also central to the appeal of opium in the book. King was the master of his realm, and the "high-priest" of the opium "cult," but the priestess of the temple was the half-Burmese "lady of the poppies," Mahâra, who represented the seductive, sensual aspect of opium.[101] Her lure was strong, but like the other denizens of the Cave, she was just the tool of a greater power. The force behind the global opium syndicate was the mind of Mr. King. His "malignant intelligence" animated the entire enterprise, and his insidious omnipresence and omnipotence made him a formidable foe. Fu Manchu, at least, had a body that could be seen and attacked—he was powerful, but still human, after a fashion. With Mr. King, on the other hand, Rohmer created a villain that, although embodying Chinese cunning and malevolence in a figurative way, possessed no literal body himself. "The Spirit of Opium," as Gaston Max dubbed King, would have no power, no existence, were it not for the decadent sensuality and moral turpitude of the British men and women that voluntarily surrendered themselves to vice.

This was the central conflict of the novel, not between Gaston Max and Mr. King, but between the two cultures that they represented. The book pitted a masculine Western morality against a feminine, decadent Eastern culture, the latter conceptualized as a terrifying blend of Oriental sensuality and Chinese cunning made manifest in a globe-spanning criminal syndicate.[102] There was no middle ground, no possibility of cooperation or assimilation—cultural, sexual, or otherwise.[103] There were no moral Chinese characters, no industrious, hardworking "coolies," and anyone not wholly of "the West" was suspect, be they Greek, Egyptian or, worst of all, the product of an interracial union (i.e., Mahâra).[104] Nor could there be legitimate Chinese businesses in Rohmer's novel—the only purpose of "Kan-Suh Concessions," an import warehouse in Limehouse, was to serve as a front for the Cave of the Golden Dragon.

The war was never explicitly mentioned, but the struggle against foreign elements in London constituted the crux of the book's plot. Just as the war had prompted the extension of the state's authority over the regulation of everyday life and justified the expansion of the laws governing aliens, the portrayal of law and public authority in *The Yellow Claw* strongly suggested that equally drastic measures were necessary if the morality of the capital and its residents were to be preserved from Chinese corruption. The key figure in Rohmer's portrayal of law and its role as a force to safeguard the integrity of Britain was the Cave's valet, Luke Soames. Although Gaston Max was the hero of *The Yellow Claw*, Soames was the primary protagonist and the most fully developed character in the story. Twelve chapters, a fifth of the entire book, were devoted solely to his induction into the King syndicate and to his internal struggle with his own greed, ambition, and fear. Soames, a former cabin boy and ship's steward, was the one major working-class character in the book and the only one who had the opportunity to make a moral choice. These choices were determined largely by his fear of authority, that of Mr. King on the one hand and of the law on the other. Soames was initially dismissive of the law, for such was the power of his mysterious new master that it dispelled the "old furtiveness" that was part and parcel of his petty criminal past.[105] His feeling of security vanished rapidly, however, when he overheard two Scotland Yard detectives discussing the search for him and Mr. King. The omnipresence and omnipotence of the police quickly replaced that of Mr. King in Soames's mind.[106] Once Gaston Max, who had infiltrated the Cave of the Golden Dragon in the guise of an opium habitué, revealed to Soames how quickly the police net was closing around Mr. King, Soames realized that his safety as part of the syndicate was only illusory and that state authority reigned supreme in the metropolis. "The law, after all, was omnipotent," he decided, "and of all masters was the master to be served."[107]

Rohmer's portrayal of a harsh and invasive system of police surveillance and law enforcement reflected the wartime investigation, prosecution, and punishment of those suspected of spying or treason.[108] In this context, *The Yellow Claw* was both a critique of the restraint still practiced by judicial authorities and a goad for the employment of more ruthless tactics. In order to preserve British masculinity from foreign vice and corruption, Rohmer suggested in the *The Yellow Claw* that the enforcers of law must not shy from draconian measures.

Above all, "the judicial folly which ties the hands of Scotland Yard" must be discarded.[109] The battle against an international Chinese criminal syndicate bent on corrupting the very heart of the nation and empire could not be left to the magistrates of "a silly bench," not when such men had been content to release one of King's chief henchmen, arrested for smuggling hashish from Britain to Egypt, with merely a fine.

The Yellow Claw concluded with a botched police raid on the Cave of the Golden Dragon. In the process, all of King's henchmen were killed, mostly by King himself, but the fate of the Chinese mastermind remained unresolved. We never see King's face—throughout the book, the villain manifests himself only as a pair of murderous hands, accompanied by the smell of decaying roses—nor do we witness his death. Many viewers of the 1921 film adaptation, including the critic for the *Times*, found this ending unsatisfactory. "A film audience loves a mystery," he wrote, "[but] a mystery that remains a mystery is too aggravating to be entirely popular."[110] This ambiguous finale, however, was appropriate both for the character Rohmer had created and for the time in which he was writing. Ultimately, Mr. King was not a corporeal being. He was "the Spirit of Opium," corruption made manifest, "a thing diseased, leprous, contagious," physically debilitating and spiritually oppressive.[111] And, like moral corruption and narcotics addiction, he could not be killed or defeated forever, only contained and prevented from spreading through constant vigilance and the swift application of vigorous justice. In an era when the outcomes of national and racial conflicts were thought to be determined not by the strongest guns but by the strongest spirits and the healthiest bodies, there could be no enemy more timely or more terrifying.[112]

The Yellow Claw highlighted the reciprocal relationship between law, press, and literature in framing the issues of race and vice in the wartime metropolis. Rohmer's inspiration came from the introduction and implementation of DORA 40b in the East End and the press stories its enforcement had generated. And the power of the author's narrative came from the portrayal of illegal narcotics use as a dire threat to white residents and to the nation, an alleged threat that had justified the passage of the regulation itself. But the focus of the wartime anti-vice campaign in London had been on gambling, not opium, and perhaps because of this, *The Yellow Claw* did not cause a popular sensation at the time. Opium use by white Britons was a greater concern among police and Home Office officials than it was among the general public and, for officials in London, it was a lesser concern than cocaine use among white soldiers was.[113]

In the wartime metropolis, moreover, there was still little evidence directly linking Chinese residents to the corruption of white men and women, and Chinese men continued to make significant contributions in British shipping, in domestic war work, and even on the Western Front itself. Like the national press reports that had contradicted union leaders' aspersions against the Chinese, the most prominent literary portrayal of them in this period was ambiguous in its depiction of their moral impact on white residents. Thomas Burke's *Limehouse Nights* (1917) suggested that although British masculinity indeed faced a crisis, it was one that stemmed mostly from its own voluntary dissipation. Many of the familiar stereotypes of Chinese men were replicated in Burke's stories. Chinese men were materialistic and "non-moral," they "love the beauty of little girls," they are pleasure seeking but commercial, languorous and also industrious, emotionally "primitive," yet subtle and cunning, tender lovers but also sexually depraved.[114] Chinese "vices" were an aspect of the East End's demoralization, and interracial contact and sexuality were both visible elements of life there, but such contacts could be beneficial, destructive, or even banal depending upon the circumstances and the personalities of those involved. In Burke's portrayal of the East End, however, as with Rohmer's fiction and the wartime campaigns against vice, Chinese control of wealth and property were the most typical avenues by which they seduced white women or corrupted white men.

Like Rohmer, Burke confessed ignorance of the Chinese people themselves, explaining in his autobiography that his stories of Limehouse came from an impressionistic assessment of the district rather than from an intimate knowledge of it or its residents.[115] The author, by his own admission, romanticized both the East End in general and Chinatown in particular, and the appeal of the stories in his bestselling anthology lay in their combination of that romance with a gritty realism.[116] Against a backdrop of dilapidated taverns, squalid tenements, a "maze of streets," and " 'general' shops with their assorted rags, their broken iron, and their glum-faced basins of kitchen waste," Burke spun tales of love, lust, betrayal, and tragedy.[117] The intentionally romanticized aspects of *Limehouse Nights*, however, did not lessen the significance of its tales as vehicles for shaping public perceptions of Chinatown and the Chinese residents of London. This was particularly true since, as John Seed writes, "Burke seems to have persuaded at least some of his readers that they were not fictions at all."[118] Not only were the depictions of Chinese men in *Limehouse Nights* consistent with previous representations of them in law, literature, and the press, but the readership of Burke's best-selling work, which sparked a transatlantic sensation, would have been far greater than the number of Londoners (let alone Britons nationwide or Americans) who had visited the small neighborhood or spoken with its residents. Burke's stories were populated by colorful characters whose passions and plots stretched the boundaries of credulity, but not so far as to make them entirely implausible.[119] For all its nostalgia and fiction, *Limehouse Nights* remains significant not as an accurate depiction of the neighborhood but rather as both a window into the popular imagining of it and as a means by which that imagining was shaped.[120]

Burke himself often seemed unable—or unwilling—to distinguish between the Chinatown he "imagined" in the stories of *Limehouse Nights* and the one he "observed" in his 1919 journalistic retrospective, *Out and About: A Note-Book of London in War-Time*. His portrayals of the character of the district and the attributes of its Chinese population, although more subdued in tone in the latter, remained relatively consistent. In both works, Chinese men appeared as cunning, deceitful characters; in both, Chinatown was a locale where many races mingled freely; and in both, opium figured significantly in the character of the district, as did the police and the police courts. Burke even inserted some of the same characters, such as "Chuck Lightfoot," a local boxing promoter, in both his fictional portrayals and his wartime observations of the same neighborhood.[121] Perhaps the most prominent feature shared in both portrayals was the prevalence of contact between white women and Chinese men, usually through the medium of Chinese-owned businesses.[122] In contrast to the negative attention that interracial social contact would later attract in interwar London law and press reports, Burke's treatment of it in *Out and About* was remarkable for its *lack* of sensationalism. In *Limehouse Nights* as well, it was this banal depiction of the interdependence and casual social contact between the Chinese and white residents of the district that differentiated his stories from previous depictions of Chinatown and the Chinese by Rohmer, Dickens, and others.[123] Burke explicitly distanced himself from these more salacious portrayals and asserted that the district and its residents were "only awful and romantic to those who have awful and romantic minds."[124] His failure to adhere to conventional standards of middle-class morality in his stories and his blatant depictions of interracial love and cohabitation, sensual vice, and casual moral degradation contributed both to the book's notoriety and to its banning from sale by the national retail chains Boots and W. H. Smith.[125]

For all the contrasts between the unremitting, sinister villainy of Rohmer's Chinese characters and the more nuanced and ambiguous morality of Burke's in *Limehouse Nights*, there are two respects in which their portrayals of Chinese men, interracial contact, and masculinity were very much in accord. First, both authors depicted Chinese wealth and property as the primary means by which they exerted power over white men and women. And second, both Rohmer and Burke emphasized the contrast between the physical robustness and often-violent masculinity of white male characters and the subtle cunning of Chinese men. Although white and Chinese men commit acts of violence in both Burke's and Rohmer's stories, white male violence invariably took the form of pugilism or beatings, while the violence of Chinese men was more subtle and indirect. Particularly in Burke's tales, Chinese methods of attacking white men closely resembled those employed by female characters—white men used their fists, but Chinese men and white women used poison, deception, and carefully-orchestrated traps. Furthermore, in *Limehouse Nights*, Chinese men and Chinese vices such as opium and gambling were often more a threat to working-class men and to the "savagely masculine character" of the East End than they were to white women.[126] Chinese men threatened the white men of the East End in ways to which the latter could not respond effectively, using their deviousness and their wealth to wrest away the love and affection of white wives and daughters. The white men in the stories realized this threat, though often too late, and it prompted them to violent action. In Burke's East End race relations, familiarity often bred contempt, and competition bred rage between white men and their Chinese neighbors. Far from being victims, however, white women, with their greed, pride, plots, and immorality, also threatened the men of the East End.

Burke's stories also depicted the profound effects that race had on respectability, the combination of appearance, reputation, and behavior by which many subtle distinctions of status were made among working-class men and women of the East End.[127] In *Limehouse Nights*, race invariably took precedence over respectability in the assessment of social relations by the community. Each white character's public reputation was of paramount importance to him or her, but Chinese men, no matter what other trappings of respectability they may have possessed, occupied a consistently low position in the judgment of their white neighbors. In the hands of Chinese men, the attributes that would bring status to a white resident—fine clothes, property, and money—were instead often used to promote vice among white men or to lure white women into unsavory interracial unions. The prioritization of race over respectability, Burke suggested, was not the opinion of just one but the consensus of many, reinforced in East End culture and passed down from one generation to the next. In Burke's most famous story, "The Chink and the Child," he explained how the protagonist's "birth and education in Shadwell had taught him that of all the creeping things that creep upon the earth, the most insidious is the Oriental in the west."[128] In these circumstances, interracial contact occurred only at considerable cost to a white resident's respectability. The low social status of Chinese men also meant that any perceived insult they made to a white man's or white woman's public reputation was intolerable and merited immediate retribution, hence the reaction of Gracie Goodnight to being manhandled by her Chinese employer—she orchestrated his death through an "accidental" immolation. [129] Similarly, when Greaser Flanagan lost his wife to a Chinese suitor, no redress was possible, only the most brutal revenge. He tolerated his wife's many previous infidelities with other white men, but he could not stand the idea of her in the arms of a Chinese man, and resolved to murder the offender.[130]

In the final story of Burke's collection, "Old Joe," many of the themes prominent in the previous tales were brought together. The story compared the powerful, masculine morality of the previous generation of white East Enders with the decrepit, feminized, cosmopolitan degeneracy of the current age. A dissolute young Englishman, Perce Sleep, stood as a stark contrast to his stepfather, "Old Joe," who was once "the strongest man in London Docks," but now, tragically, was paralyzed by age and disease.[131] While Perce cared only for pleasure and vice, Old Joe prayed to God to give him back his strength so that he could return to the docks and earn a living for the household.[132] Perce, in order to pay off a gambling debt, accepted £3 from a Chinese man in return for arranging sexual access to Old Joe's mentally disabled adolescent daughter. Old Joe listened helplessly from his invalid's chair as his daughter, lured into a locked room by Perce, was sexually abused by "a large stooping Chinky, flashily dressed in East End ready-mades," a figure whose outward English appearance masked his inner Chinese depravity.[133] In the end, Old Joe's wish was granted. His realization that his own stepson had arranged the brutal violation of his daughter by a Chinese man roused him from his torpor. The face of the Chinese assailant was "lit with horror" as he looked over Perce's shoulder, and Perce, turning, was granted his final vision. "The giant corpse standing on its feet, towering above him, one huge arm stretched to his own white gills, the other, in the joy of returned strength, clutching the long lean knife from the supper-table."[134] Thus did Burke's famous anthology end, with the dramatic resuscitation of East End masculine morality both to punish Chinese depravity and to discipline its own degenerate male progeny.[135]

In their considerations of Londoners' flagging morality, the perceived decline of British masculinity, and their suspicion that Chinese immigrants were contributing to both, Burke, Rohmer, and many of the judicial officials and police in the metropolis were very much in accord. This confluence is not surprising—it was from police reports, court cases, and the official statements of judicial authorities that the chroniclers of Chinatown, both literary and journalistic, often took their cues. Rohmer's conversations with a London police inspector had first put him on the trail of the mysterious "Mr. King, " and in *Out and About*, Burke excerpted a newspaper report of a Thames Police Court case from the 1890s as his most specific evidence for the vice and "Eastern filth" that had once constituted "the glamorous shame of Chinatown."[136] Both authors also openly confessed to having little substantive knowledge of the Chinese men about whom they wrote. But through the sensationalized retelling and reimagining of Chinatown and its residents in fiction and newspapers, a broad reading audience was exposed to the hazards of interracial social contact and sexuality, to the vice and immorality of London's Chinese population, to the corruption spread by Chinese wealth and property ownership, and to the degeneration of British masculinity that was the purported result.

Conclusion

In contrast to the prominent literary portrayals of Chinese-run gambling and opium smoking among white residents of London and the suspicion expressed by police officials, investigations produced no definitive evidence that either had become common practices among soldiers or the rest of the white population in Limehouse, the East End, or anywhere else in the metropolis. The enforcement of opium regulations by police and judicial authorities in London reflected this. In contrast to the events in Liverpool, opium prosecutions in London remained infrequent, and the fines levied against those convicted were relatively small. Two suspects arrested for opium smoking in June 1917 were fined £3 and £10, respectively. The larger fine in the second case was probably due to the defendant's violent resistance to the investigation.[137] As the war dragged on, however, the campaign against gambling in the East End continued unabated. Police raids against Chinatown gambling houses persisted throughout the final years of the war even though there was no evidence that soldiers, officers, or any other white Britons, for that matter, ever frequented them. One raid on a Pennyfields fan-tan parlor in June 1917 netted Superintendent Boxall of K Division five suspects, along with two pistols and £323.[138] Giving evidence before the magistrate H. L. Cancellor of the Thames Police Court, Boxall declared that "for years he had experienced heaps of trouble with the Chinese colony, and they were a 'confounded' nuisance to the neighbourhood."[139] The fines in this case were substantial—collectively, fines of £225 or several months' imprisonment were levied on the five principle suspects—but no recommendations for deportation accompanied the verdicts.

By the end of 1917, judicial attitudes had clearly hardened against Chinese gambling. October saw the arrest of fourteen Chinese residents in a single raid and the first instance of an East End magistrate recommending deportation on these grounds.[140] In contrast, another East End Chinese suspect arrested for smoking opium in January 1918 was fined only 10s.[141] March 1917 also witnessed a revival of violence between rival Chinese factions in Limehouse. The events followed the same pattern of fierce but nonfatal combat as other instances of internecine Chinese conflict had in the past.[142] The sentences of de facto deportation subsequently handed down by the presiding justice at the Central Criminal Court mirrored those given by police court magistrates in prewar occurrences of such violence. Mr. Leycester bound over two defendants to keep the peace, and jailed the other eight until ships could be found for them. "They must remain in prison meanwhile. That will do them no harm," another court official declared, prompting laughter from those in attendance.[143]

In tandem with the harder line taken by London magistrates, officials at the local, metropolitan, and national levels expressed increasing concern, in the closing years of the war, about both the morality of Chinese men residing in Britain and the impact of Chinese labor on public order. At the height of the war, both metropolitan and Home Office officials had acknowledged the value of Chinese maritime labor, to the point of chastising police officials in Cardiff and Liverpool whose harsh policies were obstructing Chinese employment.[144] Even so, the government went to considerable lengths to monitor the numbers and movement of Chinese aliens, and even implemented fingerprinting as a means of identifying individuals.[145] Limehouse, because of the rapid growth of its Chinese population and the tendency of Chinese seamen who had been driven out of Liverpool and Cardiff by harsher regulations to congregate there, was a subject of particular concern.[146] Officials in Scotland Yard expressed their dismay at the difficulties of keeping track of a Chinese population there that had swelled to 4,000 registered individuals, many of whom they suspected were avoiding the stipulations of the Aliens Restriction Order by employing multiple names and a variety of identifying documents.[147] By mid-1918, with the need for Chinese maritime labor waning, Home Office officials were declaring their adamant opposition to further increases of the Chinese communities of Britain's port cities. When the powerful shipping magnate Alfred Holt wrote to the Ministry of Shipping that a steady stream of inexpensive, competent Chinese sailors arriving regularly from Hong Kong would serve as an effective counter against the demands of British seamen for higher wages, the government sternly refused. Bleak memories of anti-Chinese union agitation in the prewar period remained fresh in the minds of Home Office officials. "It is an insidious move on the part of Hold & Co," John Pedder wrote, "who were the chief offenders in the old days when British Merchant Shipping was being overrun with Chinese."[148]

Pedder, the assistant secretary to the directing minister of the Home Office, had been a key figure in the enforcement of the original Aliens Act of 1905. He was joined in his resolute opposition to further Chinese immigration by William Haldane Porter, who had served as His Majesty's Inspector of Aliens since the passage of the act.[149] For Pedder, Porter, and others in the Home Office, the hostility of the NSFU, the need to find employment for white seamen, the logistical challenges of monitoring Chinese seamen once they arrived in Britain, and their reported penchants for gambling and opium use all made any increase in their numbers wholly undesirable. Porter also strongly advocated any arrangements that would decrease the current population. "Chinese seamen again!" he exclaimed in one memo, which criticized the Ministry of Shipping's failure to make adequate arrangements for the repatriation of Chinese munitions workers. "When we return to peacetime, we must make a strong effort to get the matter of Chinese seamen settled once and for all."[150] In the meantime, Porter and other officials in the Home Office and Board of Trade agreed that strict enforcement of the laws and regulations governing immigration, the movement of friendly aliens, and maritime employment were the best counters to any possible increases in the Chinese presence or disturbances to public order on account of them.

Considering the violent racial disorders that lay just over the horizon, the words of one Board of Trade official in November 1918 seem prophetic. "With the conclusion of hostilities and probable demobilization of British seamen from His Majesty's Forces in the near future," the Assistant Secretary of the Marine Department wrote, "it is even more desirable than hitherto that these Chinese seamen should not be returned to the United Kingdom for employment."[151] Porter, never one to mince words, put it more bluntly. "We may anticipate trouble," he told his superiors that same month, "when conditions become normal, from the Sailors [*sic*] and Firemen's Union over 'chinks.'"[152] But he was wrong on two accounts. The concern with Chinese residents had already spread well beyond the NSFU to become a serious issue for Home Office officials, magistrates, and police, and a popular topic in journalism and fiction. Discussions of Chinese residents and interracial contact had also expanded beyond labor issues and into the realm of morality and the possible spread of gambling and opium smoking among white residents in London. The growth of the Chinese population in Britain, albeit temporary, and the consequences of its contact with British men and women, formerly prominent issues in imperial race relations, had become domestic concerns. In response, laws designed to protect the security of the nation against hostile aliens and to preserve the morals and health of its soldiers and citizens had been employed to investigate and arrest Chinese men, and even to deport them without trial.

Porter was also mistaken in assuming that postwar conditions in Britain, with regard to race, gender, law, and labor, would simply return to "normal." Just as the outbreak of war had presaged alterations in the social, cultural, economic, and legal context of race relations in London, its conclusion and the subsequent return of millions of demobilized soldiers and sailors to Britain would once again herald change. By November 1918, the war in Europe was coming to a close, but the legal campaign against vice, immorality, and the Yellow Peril in London was far from over.

Chapter 5

East (End) Meets West (End)

In the immediate postwar period, threats of racial and gender disorder, and of the sinister power that both Chinese men and degenerate white women could hold over other white Britons, were at the center of the judicial, journalistic, and literary discussions of Chinatown. This refocusing of attention on Chinese men and their activities in London was neither sudden nor inevitable, but evolved over a series of highly visible court cases. The direst threat attributed to Chinese men emerged not from *their* opium use and gambling, activities that had been so central to earlier portrayals, but from their alleged encouragement of West End debauchery and their co-optation of white women into their schemes. Social contact between white women and the racial other had been a longstanding concern in the empire, but in the interwar period, it became an increasingly volatile issue in London.[1] Court trials, press reports, and popular fiction all helped popularize the fear that corrupted white women were helping to forge sinister connections between the decadence and wealth of white West Enders and the vice of Chinatown. The conflation of opium and cocaine into a sinister "dope" culture controlled by Chinese men and their female agents proved to be an especially potent justification for judicial intervention and public scandal-mongering. At issue was not just the power and influence of Chinese men in the metropolis but the independence and agency of white, working-class women as well—the latter a concern that women's changing roles in the wartime period had brought to the fore in British society.[2] The explicit focus on property and commerce in these circumstances also highlighted how issues of race, gender, geographic mobility, and interwar economic tensions were intertwined.

Even as court trials and their literary and journalistic reinterpretations suggested that Chinese men, often with the aid of white women, were actively corrupting other white Londoners, the legal evidence for such connections remained scant and judicial opinion was far from unanimous. Some magistrates openly decried the pernicious influence of Chinatown and its residents, while others dismissed both journalistic sensationalism and the statements by their colleagues that fed into it. Nevertheless, prominent court cases, press reports, and popular fiction helped establish the idea that the small Chinese population of London, and those white women associated with it, posed a grave threat to white Londoners. Public depictions of Chinatown helped to rewrite the imagery of vice and the standards of morality along racial lines and to clarify the racial geography of the metropolis. These trends had been part and parcel of British portrayals of Chinese residents of London since the nineteenth century, but their prominence and significance increased substantially in the interwar period.[3]

"Visits to Chinatown": Narratives of Moral Justice in the Gibson Inquest

The court case that inaugurated the next public furor over Chinatown, a coroner's inquest into the death of William Gibson Jr., took place on August 14 and 23, 1918. Gibson, the son of a noted international shipping and textiles magnate, had been found dead in his West End flat after a night of narcotics use.[4] During the inquest, statements by the witnesses, the Marylebone coroner, a scientific expert working for the Home Office, and the police all highlighted the connection between Chinatown, opium, and the conduit of drugs and vice that allegedly connected the Chinese residents of the East End to the white residents of the West End.[5] The two principal witnesses in the case—James Martin, the chief clerk of the Gibson shipping firm, and Gertrude Wilson, Gibson's mistress—both testified that Gibson, on the night before his death, had spoken to them of his recent visit to Chinatown, and Wilson told the court that "she knew he went there to get opium pellets."[6] The deceased, according to Martin, was "fond of going to queer places to see strange sights" and had related to the clerk that he often went to the East End to "see life." Martin also testified that, two days before Gibson's death, "a Chinaman" had come to call on Gibson at his office in Finsbury, but that Gibson had refused to see him. When questioned by the coroner, Mr. Webster, a scientific expert working for the Home Office, offered not just his professional assessment of the victim's drug-taking habits but also his personal opinion on his sources as well. "He believed it was common knowledge that there were opium dens in the East-end," Webster told the coroner, "but he did not know how they managed to get such large quantities of opium, which was a poison under the Pharmacy Act."[7]

Police investigations into Gibson's death had focused on "various Chinese establishments" in the East End, but were unable to confirm the reports of the deceased's visits there.[8] The *Times*'s reports, nonetheless, appeared under the headline "East-End Opium Dens" even though Gibson had died in his own apartment in the West End (Baker Street) and police had been unable to corroborate witness testimony on the matter. The coroner's inquest and the press coverage of it offered a simple, straightforward narrative to a reading audience already well acquainted—thanks to previous legal cases, press reports, popular fiction, and the wartime anti-narcotics campaigns—with the dangers of opium, the prevalence of "opium dens" in the East End, and the role of Chinese residents in the drug's importation, preparation, and distribution. All of these elements of the Gibson case were, as Mr. Webster had asserted in his testimony, "common knowledge" by 1918.[9]

The *Times*'s "East End Opium Dens" headlines on August 15 and 24 covered not just the Gibson inquest, however, but two Thames Police Court cases as well. On the same day as the second session of the Gibson inquest, the magistrate Henry Rooth had prosecuted "a Chinamen" for running an opium den at High Street, Poplar. Just as the Gibson case offered readers a stark picture of the dire threat of opium and indicated that Chinese residents were clearly to blame for its spread in London, Rooth's prosecution of the opium den proprietor reassured them that East End magistrates were well aware of the problem and were willing to employ the most potent legal weapons available. For only the second time in the history of the London police courts, Rooth recommended that the Home Office use the authority granted by the Aliens Restriction (Consolidation) Act of 1914 to designate the defendant as an undesirable alien and to deport him solely on the grounds that he had managed an opium den.[10] Although there were no concrete connections between Rooth's sharp deviation from previous judicial treatment of opium offenses in London and Gibson's death, Rooth's leniency toward Chinese opium offenders in other cases suggests that the timing of his decision was not coincidental. That the *first* instance of an East End magistrate ever recommending deportation for opium took place in the Thames Police Court on August 14, the same day on which the initial inquest into Gibson's death had been held, further lessens the odds of coincidence.[11]

The pairing of the two sets of articles in the *Times* on August 15 and 24, the first in each instance discussing the Gibson inquest and the second covering the conviction and recommendation for deportation of a suspected Chinese opium dealer, provided readers with a morally satisfying resolution.[12] The true culprits in the Gibson case may never have been found, but the public could rest assured that stern justice had been meted out to those conducting the nefarious trade in the vice that had had killed the young scion of a wealthy family. Adding to the stark moral divisions between white victim and Chinese villain that emerged from witness testimony and its journalistic representation was the relaxation of moral judgments against Gibson. As had been the case in *Rex v. Lee Kun*, the victim's transgression of popular moral standards was downplayed or ignored during the trial in favor of a narrative that highlighted the infamy of the Chinese men involved. Gibson's battle with alcoholism, for example, was presented by witnesses as proof of his perseverance, and his turn to narcotics was allegedly part of his struggle against his this earlier addiction. That the chief witness in the case was a woman with whom the deceased had been having an adulterous affair for two years was ignored entirely. The impression that vice and immorality were the purview of the Chinese race in general was further emphasized by the *Times*'s failure to name any of the Chinese men that appeared either as suspicious characters in the Gibson inquest testimony or as defendants in the Thames Police Court cases—stripped of the individuality granted to the white victim and witnesses, the former were all merely "Chinamen."

But the creation of a moral narrative where the sins of the victim were overlooked and stern justice was delivered (albeit vicariously) to Chinese peddlers of vice was the least of the misleading impressions that were publicized during the Gibson inquest. Expert medical testimony proved that, contrary to the statements made by witnesses and reinforced by the *Times*'s suggestive coverage, Gibson's death was more likely to have been caused by morphine than it was by opium. Despite the repeated and prominent discussion of "opium dens," there was no definitive evidence that he had used any opium at all on that fateful night. The autopsy revealed large quantities of morphine in Gibson's system, but only trace elements consistent with opium use, and Gertrude Wilson had witnessed Gibson injecting a substance that could have been either refined opium *or* morphine, but not smoking or consuming opium, on the night of his death.[13] It was only at the second day of the inquest, on August 23, after witnesses testified that Gibson had contacts with Chinese men and had visited Chinatown to buy opium, that the medical expert, Dr. Spilsbury, reversed his initially ambiguous findings and told the court that Gibson's death was attributable to "opium poisoning."[14]

Despite the lack of evidence that opium had caused Gibson's death, both the police and the coroner aggressively pursued the alleged involvement of opium and the connections to Chinatown and its residents. But they made absolutely no attempt to trace the origins of Gibson's morphine supply, and its possible role in his death was barely acknowledged. Such a line of inquiry would certainly have shattered the racial morality play set up by the inquest and the *Times*'s reporting of it in conjunction with the trials and deportations of the two other Chinese defendants. The consumption and distribution of morphine, although long identified as a problem in British society, had never been prominently connected in public discourse with the Chinese residents of London, and rightly so.[15] The conversion of raw opium into its smokable state (aka "cooking opium") was a relatively cheap, simple process. The refining of raw opium into morphine, on the other hand, was a far more complex and delicate affair that required both specialized equipment and a considerable knowledge of chemistry—neither of which were readily available to Chinese men in the East End.[16] Any attempt to establish the source of Gibson's morphine would most likely have implicated a white chemist, legitimate drug manufacture, and British government policy. British manufacturers had been mass-producing morphine refined from imported Indian opium for more than a decade by this time, and thousands of pounds of the narcotic were distributed every year for legitimate sale by licensed chemists around Britain.[17] Almost without exception, those prosecuted for the illegal sale of morphine in the preceding years had been white chemists who had either accidentally (according to their testimony) sold morphine beyond the proscribed boundaries of distribution or had been supplementing their legitimate income with black market sales on the side.[18] Morphine, although dangerous, was nonetheless solidly within the purview of established medical authority, and the majority of its distribution and use in Britain and abroad, according to most observers, was for legitimate purposes.[19] Opium smoking, on the other hand, was consistently described in this period as a Chinese vice, and illicit opium-selling in Britain as a Chinese business, no matter who else was involved.

The Gibson case and the trials of the two alleged opium den proprietors held dire implications for both the judicial treatment and public perception of Chinese men in London. For the first time, Chinese vice in the metropolis had been publicly held responsible for the death of a prominent white Londoner. By focusing on opium and Chinatown and ignoring evidence that contradicted this interpretation, police, prosecutors, and the press offered dramatic proof that Chinese vice was spreading from the East End to the West End. Two Chinese men had subsequently been deported for opium crimes that previously, even during the height of the wartime narcotics campaign, had only merited fines in London courtrooms. Police testimony and reports in the *Times* also suggested that the Gibson inquest and the simultaneous East End "opium den" trials were aspects of an even greater danger posed by London's Chinese residents. Although the prosecutions of the alleged opium den proprietors were reported in much less detail than the Gibson inquest was, the *Times* included one specific feature of the August 15 trial—the police witness's assertion that the Chinese defendant was not acting alone but as "the agent of an opium syndicate."[20] In the opium prosecutions that accompanied the Gibson trial, and in other trials and press reports that followed, the linkage of Chinese internationalism with the spread of illicit narcotics use and gambling among white Londoners dramatically emphasized Chinatown's sinister influence on the metropolis and helped justify further judicial and police intervention in the district. The opium trials of August 1918, however, were eclipsed in the immediate aftermath of the war by an even more sensational set of court cases that brought the connection between Chinese men, Chinatown, vice and crime, and the dire threat that they allegedly posed to white Britons to the attention of a national audience.

"A Circle of Degenerates": Ada Ping You, Billie Carleton, and the Spread of Vice in the Metropolis

On the morning of November 28, 1918, Billie Carleton (aka Florence Stewart), a London actress and photographic model, was found dead in her West End flat. The initial set of trials surrounding Carleton's death took place in December and focused on three primary suspects, Reginald de Veulle, a friend of Carleton's; Ada Ping You, a Scotswoman and associate of De Veulle's; and Len Ping You, Ada's Chinese husband. All three were charged and convicted of violating DORA 40b, which prohibited the possession or sale of opium and cocaine by unlicensed persons. But their trials and sentences varied widely, demonstrating the complex ways in which issues of race, gender, and morality could help determine how law was enforced in interwar London. Their trials, under the provisions of DORA, also highlighted both the powerful legal and cultural legacies of World War I and the role of courtroom discourse in constructions of race, gender, and the racial geography of the metropolis.

Reginald de Veulle was ultimately held responsible for providing the cocaine (originally bought by a third party, Lionel Belcher) that, according to the arguments and testimony that emerged during the trial, had killed Carleton.[21] He was charged with manslaughter and DORA violations and, after a lengthy and well-publicized coroner's inquest and jury trial in the Central Criminal Court, which lasted into April of 1919, he was acquitted of the former and pled guilty to the latter. De Veulle, whose involvement in the cocaine traffic and provision of the drug to Carleton had been corroborated by multiple eyewitness accounts, was sentenced to eight months in prison.[22] Ada Ping You, in contrast, was convicted of supplying Carleton with opium, which had not been instrumental in the latter's death. Indeed, there was neither any opium in Carleton's flat nor any signs that she had recently taken the drug—witness testimony indicated that Carleton had quit smoking opium several weeks before her death. The case against Ada Ping You, on the whole, was poorly supported by the available evidence. The only witness called by the prosecution was the arresting policeman, Detective-Inspector John Curry of New Scotland Yard. Not only did the prosecution admit that there was insufficient evidence that Ping You had actually supplied opium to Carleton, but when Curry was asked by the presiding magistrate to substantiate the claim that she had been paid to prepare opium (not supplied by her) for Carleton and others to smoke, his response was vague and evasive.[23]

The charges against Ada Ping You were so unsubstantiated by specific evidence that even the timing of her alleged crime could not be properly established. As could best be determined by Curry's testimony in the trial, her only direct contact with Billie Carleton had taken place on either September 7 or September 14, nearly two months before the latter's death.[24] Despite the lack of any tangible connection between Ada Ping You, opium, and Carleton's death, and despite the overall weakness of the legal case against her, after a trial at the Marlborough Street Police Court that lasted only a few hours, the magistrate Frederic Mead summarily convicted her of DORA 40b violations. He then sentenced her to five months imprisonment with hard labor.[25] Len Ping You, who had had no direct contact with Carleton and no specific involvement in any of the events surrounding her death, but who had allegedly sold cocaine to De Veulle on an earlier occasion and had been arrested with both opium and opium-smoking utensils in his possession, received a £10 fine.[26]

The formal strictures of the law were a poor justification for Ada Ping You's swift and calamitous trial. The reasons why, among the many men and women implicated in the Carleton affair, she was singled out for such a fierce penalty lay in the specific circumstances of her involvement, in the strategies employed by the prosecuting counsel, in the attitude of the presiding magistrate, and in the timing of the case. Of all those who went to trial following Carleton's death, it was Ada Ping You's actions that, according to both the prosecution and the sentencing magistrate, most severely transgressed racial boundaries and gendered moral expectations. The success of the prosecution's case lay in their focus on her violation of gender norms by her active participation in the corruption and demoralization of white men and women and on her breach of racial boundaries by her marriage to a Chinese man who was a known opium addict.

The case against Ada Ping You was presented by the police solicitor Herbert Muskett, who had been instrumental in the conduct of the wartime anti-gambling and anti-cocaine campaigns. Although he asserted in his closing arguments that he wished to present the facts of the case "in as colourless a manner as possible and to avoid the unnecessary introduction of any sensational or realistic matter," his conduct during the trial belied this claim.[27] Muskett's successful prosecution of Ada Ping You, on the contrary, revolved around his emphasis on her villainy and sexual depravity. Building on the evidence that Lionel Belcher, another associate of De Veulle's and Carleton's, had given on the first day of De Veulle's trial in the Westminster Coroner's Court, Muskett's opening statement in Ada Ping You's trial lingered on the most salacious details surrounding Carleton's death. "Certain events pertaining to the case took place . . . a month or two ago," he told the court, "on that occasion disgusting orgies took place extending from Saturday night until early in the Sunday afternoon."[28] These "orgies" referred to the communal opium-smoking parties held by De Veulle, Carleton, and others at various flats in the West End. There, it was reported, participants had changed into pajamas (for men) and nightdresses (for women), and smoked themselves into a dreamy torpor.

Following Muskett's introduction of the term, "disgusting orgies" became a catch phrase for the remainder of both Ada Ping You's trial and De Veulle's. It would be endlessly repeated by judges, prosecutors, and the press across the course of the next few months to denote the moral degeneracy and sexual debauchery associated with the Carleton affair. At these "orgies," Muskett argued, Ada Ping You had been the central figure. "There could be no doubt that the woman was a professional preparer of opium," he told the court. Using the testimony of Belcher and the secondhand evidence provided by Detective-Inspector Curry, Muskett painted a dark picture of Ping You's careful orchestration an of an opium-smoking party held at De Veulle's Piccadilly flat in early September.[29] At the center of a "circle of degenerates," Muskett said, "Mrs. Ping You officiated. She had an opium tin and the lamp, the opium needle, and all the accessories. She prepared the opium."[30]

Both Muskett and Curry also emphasized Ada Ping You's transgression of racial boundaries through her marriage, reminding the court on several occasions that although she was born a Scotswoman, she had married a Chinese man and now lived in Limehouse. Their determination to highlight this particular aspect of her identity was evident even in the language with which they referred to her and her circumstances—the prosecution's testimony consistently omitted both Ada Ping You's Scottish first name and her husband's English sobriquet, referring to her as "Mrs. Ping You" or "Mrs. Lo Ping" and to him merely as "a Chinaman." It was on this question of race and gender norms that Ada Ping You's defense, mounted by Barrington Matthews, also rested. According to Matthews, Ada Ping You was, like Carleton, an innocent young girl, and she had been led astray by the corrupting influences of her Chinese husband, who was hopelessly addicted to opium. "She had been married for the past 3½ years to a Chinaman," he told the court, "and one could well appreciate what her surroundings had been since her marriage . . . she was taught how to prepare opium by her husband."[31] The strength of the moral case made against the defendant stood in stark contrast to the weakness of the legal evidence against her. Muskett's arguments, Curry's testimony, and Matthews's defense were all in agreement that Ada Ping You had *not* supplied the opium that had been smoked at De Veulle's flat. There was no evidence that she had ever directly supplied Carleton with either opium or cocaine, as Muskett himself readily admitted to the court.[32] Nor was there any legal precedent for harsh punishment in such circumstances. The police court trials that took place during the Gibson inquest had set the precedent for the deportation of Chinese men for opium-related offenses in London, but as of December 1918, none of the small handful of white Britons arrested on opium charges had been imprisoned, and the highest fine imposed had been for £50.[33]

What the court had to decide was whether Ada Ping You's role in the circumstances surrounding Carleton's death—circumstances that were, according to Muskett, "squalid, deplorable . . . and disgraceful to modern civilization"—justified the imposition of a harsh sentence, and it was on this issue that the arguments of both the prosecution and the defense ultimately focused.[34] Both Muskett's prosecution and Mat-thews's defense rested on the same essential point—although Ada Ping You was not Chinese by birth, she had been tainted by Chinese immo-rality and Chinese vice through her marriage to a Chinese man. The questions that remained would occupy the center of the debate over race, gender, and morality in London for the next several years. Was Ada Ping You, in her adoption of "Chinese" vice, a victim or a villain? Was she an active participant in her own moral downfall and in spread-ing corruption to other white Britons, or had she simply been weak and fallen prey to the degenerative power of her Chinese husband and the social pressure of debauched West Enders such as De Veulle?[35]

The presiding magistrate, Frederick Mead, had a reputation as a moralizer who strongly adhered to a conservative view of gender roles.[36] As a consequence, Muskett's portrayal of Ada Ping You as an architect of vice and degeneration was even more alarming to him than it would have been to a more progressive (or more cynical) mag-istrate. It is worth noting, however, that the highest fine imposed previously for opium offenses in London had also been inflicted upon a white woman accused of running an opium den in the West End. But a different magistrate (Graham Campbell) at a different police court (Bow Street) had presided over that trial, indicating that there may have been a growing consensus among magistrates on the need for stern sentencing in such circumstances.[37] While he considered his verdict, Mead could be certain that his pronouncements would carry significant weight in the public discussion of Carleton's death and the rapidly expanding scandal it had generated. Ada Ping You was the first of the three primary defendants in the Carleton trials to receive a sentence, and the court proceedings had been closely observed by both the press and the general public. The connection between Car-leton and the theater world, the latter a perennial object of popular fascination and public scandal, vastly increased the attention focused on the cases. Not only were the trials covered, in detail, in a variety of London newspapers, but crowds gathered daily outside the court-rooms where they took place and included in their number "several well-known actresses and actors."[38]

It was in this highly charged environment that Mead delivered his scathing indictment of Ada Ping You. Openly dismissing the legal nice-ties of the case, Mead declared that that "there is no doubt that she took a leading part in the most disgraceful proceedings on the night in question [i.e., the opium-smoking party two months before Car-leton's death]. She acted as the high priestess at these unholy rites."[39]

The magistrate also made it clear that he was delivering judgment not only upon Ada Ping You but also upon everyone else involved in the opium traffic. "I suppose one cannot shut one's eyes to the fact that this indulgence in opium is prevalent," Mead told the court, "and I consider an example is required." The message behind his sentencing of Ada Ping You to five months with hard labor was not likely to be lost on any who observed the trial or followed its course in the papers that covered it, nor was Mead isolated in his judicial assessment of the defendant's transgressions. When Ada Ping You appealed her sentence, Sir Robert Wallace, Chairman of the London Sessions, sharply dismissed her application. "The offense was a very serious one," he told the court, "and must be put down."[40]

The statements made about the immorality, criminality, and degeneracy of Ada Ping You by Muskett, Mead, and others involved in these trials stood in stark contrast to the public portrayals of Billie Carleton. Her transgressions of law and popular moral standards, like those of William Gibson Jr. before her were redeemed in the press both by her death and by the greater sins of those around her, all of which were brought to light in the prosecutions that followed the actress's controversial demise. Over time, Ada Ping You and De Veulle—the latter portrayed by the prosecution as a feminized degenerate—shouldered the mantle of the villains in the press coverage and the popular retellings of the Carleton affair. Carleton's respect for racial boundaries was central to her redemption in these portrayals. Unlike Ada Ping You, she was never accused of violating the popular taboos against interracial sexuality and therefore remained, according to the *World's Pictorial News*, the "very essence of English girlhood."[41]

Despite the determined vilification and harsh punishment meted out to Ada Ping You by Muskett and Mead, the demonization of opium and opium smoking remained far from universal in late 1918, even in the fraught atmosphere of public scandal surrounding the Carleton affair. The contrast between the prosecution and sentencing of Ada Ping You and that of her husband, Len Ping You (aka "Lo Ping You"), further demonstrated that the judicial treatment of such crimes could vary widely depending upon the specific circumstances of the case and the presiding magistrate's views on race, gender, morality, and vice. Even as Mr. Mead was declaring Len Ping You's wife to be a "high priestess of unholy rites" and sentencing her to five months imprisonment with hard labor, Len Ping You himself, who had been arrested at the same time and was charged with similar crimes, was experiencing a very different type of justice before the magistrate Henry Rooth at the Thames Police Court. Len Ping

You's defense, mounted by F. Russell Davies, relied on the defendant's race, his health, his alleged moral perseverance, the power that opium addiction held over its victims, and the small amount of opium found in the police search of his home. Davies also told the court that Len Ping You had consumption (i.e. tuberculosis) and that he was diligently trying to quit the habit of opium smoking. "Chinamen held opium to be beneficial," he emphasized, "that might account for the prisoner's having taken the drug to excess at one time."[42]

Rooth's ultimate decision in Len Ping You's case was as notable for its leniency as Mead's thundering indictment of Ada Ping had been for its severity. When Rooth had adjudicated an opium case against Ten Chan, a Chinese citizen, on December 21, 1918, he had insisted that opium's status as the "national vice" of the Chinese had to be taken into consideration in sentencing practices, an assertion that he repeated in delivering judgment against Len Ping You.[43] Rooth also implied that, although he was well aware of the scandal surrounding the case, he considered such circumstances to be extraneous, and he refused to take them into account.[44] He imposed a £10 fine and, despite urgings from the prosecution, adamantly refused to recommend the deportation of the defendant. This was precisely the same course of action that the magistrate had followed when the police representative had made a similar demand in the Ten Chan case two weeks previously.[45] In Ada Ping You's case, weak, largely circumstantial evidence of what both prosecutor and magistrate had portrayed as a heinous act of propagating vice to white Britons had earned her the maximum possible sentence. In her husband's case, indisputable evidence of a much lesser sin of private drug use had brought him what amounted to a slap on the wrist. In both cases, the charges themselves had been almost identical.

The trials of Ada and Len Ping You highlighted how important issues of gender, race, and subjective assessments of vice and immorality were to the enforcement of law in interwar London. They also demonstrated how racial and national identity—particularly in relation to gender—could be constructed in British courtrooms in a variety of ways, depending upon the circumstances of each case and the predilections of counsels and magistrates. Matthews had claimed that Ada Ping You's marriage to a Chinese man had hopelessly corrupted her. Just as British naturalization law insisted that British women who married foreigners forfeited their legal identity as citizens, he suggested, with his arguments, that Ada Ping You had sacrificed her racial identity as well, falling prey to "Chinese" habits.[46] Matthews's defense of her depended upon a portrayal of Len Ping You as corrupting and seductive in a manner stereotypical of his race and of Ada Ping You as weak and malleable in a manner stereotypical of her gender. Muskett and Mead, on the other hand, had emphasized Ada Ping You's power and agency, and suggested that her willing corruption of other white Londoners was unnatural and "unholy."

In contrast to the debate over race and gender that was central to Ada Ping You's trial, Len Ping You's racial identity was never questioned. Davies and Rooth both denied that he was in any way British, despite his marriage to a Scotswoman and his long residence in London—Len Ping You was only twenty-five and had lived in Britain for more than half his life. In spite of these mitigating factors, Davies insisted—and Rooth obviously agreed—that Len Ping You remained Chinese and was thus vulnerable to the moral and physical failings thought to be typical of his race. A propensity for vice and a taste for opium, they asserted, were among these inherent characteristics. Regardless of whoever chose to smoke opium, Rooth asserted that it remained first and foremost the "national vice" of the Chinese. According to this assessment, Len Ping You, unlike his wife, had not transgressed against the standards of racial morality at all but instead had remained entirely true to form. Underpinning all these debates was the assumption that Britons and Chinese, in character and culture, in body and in spirit, were fundamentally incompatible. Unions could be formed, but only at the cost of a white woman's moral and racial status. In interwar London courtrooms, as in the empire, a moral, consensual marriage between a white woman and a non-European man was all but unimaginable.[47]

Marek Kohn, in his brief description of these trials, has pointed to their significance in demonstrating the range of judicial opinion on narcotics.[48] But such diversity of opinion had characterized the portrayal and prosecution of drug use in the East End for more than a decade by this time. Of far greater significance was what the language of trial participants and the response of journalists and the reading public revealed about the evolving views of race, gender, and interracial sexuality in the interwar period. The impact and longevity of the terms and images employed by witnesses, magistrates, police, and attorneys also highlighted the influence of courtroom narratives in shaping those views. Perhaps most significantly of all, from the standpoint of law in London, the courtroom retelling and reshaping of the events surrounding Billie Carleton's death—retellings that often adhered more closely to racial and gender stereotypes than they did to reliable evidence—offered a powerful justification for the extension of wartime emergency powers into the interwar period. By February 1919, London magistrates were openly calling for just such measures.[49] The wartime portrayal of illicit narcotics use as a threat to the nation had added further impetus for the continued employment of these powers. The war may have ended, but the vice it had spawned, as the Carleton affair dramatically demonstrated, clearly had not. DORA 40b remained the ideal judicial weapon in this context since it allowed for the selective prosecution of those involved in the illicit narcotics trade without restricting the highly profitable (and politically significant) medical narcotics industry. Used in conjunction with the laws on aliens, it granted magistrates both powerful authority and considerable discretion in cases involving Chinese defendants and their white compatriots.

"Lo Ping's Shuttered House": Interwar Chinatown in Journalism and Fiction

Even before Ada Ping You was sentenced, Chinatown and its residents began to experience negative repercussions from the scandal generated by Carleton's death and the subsequent court trials. The trials of Reginald De Veulle, Ada Ping You, and Len Ping You prompted a new phase of sensationalized reporting, the worst and most sustained yet, on the district and its residents. The *Times*, which was among the worst culprits in the exaggeration—or, at times, outright fabrication—of associations between Chinatown, the corruption of white women, Carleton's death, and opium, delivered its chronicle of De Veulle's extended trial for manslaughter and DORA violations under suggestive bylines such as "visits to Chinatown" and "opium orgy" or, in Ada Ping You's case, "Charge of supplying drugs to Miss Carleton" and "High Priestess of Unholy Rites," all of which were drawn directly from the statements made by prosecutors and magistrates in court.[50] The sinister romanticizing of Chinatown, a district whose reputation for vice and degeneracy had by this time, according to Thomas Burke, far outstripped its reality, was once again in full swing.[51]

The new focus of press coverage mirrored the emphasis Muskett and Mead had placed on interracial sexuality and the transmission of vice from the East End to the West End. The *Daily Chronicle*, a popular, Liberal, London penny daily, was the first to publish a story from "the heart of Chinatown" in the wake of the Carleton affair.[52] Its December 14, 1918, article titled "Lo Ping's Shuttered House"—referring to the home of Ada Ping You and Len (aka "Lo") Ping You—described the neighborhood in the most lurid terms.[53] The house itself, the *Chronicle*'s account asserted, "almost hides itself away under the railway arch as if anxious to escape the light of day."

According to the reporter sent to investigate, the surrounding scene was notable primarily for its squalor, its population of mixed-race children, and the status of white observers as perennial outsiders in Chinatown. The whole district fairly radiated an air of cunning and inscrutable mystery. "Outside, some children, half English, half Chinese, were playing in the dimly-lit gutters, and around them Chinatown went its way, apparently unconcerned with the sensational story in which No. 24 now figures. But it was true Oriental indifference," the report claimed, "which means Chinatown was very much alive to all that was going on." The *Chronicle* reporter, according to his account, was spotted as "a stranger" as soon as he arrived. Following this identification, Chinese onlookers interrogated him as to his business and closely watched him as he made his inquiries. The local residents proved particularly unhelpful in this regard, he claimed, as "'me no speak Englis' was the invariable answer given to the stranger within the gates."

The *Chronicle*'s report concluded with two assertions. The first was that, regardless of interracial marriage and decades of persistent social contact between the English and Chinese residents of the district, the cultural boundaries that separated the two groups remained largely impenetrable. "The English people who live among the Chinese of London know little of their doings," the paper reported, "though the Oriental marries up with English women he has little to do with his English neighbors." The second assertion was that the Carleton scandal was only the tip of the iceberg and that, although Chinatown held a host of dark secrets, the cunning nature of its residents ensured that the current methods of policing and investigation were unlikely to reveal them. [54]

The *Star*, a popular evening paper, was the next to publish a lurid Chinatown exposé, "The Evil Trade in Opium: English Girls as the Chinaman's West End Agents." The paper had a history of lively reporting and innovative content, and this, along with its radical stance, gave it a broad appeal, particularly among London's working class. It had also been notable for taking the Metropolitan Police to task for their failure, during the Jack the Ripper murders, to contain crime and immorality in the East End, though it was hardly isolated in its criticism.[55] The *Star*'s account, which began with a reference to the Carleton affair, emphasized the inherently corrupting aspects of race-mixing and the spread of degeneracy from East End to West End through Chinese direction and female agency. The author, "C. R.," also modeled his main characters on the same archetypes that counselors and magistrates had tried, with varying degrees of success, to apply to Len Ping You, Ada Ping You, and Reginald De Veulle—the immoral Chinese man who first shares his wicked habit, his initial female conquest who later spreads the vice, and the wealthy, debauched male degenerate who is their ultimate target. C. R. even claimed to be personally familiar with the three people who had originally introduced opium smoking to the East End. They were, according to him, a Chinese man named "Ching" and two Englishwomen "who had become so Chinese through constant association with 'Ching' that they had earned the sobriquets 'China-Faced Nell' and 'Chinese Bertha.'"[56]

It was these three conspirators, the author claimed, who, after "laborious years" and "carefully laid plans," had brought the market for opium from the East End to the West End. Ching's initial conversion of Nell and Bertha, and their subsequent dissemination of opium smoking more broadly in the East End, had been so lucrative that he had rapidly expanded his operation by recruiting impoverished young white women. More frightening still, the author's account claimed that this sinister plot by Chinese men and their female agents had been underway for four decades already, and even that Ching, its original instigator, remained a prominent figure in the London drug traffic. The global propagation of corruption by this seemingly immortal villain and his expansive network of white female thralls completed C. R.'s narrative of Chinese vice.[57] "It is present in all big cities," he warned readers. "The existence in the East-end of London alone of hundreds of these women living on food many Englishmen cannot buy, taking the best seats at the theatres, and living in well-appointed homes in the West-end, proves the magnitude of this traffic." A further network of maritime smugglers worked with local buyers and distributors—some who worked at the docks and some who "never leave their little grocery shops down Limehouse way"—to sustain the opium industry in London. "Amazing fortunes have been amassed by Chinamen in this illicit trade," the author concluded.[58]

Through the *Star*'s account, we can trace the evolution of negative Chinese stereotypes in the wake of wartime anxieties over moral and physical degeneracy in the capital and in the aftermath of the Carleton trials, which highlighted the Chinese contribution to these phenomena. C. R.'s account relied upon the images of Chinese corruption and vice that had been generated in court cases, popular fiction, and press reporting over the past two decades and merged them with race and gender issues popularized by the Carleton case, most particularly Chinese men's use of white women as agents of corruption and the sinister transfer of Chinese vice from the East End to the West End through the latter. C. R.'s description of the opium use as a "cult" and a "scourge" that spread, virus-like, from the initiated to the innocent, further invoked the impression of disease and degeneration. His descriptions also built on the popular stereotypes of Chinese residents as heathen, secretive, and connected to one another and to other Chinese communities across the globe through clandestine networks of vice. In this incarnation, the fear of Chinese invasion that had been central to the Yellow Peril discourse when China remained a threat to British imperial hegemony in Asia was giving way to fear of the Chinese immigrant community as a contagion that infected the social body of British society and was then transmitted from one host to another.

At issue was not just the power of Chinese corruption but also the weakness of British morality and the growth of Chinese wealth and commerce in the East End, two trends that similarly played on wartime concerns. The spread of Chinese vice in London had been facilitated, according to the author's account, by the moral degeneration of British masculinity that had been a central justification for the wartime narcotics prohibition laws and the campaign waged against gambling and drug use in the West End. The account printed in the *Star*, a paper that was popular among working-class readers who were experiencing firsthand the uncertainties of the interwar economy, also highlighted the economic facets of racial tensions in the East End. One of the most deplorable aspects of the illegal opium trade, C. R. had asserted, was the contrast between the wealth, comfort, and luxury supposedly enjoyed by the Chinese traffickers and their female protégés and the impoverishment of many honest Englishmen, who could not even afford the food that the former purchased, let alone the "best seats in the theatre" or the "well-appointed homes in the West-end."

Although the trials of the Kelly gang, a robbery group led by an American and his two female accomplices, and the arrest of two police impersonators who used false opium accusations to extort money, provided evidence of criminal conspiracies *against* Chinese men in the East End, reliable evidence of criminal conspiracies conducted *by* them in late 1918 and early 1919 remained sparse. [59] There was no concrete proof of the "Ching" syndicate described by the *Star*, for example, but the image of a Chinese mastermind coordinating a worldwide criminal organization from the East End was a popular one by this time. The Chinese involvement in the cocaine trade—an assertion that had gained publicity (but had never been decisively proven) by Muskett's case against the Ping Yous—was also gaining traction in public discourse. Opium and cocaine were increasingly conflated, particularly in fiction and the popular press, into a broader "dope" culture that allegedly connected the East End to the West End via wealthy Chinese suppliers and their debauched female accomplices.[60]

No Chinese drug kingpins had been discovered yet in London, however, and the first arrest of a Chinese man on cocaine charges would not take place until 1922, nor were clandestine "dens" fitting the lurid descriptions in press and literature ever uncovered in the East End.[61] Despite relatively scant evidence that opium posed a serious danger to white Londoners, the arrest of Chinese men for opium crimes became a more common occurrence in late 1918 and early 1919. The Metropolitan Police, who adopted aggressive tactics in the wake of the public outcry over the Carleton affair and amidst reports in the national press that China was producing increasing amounts of opium, arrested a number of Chinese men for smoking opium in boardinghouses and in private homes. The trial following the most serious of these raids took place on January 22, 1919, at the Thames Police Court. The raid, which was conducted at 30 Salter Street, began when Police-Inspector Knowler smelled opium outside the residence. The police subsequently seized three men and some material evidence, which consisted of the utensils for smoking opium, but no narcotics. The first question put to the arresting officers by the presiding magistrate, H. L. Cancellor, was whether Ng Ah Chung, the Chinese subject who held the lease on the property, was acting alone or as part of a broader opium concern. Upon being informed that Chung was the sole principal, that the house had been raided twice previously, and that it was a "regular opium den," Cancellor fined Yew Kim and Ah Foo, the two other suspects, £5 and £2, respectively. Chung, who stood accused of both allowing his property to be used for opium smoking and of attempting to bribe a police official, was remanded until a later date.[62]

Also coming up for trial that day before Mr. Cancellor were Kim Kitt and Jim Chow, who had been seized in police raids as well. The former was charged with allowing his premises to be used for opium smoking and with possession of prepared opium. Questioned by the magistrate, Kim Kitt simply replied that "the place was nothing more than an opium den. There was only one pipe." His response did little to mollify Cancellor, who not only sentenced him to six weeks imprisonment but recommended him for deportation as well. In citing his justification for such harsh treatment, the magistrate emphasized the danger that opium posed to the West End, even though there was no evidence whatsoever, beyond the Carleton affair, that this transferral was taking place or that any white Londoners had visited either Kim

Kitt's house or Ng Ah Chung's. "This sort of thing has got to be stopped," Cancellor announced to the court. "It starts in the East End and sometimes, as we know, spreads to the West."[63] Jim Chow, who had been charged merely with possession of the utensils for opium smoking, was fined £3 or eleven days' imprisonment. The following week, Cancellor delivered an even more forceful diatribe against opium use when Ng Ah Chung appeared for trial on the remanded charges.[64] He linked the defendant's actions with international Chinese criminality, and announced in court that "legislation seemed to have been needed all over the world" to stop the opium traffic. The relatively moderate legal treatment of such offenses, Cancellor continued, must be discarded in favor of harsher methods. He sentenced the defendant to six months' imprisonment and recommended him for deportation.[65]

Not all East End magistrates shared Cancellor's views on the necessity of fiercely punishing Chinese men arrested on opium charges. Judicial and police attitudes toward opium smoking in Chinatown, as had been the case with the response to Chinese immorality and criminality in previous years, varied considerably depending upon the individuals involved and the broader circumstances surrounding each case. One factor mitigating the punishment of Chinese men for such crimes was that, in the months immediately following the Carleton case, no further evidence appeared that the corruption of white women by means of cocaine or opium were common occurrences in Chinatown, and there was no solid evidence that the habit of smoking opium was spreading beyond the Chinese residents of the East End. To Henry Rooth, Cancellor's colleague in the Thames Police Court, for example, opium use remained a Chinese habit, and he adamantly refused to bow to public pressure to treat Chinese opium smokers any differently than he had before the Carleton affair. "There is great public outcry against you people for smoking opium," he told one Chinese defendant in January 1919, "because it is thought it works from East to West with disastrous results. I have to bear in mind that you were born in a country where this was, I suppose, part and parcel of your education." Rooth then announced that he was "not going to truckle to public opinion" and imposed a fine of 20 shillings.[66]

Even in the wake of the Carleton affair and the subsequent public outcry, no judicial consensus had been reached on opium offenses committed by Chinese residents. Gambling in Chinatown and cocaine use in London, on the other hand, both identified during the wartime period as threatening to the physical and moral integrity of the metropolis, continued to attract concerted police attention and broad judicial antipathy. On December 30, 1919, three Chinese defendants who had been caught playing fan-tan were fined a total of £140 in the Thames Police Court for managing a gaming house in Pennyfields. The acting police superintendent of the division added that the police were experiencing "great difficulty" suppressing Chinese gambling and that "police notices, printed in Chinese, had no effect."[67] Meanwhile, cocaine arrests continued to mount, with more than a dozen individuals, divided evenly between men and women, tried in the London police courts between December 1918 and March 1919. The defendants, almost without exception, received heavy sentences from London magistrates. It was not uncommon for those convicted to be punished with six months' imprisonment, the longest sentence permitted for such crimes under DORA 40b, which remained in force despite the conclusion of the war. The significance of these arrests was amplified by impassioned articles in the *Times* and dire warnings from medical experts that "cocaine spells death."[68] Such caveats alerted readers to the hazards of the burgeoning "cocaine cult" and were accompanied by demands that the British government take decisive steps to join the international campaign against its spread. By late February, one prominent London magistrate, Edmund D'Eyncourt of the Marylebone Police Court, had joined the public outcry and was openly calling for the extension of DORA 40b into peacetime so that the cocaine menace could be dealt with effectively.[69] A threat to the nation's strength and morality in wartime was rapidly becoming, in public discourse, a dire threat to its health and sanity in peacetime.

Despite Cancellor's ominous pronouncements about the transmission of drugs and vice from the East End to West End, with the exception of the Carleton affair, there appeared to be no discernable link between the opium traffic and the cocaine traffic, or between Chinese men and cocaine. There was no further evidence that Chinese men were corrupting white women by means of either drug, and not a single white Londoner had been found during any of the raids on East End opium dens. The majority of cocaine arrests had taken place in the West End and had been tried at the Bow Street Police Court (just north of Covent Garden), the Marlborough Street Police Court (Chelsea), or the Marylebone Police Court. Not a single Chinese man had been arrested for such offenses—all the defendants had been white, and all but one had been British—and none of the cocaine involved had ever been traced back to an East End source.

In this climate, where fact did not support popular suspicion, fiction would suffice. Investigations, arrests, and prosecutions following the trials of the Ping Yous and De Veulle had failed to reveal connections between Chinese men, cocaine, and the corruption of white women or further evidence of the transmission of vice from the Chinese in the East End to white Londoners in the West End. But such connections were a central feature of Sax Rohmer's newest novel, *Dope: A Story of Chinatown and the Drug Traffic*. The sensational bestseller, first published in both London and New York in 1919, drew strongly on the entire gamut of negative Chinese stereotypes that had been popularized in Britain and the empire across the previous two decades. Just as Rohmer used events in London courtrooms, press reports of Chinatown, and statements by police and judicial officials—sometimes even to the point of quoting the latter verbatim—to develop the plot and characters of *Dope*, his portrayals of the narcotics trade and the roles played by both white Britons and Chinese would subsequently filter back into the attitudes of magistrates, police, and reporters. And, like the romanticized "opium dens" depicted in press and literature that had found a prominent place in the language of East End magistrates and police, the search for a Chinese criminal mastermind and a "syndicate" of vice, as depicted in Rohmer's novel, would occupy the attention of journalists, police, and magistrates in the years that followed.[70]

This reciprocal exchange between law, press, and literature had been part of the portrayals of Chinatown and its residents for several years already—Fu Manchu and Mr. King, for example, well predated *Dope* and served as models for its Chinese villain, Sin Sin Wa. But the increasing prominence of the police investigations and trials involving the district in the interwar period made it an even more fruitful (and remunerative) subject for journalists and fiction writers alike. In 1911, according to Rohmer, the market had been ripe for a Chinese villain. By 1919, the author felt that the time was equally fortuitous for a Chinese villain who was truly *of* Chinatown. According to his biographer, in the wake of the Carleton scandal, Rohmer viewed the writing of a second book on the drug traffic as both a "profitable assignment" and a "public duty."[71] The book was adapted to take full advantage of interwar racial and gender anxieties and the increasing prominence of the "dope scene" and West End decadence in public discourse. But the previous themes from Rohmer's wartime book on the drug trade, *The Yellow Claw*, were very much in evidence as well. As in *Claw*, the storyline of *Dope* revolved around an international drug cartel and the masculine agents of state authority arrayed against it. Similarly, decadent, corrupted women were the primary agents by which the drug habit was spread, though the ultimate source of the evil was a Chinese mastermind. Of the book's two main villains, one was a Chinese "crimp" who ran a boardinghouse and opium den in Chinatown, while the other was a mixed-race seductress who lured West End dilettantes to the East End with the promise of drug-induced ecstasy. In *Dope*, Rohmer also revived some of the imperial themes of the original Fu Manchu stories, vividly portraying the effects, both positive and negative, of foreign sojourns on British masculinity.

Dope took the complex and often ambiguous evidence that had emerged from the Billie Carleton affair and retold the story in stark moral terms, restructuring the scandal in a fashion that adhered even more closely to popular racial and gender stereotypes than the trials and the press reports of them had. Rita Dresden, who represented Billie Carleton in the novel, was a debauched actress who fell under the influence of a West End drug-taking set. The character of Lucien Pyne was modeled on Reginald de Veulle, and as with Dresden, Rohmer translated the images presented in the press coverage of the scandal with little alteration. Dresden was a relative innocent, weak, but not sinister, while Pyne was a feminized society aristocrat, jaded and cynical. But Pyne's decadence, which was the result of his exposure to the Orient, was countered by Seton Pasha, a paradigm of English masculinity. In contrast to Pyne, whose time in Malta, India, and Burma corrupted his soul, Pasha was a heroic figure, an "*Arabian Nights* myth."[72]

The character of Lola represented Ada Ping You, but Rohmer dramatically departed from the real-life figure in this instance. Whereas Ada herself was Scottish, the author refashioned her into a distinct racial other. Lola, a "Cuban-Jewess," was doubly corrupted, first by her mixed-race background and second by her marriage to a Chinese man (Sin Sin Wa). Rohmer drew on Mead's courtroom comments verbatim in his description of Lola as "the officiating priestess" of the opium cult.[73] But the most drastic transformation wrought in *Dope* was that of Len Ping You, from a consumptive who was trying to wean himself from the opium habit into the diabolical Sin Sin Wa, a Chinese criminal mastermind.[74] The campaign of Lola and Sin Sin to enslave white Britons through drug addiction was every bit as grand as Fu Manchu's machinations, but more closely resembled the subtle corruption of Mr. King from *The Yellow Claw*. As with King's plots, the villains of *Dope* were supported by a global criminal syndicate based in Chinatown.[75] But the storyline of *Dope* focused distinctly on the increasing racial and cultural cosmopolitanism of London and on the threat that the influx of foreigners to the West End posed to white Britons. The central locale of evil in *The Yellow Claw* was Mr. King's secret Limehouse lair, while the corruption in *Dope* moved easily between the East End and West End. And the spread of foreign influence and presence from East to West had been accompanied by the spread of Chinese vice and decadence. The most salacious indulgences described in *Dope* did not take place in private, underground rooms frequented by habitués, as was the case in *The Yellow Claw*, but in a Duke Street flat in Mayfair.[76] The address was no coincidence—the opium-smoking party depicted in *Dope* was identical to the "disgusting orgies" described by Muskett in the De Veulle trial, and Rohmer's setting was only a few blocks north of De Veulle's real-life address.

Whereas class differences among the British characters had been more evident in *The Yellow Claw*, ethnic and cultural distinctions among the white principals was a more prominent feature of *Dope*. Rohmer's main working-class character in *Dope* was an Irishman who, as a police detective, was himself an extension of the state apparatus that had so terrified Soames in *The Yellow Claw*. In contrast to the sharp political and social tensions that had characterized recent Anglo-Irish relations, "Red" Kerry was fiercely committed to protecting the English inhabitants of the West End from the "foreign" threat. In *Dope*, moreover, Rohmer portrayed in a positive light the same racial features that had previously marked those of the Celtic fringe as deviant and disruptive foils to proper Anglo-Saxons.[77] The policeman's lack of emotional control and his tendency toward rage, which even his colleagues found intimidating, and his wife Mary's mystical clairvoyance were neither threatening nor heretical, but were both potent weapons against the Chinese menace. Rohmer thus subsumed the ethnic and cultural divisions between the Irish and the English in their united effort against the more formidable, and more alien, racial other represented by the Chinese villain, Sin Sin Wa.[78]

Kerry, Mary, Scotland Yard, and Seton Pasha battle both Chinese villainy and those Britons whose racial and national identities had been corrupted by their association with Chinese men and their adoption of "Chinese" vices. The process of racial transformation experienced by corrupted Britons was similar both to Dickens's descriptions of the effects of opium smoking in *The Mystery of Edwin Drood* and to the arguments made by Muskett and Matthews in Ada Ping You's trial. Corruption was an inevitable consequence of close interracial contact in these circumstances, as was evident in Rohmer's description of Cyrus Kilfane, a wealthy West End opium addict: "Long familiarity with China's ruling vice and contact with those who practiced it had brought about that mysterious physical alteration—apparently reflecting a mental change—so often to be seen in one who has consorted with Chinamen. Even the light eyes seemed to have grown slightly oblique; the voice, the unimpassioned greeting, were those of a son of Cathay."[79] The effects of the drug, according to Rohmer, were highly race-specific. For Asians, opium use was a form of cultural nostalgia—smoking evoked the sights, sounds, and smells of their homes.[80] But the effects on Europeans were much more drastic. For them, opium was a "potent necromancer" that robbed them of both self-control and judgment, two key moral attributes of the British middle class.[81] Gender was also essential in determining a user's reaction to drugs.[82] Although there were several male opium addicts in *Dope*, the women were far more prone to addiction and excess. Their use of the drug was portrayed as a more serious violation of moral and gender norms as well. Opium smoking, Kerry declared at one point, is "bad enough in the heathens, but for an Englishwoman to dope herself is downright unchristian and beastly."[83] Rohmer portrayed bohemian, artistic women as particularly susceptible to the temptations of vice due to their "pleasure-loving" and their "insatiable curiosity, primitive and immoral."[84] The male drug users in *Dope*, even those who had been longtime addicts, were still capable of maintaining some semblance of self-control in the face of their desires. For women, on the other hand, the path of drug use led inevitably to their utter enslavement.[85] Drug use, for them, was "a form of mania," one medical expert told Kerry, and prompted them also to become cunning liars in order to conceal their addiction and pursue its satisfaction.[86]

In contrast with the discussions of drug use and addiction that were equally evident in *The Yellow Claw*, the portrayal of these issues in *Dope* conflated opium and cocaine use. Both were subsumed under the umbrella term "dope" in their distribution and consumption and in the views of legal and medical authorities toward them. Although Sin Sin Wa and Lola dealt primarily in opium, they also supplied cocaine and a variety of other drugs to their clientele through an intermediary in the West End. This conflation of cocaine and opium contradicted the legal patterns of narcotics crimes in Britain, but it was very much in line with Herbert Muskett's prosecution of Ada Ping You and Reginald De Veulle. In both trials, although cocaine was the culprit behind Billie Carleton's death, the "opium cult" supposedly fostered by the two principals and Len Ping You had been central to the prosecution's case. Considering the different histories of the two substances in both Chinese and British society, the absence of any tangible connection between the Chinese and the cocaine trade, and the public hysteria over wartime cocaine use, the importance of this commingling cannot be overestimated. In interwar public discourse, association with Chinese men left women open to accusations of immorality and corruption. But the association of Chinese men with cocaine exponentially increased their potential threat to white communities in the eyes of legal officials and worsened their villainy in journalistic and literary portrayals.[87]

Dope also foreshadowed what would soon become the primary justification for judicial and police intervention in Limehouse—the intimate involvement of women in the culture of vice. The main difference between *Dope* and Rohmer's original depiction of the drug traffic in *The Yellow Claw* was the former's focus on women's roles in the drug trade, both as its propagators and as its consumers. The most dedicated and decadent of the drug users in the book were women, not men, and Lola, not Sin Sin Wa, was the true corruptor—conniving, jealous, vain, and murderous beyond all reason or moderation. Sin Sin, motivated partly out of infatuation for Lola's putative murder victim, the beautiful Mrs. Irvin, and partly out of his fear that the murder of Irvin would bring unwanted police attention, eventually killed his wife by strangling her with his queue. This method of murder could be committed only by a Chinese man and it transformed the most prominent Chinese racial marker into a tool for violence and villainy.

But what followed this act of race-specific murder had far more disturbing implications for readers who lived in British cities where Chinese seamen remained among the most visible and prolific members of the Asian community. Sin Sin Wa, known to police as the one-eyed Chinaman, removed his queue, which had been fake all along, doffed his eye patch (also fake), cut his mustache and, in the guise of an ordinary sailor, boarded ship and vanished. Rohmer's conclusion not only "spelled failure for British justice" but also suggested that the most innocuous Chinese countenance might conceal the heart and mind of a villain.[88] As with the climax in *Yellow Claw*, the ending of *Dope* was ambiguous. Somewhere out there, the villain remained at large, and readers could only hope that Red Kerry and the other agents of British justice were up to the task of warding off the next assault. In what had become a recurring theme in Rohmer's writing, the persistence and omnipresence of this threat also justified the continued employment of wartime emergency powers and invasive police tactics.

In 1919, Thomas Burke once again offered an alternative vision of Chinatown. The Chinatown portrayed in *Out and About: A Portrait of London in War-Time* was far less salacious, and certainly less drug-ridden, than it had been in either *Dope* or his own *Limehouse Nights*. Burke also demonstrated a greater awareness of the contrast between "Chinatown" as an imagined locale and "Limehouse" as a geographic designation, whereas Rohmer and most London journalists were using the two terms interchangeably by this time.[89] But Burke's Chinatown resembled Rohmer's backdrop in three very important aspects. First, it was a cosmopolitan district where men from many ethnic and national backgrounds mingled freely.[90] Second, although the wartime laws had significantly reduced the prominence of vice, Chinatown was still a place to which white Britons came seeking the exotic, even if it was sometimes only a façade created in part by their own imaginings and encouraged by Chinese proprietors seeking to profit from it.[91] And last, Chinese property and commerce were the primary venues that brought different races together and that attracted white women, in particular, to unions with Chinese men.

In this last regard, both Rohmer's and Burke's 1919 works posed the same question: what was the significance of white women entering, in ever greater numbers, a space that in the past had almost always been constructed as a male Chinese one? The latter years of the war and the immediate postwar period had witnessed women assuming new roles and acquiring new freedoms and, to read the daily broadsheets, it seemed as if they were using that freedom in increasing numbers to visit Chinatown. There was a clear consensus among magistrates, journalists, and popular authors that such mobility could have dire consequences for them and for the British race more generally. A white woman's crossing of the invisible border into London's Chinese community threatened not only her life and her morality but her very "whiteness." Such was the power of Chinese men that contact with them led almost unerringly to the adoption of "Chinese" vices. At worst, these women could become the vectors by which such vice spread beyond the borders of Chinatown, or potent lures for others to sample its degenerative pleasures. The contrasts among how Ada Ping You, Len Ping You, Billie Carleton, and Reginald De Veulle were presented in court, in newspapers, and in fiction stood as a stark indicator of how deeply intertwined the issues of race, gender, vice, morality were in the interwar period. All these media and the issues that they addressed worked in tandem to determine the imagined boundaries of urban spaces.

The question that still remained unanswered, however, was to what degree white women who crossed these boundaries were responsible for their own actions. Were they passive agents, overcome by the power of male corruption, as Matthews had suggested in his defense of Ada Ping You? Or were they, as Mead, Muskett, and Rohmer had asserted, powerful, independent agents of degradation who willingly married themselves to Chinese vice both literally and figuratively?

Burke chose the middle ground, portraying a Chinatown where some women came for a mere brush with the exotic and decadent, while others arrived with little in the way of moral restraint to begin with. But in the wake of the Billie Carleton scandal, Burke's moderate vision held little attraction for readers. What had seemed scandalous and shocking in 1916 was now quaint and tepid. In contrast with their wartime writings, in 1919, it was Rohmer's *Dope* that became a popular sensation, while Burke's *Out and About* remained relatively obscure.[92]

In the immediate postwar period, the issue of West End decadence and women's roles in the drug trade became urgent concerns to magistrates, police, and other state officials. At the same time, magistrates' attention, journalistic coverage, and popular fiction all began to converge around the issues of women's narcotic use, interracial sexuality, the degeneration of British masculinity, and the spread of decadence and vice from East End to the West End through Chinese men and their immoral female compatriots. The new metaphors of Chinese corruption, which focused on the infection of white residents and the transfer of degenerative vice—via the vectors of Chinese wealth and the white women attracted to it—to other white residents superseded the older images of invasion and conquest. The negative stereotyping of Chinese men in public discourse was also on the rise, as new crimes joined old conspiracies in a potent blend of mythmaking and racial paranoia. With the figures of Billie Carleton as a tragic victim and Ada Ping You as the "high priestess" of vice and death before them, the London press had greater motivation than ever before to observe and report on the affairs of Chinatown. The British state, in turn, had greater justification than ever before to intervene. The laws that had been expanded and mobilized from 1916–18 to protect British masculinity, a vital wartime resource, would soon be deployed in London to protect one of society's most valuable peacetime commodities—white womanhood.

Chapter 6

"This Plague Spot of the Metropolis," 1919–21

Between 1919 and 1921, mob violence, popular hostility, press sensationalism, and judicial action against the Chinese residents of the East End reached new extremes. The strands of anti-Chinese sentiment expressed by different groups in Britain and the negative stereotypes generated domestically and in the empire converged, triggering a full-blown "moral panic" in London. [1] The focus of attention was not the itinerant Chinese seamen who had attracted so much attention in the past. The size and significance of that group, after a brief surge during the war, had diminished considerably, though union leaders continued to argue that their employment in British shipping undermined the status and welfare of British seamen.[2] In the interwar period, the growing population of long-term Chinese residents and Chinese business owners became the center of controversy.[3] In the wake of the 1919 race riots, their commercial activities were linked publicly to interracial social contact and sexuality in the East End, to the alleged increase of gambling and narcotics use among white residents, and to the physical and moral decline of the metropolis as a whole. In response, magistrates, police, and white working-class men all sought, through means legal and extralegal, to restore what they viewed as the proper racial and gender order in the East End and, by doing so, to return both Chinese men and working-class women to positions of subordination.

Although official statements and press reports explicitly linked vice in Chinatown to the well established anxiety over international conspiracies, concerns about the "morals of Chinatown" were situated locally, revolving around the pernicious moral influence of Chinese wealth and Chinese-controlled businesses in the East End. The growth of popular anti-Chinese sentiment during this period was leant further impetus by a deepening economic recession and by the mounting opposition of elected officials in the East End. While the final result of the interwar surge in racial hostility fell short of legal segregation, the violence, police raids, prosecutions, deportations, and sensationalized press reports insured that Chinese residents would remain outsiders—legally, socially, and culturally—in both the metropolis and the nation for years to come.

The 1919 Riots

The negative stereotypes of Chinese men and the increased police and judicial focus on Chinatown emerged in the context of heightened racial tensions throughout Britain in the interwar era, with 1919 being a particularly tumultuous year. The public furor generated by Billie Carleton's death was just beginning to die down when the nation was rocked by racial violence on an unprecedented scale. The 1919 riots, which took place in London, Liverpool, Glasgow, Cardiff, Salford, South Shields, Hull, Newport, and Barry between April and August, were among the most serious racial disturbances to ever occur in Britain. Reflecting the general scholarly neglect of domestic race relations in this period, however, there have been very few studies made of the events surrounding the riots, and existing scholarship has focused almost exclusively on violence against black men in Liverpool.[4] Anti-Chinese violence, the metropolitan occurrences of rioting, and the role of anti-Chinese sentiment in interwar race relations have yet to be explored. There is insufficient evidence that anti-Chinese sentiment in the East End was a *direct* precedent for anti-black stereotyping, working-class hostility, and popular violence in the interwar period. But the encoding of the racial threats posed to white women, white labor, and the interwar social order by the visible presence of black men in the metropolis found more fertile ground that it otherwise would have thanks to the recent controversies over Chinese labor and immigration.

In the broader context of attitudes toward race and immigration, the negative stereotyping of Chinese and black residents was also related to anti-immigrant sentiment against both Irish and Jewish residents of the metropole. The public outcry against interracial sexuality and job-stealing leveled against black men in the interwar period, for example, had been a prominent part of negative Chinese stereotypes in London for more than a decade before the 1919 riots, of anti-semitism since the late nineteenth century, and of anti-Irish sentiment since the mid-nineteenth century.[5] All four groups had a long and complex history in the evolution of British public discourse on race and nation, but the hostility against the Chinese and black populations in Britain was more directly related to the recent (i.e., nineteenth-century) history of colonialism and racism in Asia and Africa, and the hostility against them was more disproportionate to the size of their populations in London. Although the prejudice against both Jewish and Irish immigrants—particularly on economic grounds—was still very strong in Britain, both groups had more successfully integrated into the general population than Chinese or black residents had, in part because the popular prejudice against intermarriage between them and British women was not as powerful. The growing popularity of racial categorizations that conflated differences between European cohorts in Britain and the empire into a homogenized "white" identity from which groups defined as "yellow," "black," "coloured," "Asian," or "Oriental" were explicitly excluded also exacerbated the sense of difference between white Londoners and the latter.[6] The cultural, social, and economic aftereffects of the war played a significant role in British racial dynamics as well. Examining the 1919 riots from a metropolitan perspective highlights these afteraffects, the domestic social and cultural legacy of British colonialism in Asia and Africa, and the persistent influence of gender issues in metropolitan race relations.

The first instance of interwar racial violence that garnered public attention took place in mid-April, but the highpoint of the disturbances was the second half of May.[7] The *Daily Chronicle*, which had printed the first Chinatown exposé in the wake of the Carleton scandal, attributed the violence in Limehouse to antipathy against interracial sexuality rather than to economic tensions. According to the paper's coverage, local residents claimed that "many young girls have been decoyed by the coloured men, who have lavished money on them," an assertion that echoed the accusations made against Chinese men in previous years.[8] In contrast to this and other similar reports in the *Times* and the popular London press, Jacqueline Jenkinson and other historians who have studied the riots in Liverpool have argued that the issues of interracial sexuality and racial tension were overemphasized in press coverage and that the true cause of the violence often lay in economic competition between black and white residents.[9] Such competition was acute, while racial prejudice was already "well-internalized" and "entrenched," and popular concern over interracial sexuality was, similarly, "perennial."[10] Racism and opposition to interracial sexuality, Jenkinson surmises, were important background contexts for the 1919 riots but they were not the primary catalysts.

While competition for jobs and housing was certainly a central issue in the London disturbances, any explanation of the riots that rests on an ahistorical view of racial prejudice and the anxiety over interracial sexuality—and therefore dismisses both as central causes—is unsatisfactory for a number of reasons. First, it fails to acknowledge that public concern over interracial sexuality in London, thanks in part to the Billie Carleton trials and the broad publicity that they had received, was at a high point in mid-1919. The Carleton trials, sensationalized newspaper stories about Chinatown, and the publication of Sax Rohmer's *Dope* all fostered popular anxiety over physical and moral degeneracy in the capital, as did the stream of returning wounded, disabled, and disfigured veterans.[11] Second, such arguments do not explain why many other prominent minority groups in the East End—Jews, Poles, and Russians, in particular—who were present in greater numbers and who had been similarly accused of job-stealing and profiteering during the war were not attacked as well.[12] Third, explanations for the riots that focus on economic factors do not take into account the rampant upsurge in racialized nationalism that characterized the war years. To achieve victory in World War I, Britain had drawn upon the manpower and resources of the empire to a degree not witnessed since the Napoleonic era.[13] The extraordinary contributions of the white settler colonies to the fighting forces stood as a testament to the persistent strength of imperial bonds, but also reinforced concepts of Britishness and British masculinity that subsumed discrete colonial identities under a common racial and imperial one.[14] The tendency of working-class Britons to draw stark distinctions, often down ethnic lines, between insiders and outsiders—at the local, national, and imperial levels—and to subject the latter to abuse or violence did not simply vanish when the war ended.

Lastly, any explanation that downplays either race or interracial sexuality in favor of economic competition obscures the essential interrelation between them as motivations for the violence and as factors in court cases and press reports. Following the precedents set by anti-Chinese sentiment and violence in the previous decade, black men in London were portrayed as denying white, working-class East Enders their "rights" to employment, housing and property, and sexual access that they insisted their wartime service had earned them. Subsequent to the riots, a similar argument that wartime service had earned British men protection against "Chinese labour" would be employed in parliament by Joseph Havelock Wilson MP (South Shields, Liberal) to support the strengthening of Britain's immigration laws.[15] It was this threat to the three pillars of masculinity—a threat that combined racial, gendered, and economic elements—that often prompted violence against black men, just as it had motivated hostility and violence against Chinese residents, and negative portrayals of them in public discourse, in previous years. The mutually reinforcing character of the racial, sexual, and economic anxieties that motivated violence by white Britons emerges clearly when one examines the attacks made against Chinese men in 1919.

At the height of the London disturbances in mid-June, a mob attacked a Poplar house recently occupied by two Chinese men and their white wives. The specific catalyst of the violence had been reports that F. Francis, a local landlord, had evicted a demobilized soldier and his wife in order to rent the property to the interracial couples. In response, an infuriated mob assaulted the two women—one who was the wife of a man named Luck Sing—and then piled their furniture in the street and set it ablaze. The *Star*, consistent with its previous sympathy toward labor interests, asserted that the rioters had been motivated by their resentment against Chinese residents for taking the jobs vacated by white men who had gone off to war, for "forming alliances" with white women, and for paying exorbitant sums in order to secure housing.[16] In short, white veterans had returned to the East End to find that their sacrifices in the war had earned them no privileged place in their communities. Employment, wealth, female companionship, and housing had all been secured by Chinese interlopers in their absence. Reports that these interlopers had publicly flaunted their access to women and property to an intolerable degree appeared in a broad spectrum of the British press, from evening papers like the *Star*, to more established national papers such as the *Daily Telegraph*, to those with a primarily local audience such as the *East End News*. As with similar newspaper coverage of the anti-black riots in Liverpool, these explanations exonerated the men who had attacked the wife of Luck Sing—they had only been protesting the denial of their entitlements as both white British men and veterans.[17] The Chinese contribution to the war effort, like that of Indians and black Britons, was ignored in such accounts, and the demographics of Chinese residency in London highlighted the gross distortions that were inherent in these representations. According to the census records, Chinese residents and Chinese-owned businesses had both multiplied across the course of the previous decade, and the war had certainly seen a substantial increase in the number of Chinese seamen employed aboard British ships.[18] London County Council surveys and census records also revealed severe overcrowding in the East End and in Poplar in particular.[19] But the Chinese population in London was still officially reported at less than a thousand individuals. As had frequently been the case in the past, the small Chinese population had aroused hostility out of all proportion to its numbers.

In such fraught circumstances, the Poplar landlord whose alleged decision had sparked the riot was eager to divorce himself from any association with the Chinese. He publicly declared that the reports of his eviction of a demobilized soldier in favor of a Chinese tenant were utterly false. On the contrary, in a statement printed in the *East End News*, Francis insisted that he had "turned out a CHINAMAN tenant from a house and shop in North-street, to take in a demobilized soldier to open a business."[20] "I have NO Chinaman tenants," he further stated. Whether Francis was telling the truth or simply trying to prevent further damage to his properties, both the rumor and the violence it had triggered proved exceedingly difficult to quell. Following the attack on Luck Sing's wife and home, a crowd smashed the windows of a Chinese laundry, and according to one report in the *News*, "there was some talk of wrecking the whole of the Chinese quarter."[21] The representations of Chinese drug traffickers that had been propagated in the press, in the courts, and in popular fiction in the previous year had helped to disseminate the idea that Chinese men enjoyed the privileges that were denied to white veterans. In press reports about the violence in Poplar, the stereotype of the Chinese corrupter who used his immoral gains to purchase property and the affections of white women was replicated and applied to Chinese property owners in the East End in general. Both the *Star* and the *Telegraph* also emphasized the hostility prompted by the wartime growth of the Chinese population and its expansion beyond the traditional borders of Chinatown.[22] Such descriptions paralleled reports of the "opium cult" and the alleged increases in Chinese commercial activity and influence in the West End that had been so central to the Carleton scandal—reports which had appeared in the very same papers that, in June 1919, helped to sustain this particular narrative of anti-Chinese violence in the East End.

It was only in subsequent conflicts between white and Chinese residents that competition for employment appeared to be the primary focus. Following reports that the Chinese seamen were accepting work at half the wages demanded by white seamen, further instances of violence took place a few days after the Luck Sing incident. Rumors that Chinese sailors had attacked a man "of another nationality" incensed the local white population, who again assaulted Chinese residents and smashed the windows of Chinese-owned lodging houses and shops.[23] As had been the case in 1911, the police were summoned in considerable numbers to quell the disturbances and to provide some measure of protection for Chinese residents. But even a strong police presence did not thwart "a good deal of free fighting" or prevent some Chinese men from being severely assaulted.[24] By the beginning of July, the racial violence between different groups in Limehouse had become so serious that almost the entire East End police force had been deployed in an effort to restore order.[25]

As racial violence flared in cities across Britain, anti-Chinese agitation was revived in the empire as well. In 1919, Chinese communities once again became the focus of racial hostility in Canada. Chinese residents there became the targets of mob violence by demobilized soldiers and mass raids by the police, and labor leaders demanded the extension of wartime emergency powers to monitor their movement and residency.[26] Violence between blacks and whites was similarly widespread, and 1919 witnessed racial confrontations in South Africa, Belize, Sierra Leone, and Jamaica, as well as in major U.S. cities.[27] Although there were many similarities between anti-Chinese and anti-black discourse and imagery, and there were parallels in the expressions of popular hostility in this period, the contrasts were equally significant. In Britain, these contrasts reflected the differences in the history of imperialism and colonialism in Asia and Africa, in the legal status of black men and Chinese men vis-à-vis citizenship, and in the history of racial stereotyping. China, even in 1919, was not subsumed under British and European hegemony to the same degree that much of Africa was, even though China's repeated military defeats at the hands of Western powers had allowed the latter to dictate much of China's trade policies, nor had the Chinese suffered under the yoke of slavery in the previous centuries, although they had been exploited as indentured laborers throughout the empire. The division of the Chinese community between resident aliens and British subjects, and the common practice among the former of claiming status as the latter in order to avoid restrictions on labor and residency, further complicated their legal status.

As a result of these contrasts, black men in the courts and in the press were not portrayed as posing the same *type* of racial threat as Chinese men did. Although some British officials were concerned with what appeared to be a simultaneous upwelling in black racial consciousness throughout the empire, no one suggested, for example, that there was a clandestine global syndicate supporting black men in London.[28] Neither was it publicly asserted that black men in the metropolis could draw, via insidious connections, upon the resources of other black communities in the empire to aid them in the same manner that Chinese men supposedly could. There was no black equivalent of "Fu Manchu" or "Mr. King," no African "White Lilies," "Tongs," or "Triads." Black men in this period also posed a different kind of challenge to white British masculinity and to white womanhood. The sexual threat of black men was predicated on their alleged sexual potency and savage, masculine allure, not, as was the case with Chinese men, on their commercial acumen and feminine cunning.[29]

This is not to deny that there were vital imperial dimensions to the threats allegedly posed by black labor and sexuality or that, in British racial discourse, black men had been (and still were) feminized and accused of sexual deviancy.[30] But the character of those threats at the time of the riots was based on an image of black men as "uncivilized" primitives, while the Chinese were commonly described as the products of a complex and ancient—but inherently immoral and sinister—culture that was antithetical to British society and its values. While this distinction was only an undercurrent to popular hostility, it emerged clearly among East End officials and in London press reports. J. A. R. Cairns, the magistrate who adjudicated many of the interwar Thames Police Court cases involving Chinese and black defendants, neatly summed up the difference between the two groups, as he saw them. "The black men have no stronghold. They have set up no boundaries . . . there are black men, but there is no black civilization," he wrote in his 1922 memoir. "It is otherwise when you pass further east into the region of London's Chinatown. In Limehouse you have Chinamen, but there is more. There is China's atmosphere, China's morals, China's attractions and sins and transgressions." [31] In the press reports and court cases surrounding the 1919 riots, black men were consistently described as violent, but never as cunning or organized as Chinese men had been in earlier instances of East End racial disorder, nor were black men implicated, initially, in the drug trafficking or gambling that had previously brought official attention to the affairs of Britain's Chinese communities. In short, despite important similarities in their portrayal and treatment in London's streets, its courts, and the pages of its newspapers, Chinese men and black men posed very different challenges to British masculinity, to British imperial hegemony, and to public order.

As had been the case with violence against Chinese men in the past, the black workingmen who were the focus of popular hostility bore the brunt of official blame for the incidents. But the practical impact of this for black men in Britain was mitigated by their formal legal status, by their ability to organize against wholesale persecution, by their effective public assertion of their rights, and by their networks of social support. Not only were a high proportion of black residents British subjects, but their claims to status as such also attracted less suspicion from officials than Chinese residents' did, since the latter had been repeatedly accused of making false assertions and producing forged documents in order to avoid the "language test" stipulations of the Merchant Shipping Act.[32] Language itself was also less of a barrier for black residents of Britain than it was for Chinese residents, and the former were often able to defend themselves in their own words. In letters to newspapers, petitions to the government, and peaceful mass meetings, black men in Britain asserted their membership in the nation and their right to fair treatment.[33] When John Martin, a black seaman from Jamaica, was brought up on assault charges relating to the May riots in London, he emphasized his status as a respectable British subject and highlighted his contributions to the nation through military service.[34] Exonerated in court of suspicions that he "went about with white girls," Martin was found *not guilty* and discharged. When a state-sponsored scheme of voluntary repatriation for black working men was implemented in the wake of the riots, it was largely ineffective due to lack of cooperation on their part.[35] Black residents' status as British subjects and citizens, the strategies they adopted in response to official persecution, and the failure, to that point, of politicians, the press, and union leaders to portray them as dire threats to the nation protected them from wholesale repatriation and from summary deportation.

The 1919 riots highlighted both the common threads of racial prejudice toward black and Chinese residents in Britain and the contrasts in their portrayal, treatment, and legal status. The riots also brought the issue of interracial sexuality and the threat it posed to public order to the forefront of legal discourse and popular journalism in London. In the London press, incidents of violence and disorder were blamed on social contact between black or Chinese men and white women, a narrative that exonerated white rioters of responsibility for the violence and justified the arrests of black men and the attempts at repatriation that followed.

The attacks on Chinese residents in 1919 were also significant because they revealed an upswing in *popular* racial hostility among white East Enders. The focus of violence on the issue of interracial marriages was particularly damning because without such unions, Chinese men could not assimilate and the Chinese community could not sustain itself over time.[36] As with the Carleton trials, the question of whether the white women or the Chinese and black men involved were ultimately to be held responsible for interracial contact remained unresolved.[37] But it is telling that East End press reports and the statements of police and magistrates during the 1919 disturbances generally blamed black men and Chinese men for seeking such unions, while in London police court cases in the preceding months, the discussions had been more ambiguous in assigning fault.[38] In a January 1919 case, East End police and judicial officials had even intervened to *preserve* an interracial marriage when a white soldier who had married a black woman in South Africa was arrested for lying about his marital status and for trying to conclude a second marriage to a white woman in Stepney.[39] Interracial marriage and sexuality, who should be held accountable for their increasing visibility in the metropolis, and what the proper legal response should be were all issues that would continue to preoccupy London magistrates and police, and to guide their attitudes toward Chinatown, in the coming years.

"Undesirable Companions": Violence and Vice in the East End

In the months immediately following the 1919 riots, the attention of London police, magistrates, and the press returned to Chinese gambling and its pernicious influence on white Londoners and to the reported predilection of Chinese men for violence. In a case tried before H. L. Cancellor in the West London Police court in September and October of 1919, Djang Djing Sung, a Chinese laborer, was charged with the murder of Zee Ming Wu, another Chinese man, in Birmingham.[40] The timing could not have been worse for the image of Chinese residents in Britain, since the trial reinforced many of the negative stereotypes that had been propagated up to that point in popular fiction and in the sensationalized press reports of Chinatown's affairs. The prosecution's case, witness testimony, and the magistrate's commentary all suggested that brutality and greed were inherent Chinese racial characteristics, much as they had been for Fu Manchu, Mr. King, and Sin Sin Wa. In contrast to literary depictions of Chinese violence, the victim was Chinese, not white. But the murder represented a violation of the racial geography of the metropolis nonetheless, since it had taken place in the West End, suggesting that Chinese violence, like Chinese vice, was no longer confined to the borders of Chinatown. Taken together, the framing of the prosecution's case against Djang and Cancellor's later commentary on it highlighted the racial prejudice that Chinese defendants could face before the bench and before the court of public opinion.

Djang, the prosecution alleged, had brutally murdered Zee and had then come to London with the intention of stealing £240 from Zee's post office savings box. The prosecution's case and witness testimony lingered long on the brutality of the murder, which had been committed with a hammer and a chisel-like device, on the extensive postmortem mutilation of the body, on the greed that had supposedly motivated the crime, and on Djang's alleged perfidy throughout the entire episode. According to witnesses and the prosecution, these elements made the crime distinctly Chinese. "No Englishman would be so brutal," insisted Arthur Grosvenor, the prosecutor's prime witness and the proprietor of the Birmingham boardinghouse where Djang had resided [41] The prosecution also raised the issue of deviant sexuality, asking Grosvenor if Djang had ever asked him to sleep with him. "Yes," the witness replied, "on June 27. If not, would my son?"[42] The prosecution had posed the question to demonstrate that Djang had exhibited anxiety and nervousness following the murder, but in light of the previous portrayals of Chinese men as being lecherous and sexually deviant, the implication was doubly damning.

Cancellor, in an autobiography published ten years after the conclusion of the trial, devoted almost an entire chapter to the case. He was contemptuous of Djang, whom he described as being subhuman, greedy, servile, and cunning, "more like a dog that any human being I have ever seen."[43] Far from being unique in these characteristics, Djang was, according to the magistrate, an apt representative of a "secretive race" that came from "an Eastern land where human life is a small thing compared to the injury caused by the loss of money."[44] Cancellor reassured readers, however, that in the British legal system, Djang would not face the same savagery and merciless punishment that he had dealt to his victim.[45] Djang's legal counsel and the Assize judge that would pass final sentence had been informed of his lack of English language skills and his counsel would plead for his life "with the power of persuasion which members of the English bar always use in the interest of even the meanest and poorest prisoner in a trial for wilful murder."[46]

Such pleas aside, on October 22, Djang, protesting his innocence to the very last, was sentenced to death for the murder of Zee Ming Wu. He was the first Chinese man to be executed in Britain since 1916 and the fourth, overall, since 1900. At the conclusion of the trial, Djang handed the magistrate a written statement. "I am very sorry this occurred," it read, "I can't understand English very much.

Will you please be very lenient with me as I want to go back to my wife and business, and my mother, who is very good to me."[47] Cancellor, who would meet many more Chinese defendants after his transfer to the Thames Police Court in December 1921, did not include this final coda in his memoirs.[48] Considering the magistrate's description of Djang as "a creature of the animal world," however, the rest of his chapter on "tragedy and comedy" in the police courts was oddly appropriate—it discussed trials involving dogs and cats.

Following the Djang murder trial, arrests, prosecutions, and press reports concerning Chinatown in late 1919 and early 1920 focused on the increasing presence of white Britons in the district and on the accompanying moral hazards. According to witness testimony, Chinese-owned gambling houses and cafés were attracting patronage from a broad spectrum of the London population. One London riverboatman announced in a Central Criminal Court trial that "people resorted to Chinese gambling houses from all parts of London. They came from Brentford and even from Gravesend."[49] A February 1920 Thames Police Court case highlighted the perils that Limehouse leisure allegedly posed for white Londoners. When a "well-dressed" young girl was brought before the magistrate J. A. R. Cairns on a charge of insulting behavior, her mother blamed her downfall on the attractions of "the Chinese quarter."[50] Her daughter had been "a good girl up to a few weeks ago," she told the court, but had been led astray by "undesirable companions." When her pleadings in court for her daughter to return home were met only with averted eyes and a downcast face, the mother expressed her frustration that magistrates and police had done nothing about the haunts that had lured her daughter away. "You should see those dens at Limehouse—those cafes they call them," she told the court, angrily. "They ought to be swept away." Since no charge had been leveled beyond the initial one at the girl herself, Cairns could do little except refer the case to the "lady missionary," the court's semi-official social welfare agent, "to see her with a view to her reclamation." Further reports in the London press, some of which recounted the views of local officials, emphasized the continuing tensions between Chinese and white residents in the East End over employment, housing, and interracial sexuality and marriage. They also commented on the frequency with which residents of the West End came to the East End seeking a taste of the exotic.

The increasing publicity accorded to interracial contact in the East End was matched by vociferous assertions, in both London judicial discourse and popular culture, that Chinese men and white Britons were fundamentally incompatible, particularly on matters of marriage and sexuality. In a November 1920 divorce court case, Justice Thomas Horridge, a former MP (East Manchester, Liberal), made no attempt to hide his disapproval of interracial marriage and of the Limehouse Chinese petitioner who came to his court seeking a divorce from his wife. The issue of race and cultural difference became the main topic

Figure 6.1. "London's Chinatown: Taking the Oath." The original image includes the caption: "A Scene in an East End Police Court. When a Chinaman takes the oath he usually breaks a plate-generally on the edge of the witness box, but sometimes on his head-and in East End police courts a stock of cheap crockery is kept for this emergency. As the plate falls in pieces he repeats, 'May my soul be broken even as this plate if I do not tell the truth.' Curiously enough, about the very time our artist was sketching this scene the first trial by jury conducted in China was being held in Shanghai, and when the jurors were sworn in a translation of the English version of the juryman's oath was used." (*Daily Graphic*, August 2, 1913. Courtesy of the British Library.)

of a case that was an otherwise straightforward occurrence of adultery and abandonment. The suit was brought by Chang Ping, whose wife of six years had eloped with another man, Mr. Yip. Horridge, upon learning that the wife's new partner was also Chinese, exclaimed to the court that "the woman must have a fancy for Chinamen!"[51] When the petitioner's counsel explained how Chang had given up his work as a ship's steward in 1916 to take a position as a butler, Horridge accused him of cowardice. "He thought that he would be safer on land," the justice commented, provoking laughter from the court. Horridge initially refused to let the petitioner give an oath in the English manner, despite his clear eagerness to do so. The justice suggested that, following Chinese custom, he should be "sworn on a saucer" instead (see Fig. 6.1).[52] Chang, who appeared before the court in "smart European dress," refused, and would not relent until he had delivered his oath in broken English. He further emphasized his commitment to assimilation by telling the court that he "intended to make England his home." The case subsequently turned away from Chang's status and back to a common subject in courtroom discussions of Chinese men—gambling. Asked by Horridge to supply more information about Yip, Chang replied, "'e gamble . . . 'e play anytink," again prompting laughter from those in attendance. After establishing that Yip was a saloon owner, the justice granted Chang his divorce. But acknowledgement of his legal right to a divorce under English law was not matched by any public recognition that he was any less Chinese, or any more English, because of it. Despite his engagement of English law on its own terms, his wearing of European clothing, his marriage to an Englishwoman, his insistence that he take his oath "in the European fashion," and his declaration that England was his "home," his racial identity, in the eyes of observers, remained immutable. For Horridge and the courtroom audience, Chang's attempts at assimilation and his language difficulties, faithfully reproduced in the newspaper coverage of his testimony, only made him an object of ridicule.

The supposedly unbridgeable gap between China and the West and the sinister consequences of any attempt to mingle them also remained popular topics in West End theater. In June 1920, Samuel Shipman's *East is West* opened at the Lyric after a successful run at the Astor Theater in New York.[53] The action, which took place in China and in San Francisco's Chinatown, revolved around the villainy of westernized Chinese men, their sexual depravity, and the popular revulsion against interracial sexuality. Ming Toy, a Chinese girl, is rescued from the grasp of a Mandarin and brought to America by Lo Sang Kee and an American, Billy Benson. Lo Sang, an honorable man, treats Toy with utmost respect until public scandal and the threat of deportation forces him to sell her to Charlie Yong, a wealthy and prominent member of the San Francisco Chinese community. Yong, like Sax Rohmer's villains, combined the characteristics of "East" and "West" in a menacing and potent mix. "An Americanized Chinaman," he is "at once smooth and sinister, genial and repulsive."[54] Yong is also both vicious and feminized, being "in the habit of beating the girls he bought and also of wearing wonderful American clothes." Billy Benson rescues Toy from sexual slavery and Yong's dastardly clutches, but his love for the beautiful Chinese girl is an anathema to his parents. All ends well when it is revealed that Toy is in fact an American who had been abducted and taken to China as an infant. This discovery, according to the *Times* critic, "deprived the play of all ethnological significance, but provided it with a cheerful ending."[55] With the threat of an interracial union removed, the Bensons give their blessing to the marriage and the curtain falls.

Even as the worried mother in the Thames Police Court, Justice Horridge, and the playwrights of *East is West* emphasized the hazards of interracial sexuality, the sinister results of meetings between "East" and "West," and the impossibility of true cultural assimilation by Chinese immigrants, stories on the practical outcome of romantic unions between Chinese men and white women began to appear more frequently in the press. In June 1920, the *Daily Telegraph*, which had been notable for its earlier refutation of union leaders' scandalous depictions of vice in Chinatown, printed another sympathetic account of the neighborhood. Its article, "The Children of Chinatown," portrayed the Chinese residents of the East End in favorable terms and claimed that their cultural and social assimilation was well under way. The *Telegraph*'s story also strongly contradicted the portrayals of Chinatown as a place filled with "opium dens wherein lurid dramas are continually taking place."[56] According to the author, such misconceptions stemmed from "vivid imagination and kinema [*sic*] pictures" rather than from actual knowledge of Chinatown, a district that was, on the contrary, "outwardly placid and unromantic." But the author acknowledged that the increase in Chinese-owned businesses and the establishment of a permanent Chinese population, as commented on in previous press reports, was not an exaggeration, and further recognized that these trends had caused tension in the East End.

The *Telegraph*'s portrayal of interracial sexuality and its consequences differed dramatically from previous discussions of the issue in the courts, the press, and popular fiction and theater. Although Anglo-Chinese children were a visible element in the district, the author saw nothing deplorable or immoral about interracial unions or their offspring. The children were bright and inquisitive, and the interactions between them and white children at the local state elementary school (Dingle Lane) paid no heed to racial boundaries. At the Dingle Lane school, according to the headmaster, "the Chinese youngster is treated quite as a true little Londoner." The permanent Chinese community, the *Telegraph*'s story asserted, enjoyed a positive standing among their white neighbors, largely due to the honor and fairness they brought to commercial dealings "in London as in the Far East."

Whereas previous judicial, journalistic, and literary portrayals had emphasized the irreconcilability of Chinese and British culture

Figure 6.2. Children on a stoop in Limehouse, 1928. (Courtesy of the Tower Hamlets Local History Library and Archive.)

and society, the *Telegraph*, in contrast, reported that Anglo-Chinese children had become so thoroughly assimilated that, ironically, the survival of Chinese culture itself in the district had become an issue of serious concern. The dilution of Chinese culture and the decline of Chinese language fluency among the new generation had prompted an initiative to insure that the children of mixed-race parentage were educated in "their own language," an initiative that was supported by "learned and wealthy Chinese gentlemen" and East End teachers alike.[57] In one of the rare instances of official Chinese government involvement in the affairs of Chinatown, a campaign spearheaded by Lo Chong, the Chinese Consul in London, inaugurated the teaching of Chinese language classes at the Dingle Lane school.

In regards to the issues of race, immigration, and the assimilation of Chinese residents in the East End, the significance of the article and the "educational movement" it described was twofold. First, it highlighted the degree to which children of mixed Chinese and English backgrounds were popularly viewed as retaining the racial identity of the father (the Chinese parent in the vast majority of instances) rather than that of the mother.[58] Such children may have been going to English schools, dressing as English children did, and speaking English to

Figure 6.3. A Chinese grocery store, Limehouse, c. 1930. (Courtesy of the Tower Hamlets Local History Library and Archive.)

the exclusion of Chinese, but they remained "Chinese" nonetheless. Second, the popularity of the new Chinese-language program among both children and adults indicated that the issue of cultural assimilation, at least by 1920, was not one-sided.[59] The Chinese of London were confronting a concern common among immigrant communities—how to assimilate with a local populace that was often, at best, ambivalent about such integration while still preserving some level of social cohesion and cultural tradition. The cultural, social, economic, and linguistic diversity within the London Chinese community itself made this process even more problematic. But despite the hostility and violence to which Chinese residents had been subjected in the past, many clearly had not been deterred from trying to preserve their language in the metropolis or from openly exhibiting indicators of their cultural background. The prominent display of Chinese-language signs on businesses well into the following decades offered further evidence of the tenacity of London's Chinese community in this regard (see Fig. 6.3). It is hard to determine, however, whether this last measure was driven by cultural pride; by practicality, since much of the daily business conducted by Chinese proprietors depended upon the patronage of other Chinese residents and itinerant seamen; by resignation, since the exclusion of even long-term Chinese residents from recognition as Britons was by then a decades-old phenomenon; or by commercial acumen, since the allure of Chinese restaurants, shops, and cafés to curious Londoners depended upon the persistence of the district's exotic glamour.[60]

"Moral and Physical Suicide": The Campaign against Gambling and Interracial Contact in Interwar Chinatown

The "Children of Chinatown" article, despite its reflection of a bias toward the fixed racial identity of Anglo-Chinese children, was one of the most substantial attempts thus far in the London press to paint a relatively positive picture of the district and its residents. The author demonstrated a detailed knowledge of the London Chinese community, even to the point of recognizing the cultural and ethnic variations within its population. This diversity has recently been confirmed in oral accounts given by the community's few surviving members, but remains otherwise unacknowledged in most descriptions of it both then and now.[61] The author also contradicted the popular portrayal of Chinese residents as being an exclusively male cohort. Although the presence of Chinese women was exceedingly rare, he wrote, and Chinese men were far more likely to find "an English partner willing to share his lot," Chinese women did occasionally come to London to help run their husband's business.[62]

The *Telegraph*'s nuanced portrayal proved to be the calm between storms. Chinatown soon became a subject of public anxiety and a focal point of police and judicial concern once more. A police court magistrate and his views of race, gender, and morality were at the center of the latest campaign against vice in Chinatown. At a Thames Police Court case on October 2, 1920, Doe Foon, a Chinese man who had resided in Britain for twenty years, was charged with keeping a disorderly house. Since its passage in 1751, the Disorderly Houses Act, which held legally responsible those whose property was employed to "deprave and corrupt" the public, had been used for a variety of purposes, but particularly to prosecute music-hall proprietors, brothel keepers, and the owners of gambling houses.[63] In the twentieth century, it was also employed to suppress homosexual activity.[64]

The Doe Foon case was the first instance in which the act was employed to regulate interracial sexuality. The adaptation of the law to this purpose demonstrated how closely the issues of race and gender had become intertwined in East End law and policing and in the attitudes of officials toward what constituted "vice" in interwar London. Although the two police officers who gave evidence claimed that Doe Foon's establishments were indeed being used by prostitutes to solicit business, the prevalence of interracial sexuality there was the focus of their testimony. "They saw coloured men, Chinamen, women of loose character, and young white girls there," the witnesses reported, "kissing and cuddling went on, and acts of indecency occurred. Some of the girls had half-caste babies with them."[65] One of the officers elaborated further on the general atmosphere of race-mixing that pervaded in the East End. "There were quite a number of these half-caste children in East London now," Detective Tarry told the court.[66] Black men, according to the police witnesses, had also brought their culture to the East End, and at Doe Foon's cafés, they "sometimes sang coon songs." Not content with merely fining Doe Foon £5 and recommending him for deportation, J. A. R. Cairns, the presiding magistrate, launched into a furious tirade against "the lamentable state of things" in East London. "To him, the problem was a frantic one," he declared, "why young English girls should thus commit acts of moral and physical suicide was unexplainable."

Cairns's enthusiasm for eugenics theory and his belief that the English race must be rescued from the degenerative practices of miscegenation, decadent sensuality, and other forms of moral and physical corruption guided his approach to interracial sexuality in the East End. The deplorable physical state of the population, he wrote in his memoirs, had become obvious during the recruitment drives of World War I.[67] In his descriptions of Chinatown, the magistrate expressed an unabashed loathing for the casual affairs that took place between white women, Chinese men, and black men in the cafés there. In such places, he wrote, "the hands of white girls were fouled by nameless contacts and their bosoms polluted by the lecherous touch of black and yellow hands that oozed with a sweating noisome excrement. It was degradation upon degradation, it was shame upon shame. It was despair."[68] Cairns's descriptions of Chinese-owned cafés as sites of indiscriminate race-mixing and decadent sensuality replicated the images of opium dens that had appeared previously in literary and press depictions. But Cairns could draw on courtroom accounts of white women frequenting such cafés, whereas the presence of white women in opium dens had yet to be confirmed. In the magistrate's statements and representations of these locales, the evidence provided by police reports and court testimony was thus interpreted through the precedents set by literature and sensationalized journalism.

For Cairns, the maintenance of public order and, more importantly, the preservation of both the English race and the British nation were dependant upon the segregation of white women from Chinese men and black men. Eugenics theory provided him with a "scientific" justification for legal intervention in Chinatown, and police reports of race-mixing in Chinese-owned cafés gave him a concrete target for his campaign. Other East End magistrates shared Cairns's concerns over immorality and race-mixing, and were equally willing to go to extraordinary lengths in order to prevent interracial unions. H. L. Cancellor, who would be transferred from the West London Police Court to the Thames Police Court in late 1921, later openly admitted to using his judicial authority to "stop a white woman from marrying a Chinese man."[69] Convinced that one Chinese suitor was seeking a union solely with an eye toward financial gain, the magistrate placed the woman involved, who had been charged with entering a false name in a hotel register, under the probationary charge of the police court's female missionary. The probation was granted to the young woman only on the condition "that she should not associate for six months with her Chinese lover."[70] The missionary subsequently put the women in the care of a female Salvation Army worker, who was "willing . . . to reform her, and also to keep her away from the Chinese colony." The

"Chinese lover" himself, Cancellor explained in his memoirs, "I sent to prison for a short time to keep him safely out of the way."

Following the conclusion of the trial, the magistrate was shocked to learn that the truth of the matter was far worse than he had first surmised. The woman, he explained, turned out not to have been the unsuspecting victim of Chinese perfidy but rather "the unfaithful wife of an English soldier" and a willing accomplice in her Chinese partner's intrigues.[71] But, despite his realization that she had deceived and manipulated him, Cancellor was unwilling to condemn her, and instead blamed the Chinese man. The woman, like others who had come before his court in order to "give evidence to screen their yellow spouses," had "taken lessons in the art of lying from their lords and masters."[72] Such women, he wrote, who appeared in court "always well dressed and wearing jewelry," had degraded themselves to such an extent that there was no way out of their predicament, and they knew it. "The women are so conscious of having sold their souls and bodies to their yellow masters," he explained, "that they are afraid to publish the tragedies of their lives."[73] Magistrates' descriptions, much like earlier literary accounts, portrayed Chinatown as a locale where the expected dynamics of racial hegemony were starkly reversed. There, according to Cairns and Cancellor, Chinese culture dominated and British culture was eclipsed, Chinese men were the masters and white women were the slaves, Chinese men were the purveyors of desired commodities and white men and women were its consumers, and sexual access to white women was the provenance of Chinese men and black men, while white men were left forlorn.

By portraying white women as the hapless victims of Chinese vice rather than as its purveyors, magistrates' discourse also returned such women to a position of subordination and created an implicit justification for the intervention of masculine morality via the state and its agents. Cancellor did not give a specific date for the incident he described, but by the time of his transfer to the East End in 1921, judicial intervention to halt the supposed prevalence of interracial social and sexual contact had become commonplace. Such intervention followed hard on the heels of the public scandal generated by the Doe Foon case. The trial, which brought the issue of interracial social contact and sexuality to the immediate attention of East End magistrates and the reading public, prompted a barrage of commentary in the London press over the following weeks, and Cairns's declarations would be repeated in the pages of the *Evening News*, the *Times*, and the *Daily Mail*. Stories in the latter blamed race-mixing not only for the moral corruption of young white girls and for the resulting proliferation of half-caste children, "the fathers of whom are Arabs, Japanese, Chinese, and negroes," but also for the spread of venereal disease.[74] In early October, the *Evening News*, one of the most popular of the London evening papers, referenced Cairns's statements in the Doe Foon case and demanded the legal segregation of white women from men of non-European races in Limehouse. "The ordinary machinery of the law is unequal to this new problem," their story on "the Lure of the Yellow Man" claimed.[75] "The time has come to draw a cordon around this area of London and forbid any white woman from frequenting it." The following day, the *Times* contributed its own article on "the Morals of 'Chinatown,'" commenting on the growth of interracial relationships in the East End and reassuring readers that public authorities were taking swift and decisive action.[76] As evidence of this effort, the paper reported that the Poplar borough council was "seriously concerned" with the issue and would soon be submitting a petition to the Home Office.

To what extent this alarm issued from the general population of the East End and to what extent it was generated by Cairns's statements, the concerns of police and other representatives of state or private social reform in the East End, and the subsequent hysteria fomented by the London press is not easy to determine. The involvement of the Poplar borough council, which was made up almost entirely of Labour representatives, indicated that interracial sexuality in the East End, and Anglo-Chinese unions in particular, had become a cause for serious concern among labor leaders (if not necessarily their constituency) by this time.[77] The contributions of the magistrates, the police, and the press certainly help explain why interracial sexuality became such a prominent public issue once again in late 1920. But the resentment of working-class East End residents, and of seamen and demobilized soldiers in particular, over the apparent ability of Chinese men to attract the trappings of success had established fertile ground for such anxieties. The events of the previous year had also fostered, among East End officials, an acute concern over popular racial unrest. They had witnessed, firsthand, the violence and destruction it could spawn. It is therefore hardly surprising that in the wake of the 1919 riots, which many commentators had blamed upon white men's resentment and hostility toward interracial sexuality, East End magistrates were quick to respond to the revival of public anxiety over the issue in late 1920. The popular press further encouraged such intervention by praising the magistrates and police who chose to get involved. The editors of the *Evening News* commended Cairns, in particular, for bringing to light the Chinese "merchants of vice" and their "foul places," and expressed confidence that "the public conscience will insist on their being cleaned out."[78]

By late 1920, magistrates, police, and Poplar borough council members all seemed to have reached a consensus that the "morals of Chinatown" required immediate attention. Two years after the conclusion of the war that had prompted the expansion of state authority to protect the security of the nation against the designs of enemy aliens, East End magistrates were poised to use their increased powers in order to stop the "moral and physical suicide" of white girls and, in doing so, to protect the health and wellbeing of the nation and the race against the alleged designs of cunning Chinamen. The legal protocol for summarily deporting resident aliens, once they had been convicted of a crime, had been in place since 1914. And the passage of the 1919 Aliens Restriction (Amendment) Act—a measure that had been enthusiastically supported by the opponents of Chinese labor in parliament—had made permanent the wartime augmentation of the laws governing aliens.[79] In their attempts to address the "frantic problem" of interracial sexuality, however, magistrates and police confronted a serious practical obstacle: there were no laws that expressly forbade interracial contact where no other crime had been committed. Cairns had overcome this impediment by charging Doe Foon with a violation of the Disorderly Houses Act, which had been employed in preceding decades to address public sexual immorality but not interracial sexuality in particular. With the cooperation of the Home Office, he and other East End magistrates swiftly began to employ extant laws in order to close the establishments where interracial contact allegedly took place and to expel from the country those who ran them.

The same *Times* article that introduced the Doe Foon trial to a national readership also indicated what would become the primary legal justification for decisive state intervention in Chinatown. Gambling, which had been identified by police and magistrates as a serious issue in Chinatown during the war, would be the focus of the newly revived effort to address "the Morals of Chinatown." East End magistrates had also previously associated gambling with the district's Jewish population, whose loyalty to and membership in the nation had been similarly suspect to them in recent years.[80] But with the Chinese in interwar London, the activity took on a deeper and more frightening significance. According to the Poplar borough council's report to Scotland Yard, the "alarming increase" in the popularity of the Chinese lottery game "puk-a-poo" was chiefly responsible for the "growth of relationships between Chinese and white women."[81]

Women and children, according to the *Evening News*, were particularly vulnerable to "the evil attractions" of the game. The allure of puk-a-poo was the high prizes attainable from very small wagers and, as a result, "women and even children in the district will stop at nothing to raise the small sums necessary to play."[82]

"The lure of puk-a-poo," the paper reported, had drawn a steady stream of young white women, many unemployed, to Chinese gambling establishments.[83] The temptation of "a gay life and easy money" was so strong that women were coming from as far away as Glasgow, Cardiff, and the industrial towns of northern England to congregate in Chinatown. Once they had "taken up with Chinamen," the paper reported, neither police nor parents could separate them. "Their moral sense is gone," the article informed readers, "they behave as though hypnotised by the Celestials, and seem helpless to break their spell." The result, according to the *Evening News* and other popular London papers such as the *Daily Express*, the *East End News*, and the *Evening Standard*, was an inevitable spiral downward from gambling addiction to the abandonment of motherhood—an *Evening News* reporter interviewed one woman whom claimed to have seen "a mother take the shoes off her baby's feet in order to raise money for Puckapu"—to interracial sexuality, prostitution, and the spread of disease.[84] "There has crept into the community of the East End," a report by the *Daily Express* concluded, "a 'Yellow Peril' not formed of massed battalions of saffron manned bayonets, but composed of a corruptive organized financial force backed by millions, that is undermining the morale not of the men, but of the women and children in the East End."[85]

Press reports sometimes held women partly to blame for the deplorable state of affairs in Chinatown and the figure of the "new woman" was central to the press and judicial accounts of the puk-a-poo menace. Like Chinese men's supposed usurpation of demobilized soldiers' access to property, gainful employment, and sexual status, "the new woman" also stood as a threat to traditional gender norms and as a visible symbol of the decline of British masculinity. World War I had empowered working-class and lower-middle-class women, opening up opportunities for employment, leisure, and mobility that had been largely unavailable to them before the changes wrought by "total war." [86] An article by the popular jingoistic novelist Dorota Flatau explicitly connected women's mobility and the legacy of the wartime economy with the scandalous race-mixing taking place in Chinatown. The women coming from the north, she wrote, "met Chinamen who had been engaged in munition-making, aeroplane manufacture, and other pursuits during the war," and had followed them to London.[87] Such girls, according to Flatau, were generally "of a low type" and had resigned themselves, fatalistically, to accommodating the customs of their husbands. "They like you to look flash and to go an 'ave baths and all," Laura, a mother of four children by her Chinese husband, told the author. "So long as you don't shame their face, you're all right," she explained, but any disrespect was met with harsh punishment. Moving between the two rival groups of Hong Kong and Shanghai origins, Laura told Flatau, was a particular taboo.

The majority of newspaper articles, magistrates' statements, and police declarations on the issue, however, placed the blame for interracial relationships squarely on the shoulders of Chinese men. Following the precedents set by literary and journalistic portrayals of Chinese drug traffickers, press reports claimed that the women lured into interracial unions by the appeal of Chinese gambling became "fascinated," "hypnotized," or, worse yet, "enslaved," and were therefore either unwilling to leave their new partners or incapable of doing so. Unlike opium smoking, which appeared to be confined largely to Chinese men and the West End thrill-seekers who could afford its high interwar price, Chinese gambling, according to police, magistrates, and press reports, was attracting a working-class clientele and was accessible even to unemployed women.[88] Magistrates and East End journalists insisted that the only hope of rescue for the women so "enslaved" lay in direct intercession by agents of law and order. By portraying women as being demoralized and helpless before the material enticements of wealthy Chinese men, the public outcry on "the morals of Chinatown" justified strong judicial action against interracial social contact and sexuality, but also restored working-class women in the East End to a subordinate position.[89] State intervention in Chinatown could thus simultaneously address two major sources of concern among white, working-class men and the putative advocates of East End British masculinity in the interwar period. The first was the rising social and economic status of Chinese property owners. The second was the instability of gender roles resulting from the mobility and independence demonstrated by the "new woman."

The lure of Chinese gambling proprietors and the weakness and deceptiveness of women who frequented their establishments were, according to press reports, sabotaging any hope of a return to domestic stability and white, working-class male dominance in the interwar East End. "Mothers and daughters," the *Evening News* reported, "have gambled and got into debt without the knowledge of the husband and father," and it is by this path that they "fall easily into the Oriental's coils."[90] The response of East End men to this predicament was sometimes a direct and violent one. One docker who had discovered that his wife had "pawned clothing and squandered the rent money" to fund her gambling habit "went in hot anger to the Chinese café and thrashed the Chinaman."[91] The worsening economic situation of the East End, and of Poplar in particular, added further fuel to popular resentment at the perceived collusion between Chinese men and white women to undercut white working-class men. The predominance of Labour interests in East End borough councils gave the aggrieved cohort greater leverage with which they could encourage official action on these issues.[92]

Despite concerted police efforts to ameliorate the alleged immorality of Chinatown, the press reported that they were having difficulties dealing with the recent upsurge. Police were struggling to combat West End vice at the same time and their patrols in Piccadilly and Victoria had, ironically, worsened the situation in Chinatown, it was reported, by driving "a certain type of woman eastward" out of her more common haunts.[93] Public discussions of vice in the metropolis increasingly merged images of West End decadence with Chinatown's established reputation for racial immorality to frame the latter as the new "plague spot of the metropolis."[94] Even as the West End was coming to the East End, Chinese vice was moving in the other direction as well. "Chinatown has active scouts in the West End," the *Evening News* reported, "and it caters for vice in various forms."[95] Chinese vice-peddlers had also been observed, according to the paper, in Stepney, West Ham, Westminster, and Hampstead.[96] Chinese wealth and vice were not only encouraging indiscriminate race-mixing in the East End, such reports claimed, but were also continuing to violate the racial geography of the metropolis by extending Chinese influence well beyond the borders of Chinatown.

The Chinese residents of Limehouse, by now accustomed to such spasms of public alarm and official intervention, contested the claims that they were corrupting the white women of London. One such resident, interviewed by F. W. J. Underwood for the *Daily Graphic* shortly after the publication of Cairns's comments on the "moral suicide" of white girls in Chinatown, challenged the portrayal of Chinese men that had appeared in recent newspaper articles. Speaking rhetorically, he insisted that the magistrate's assertions defied the legal evidence concerning interracial marriage: "Do you ever see a Chinaman in the police courts charged with assaulting his wife? No. Do you see Chinese charged with bigamy? No."[97] There was nothing salacious about interracial unions, he insisted. "Some of our men," he told Underwood, "steady and hard-working-people, have married white women and have been very happy and contented with them." This prosaic image of these unions was further reinforced by two of the wives in question, whom Underwood also interviewed. "He has been an ideal husband to me, and he worships his children," Mrs. Chow Lan said of her husband of fifteen years. "My home life is just like an ordinary English home." The problems of vice and unwelcome interracial social contact, she continued, were not the fault of the Chinese men luring innocent girls to Chinatown. On the contrary, Mrs. Chow insisted, it was "English girls who are out searching for men" that made the local restaurants so iniquitous. Underwood's original interviewee similarly asserted that the blame for the current Chinatown scandals lay with the white women who visited there of their own accord and, in the process, had transformed gambling and opium smoking from the discreet habits of a few into a public spectacle of rampant vice.

Chinese café proprietors responded to increased police investigation by posting signs that forbade loitering (in order to discourage soliciting by prostitutes), and those conducting gambling displayed written notices warning patrons of the possible legal penalties for their activities.[98] The Chinese residents who conducted puk-a-poo games, one paper reported, had also petitioned Scotland Yard to have the activity removed from proscription.[99] The East End magistrate Henry Rooth, however, definitively settled the issue in a June 1920 Thames Police Court case when he declared puk-a-poo to be both a lottery and unlawful gaming and its organizers therefore liable to prosecution under the Gaming House Acts and the Lotteries Acts.[100] Rooth, who had been sympathetic toward Chinese residents who practiced the "national vice" of opium smoking, was sterner when it came to their gambling. In order to avoid investigation and prosecution, the proprietors of Chinese games began conducting them on Sundays, when the execution of search warrants under the Gaming House Acts was forbidden. The culprits had been "eminently well-advised," Chief Inspector Mann, the Police Superintendent of K Division, reported, about the legal restrictions on Sunday warrants, "therefore they throw open their houses and defy all authority."[101] In response, he successfully petitioned Scotland Yard for permission to execute Sunday search warrants for such offenses—a power previously reserved for serious offenses such as treason or breaches of the peace—though they advised him that his plan to prosecute the printers of puk-a-poo gaming tickets as well was likely to be unsustainable in court.[102] Mann emphasized that the spread of Chinese gaming to the general population had made the activity "highly offensive to the respectable law abiding citizens" of the East End and justified the rapid expansion of the police campaign against it. He estimated that, at the time of his report in October 1920, there were between thirty and forty gaming houses managed by Chinese proprietors in Chinatown. Mann was particularly eager to prosecute Chinese proprietors and gamblers in order to "quash the impression that Police are sympathetically inclined towards Chinese offenders at a time when they vigorously prosecute English gaming house keepers and street bookmakers."[103]

As had been the case in the wartime anti-gambling campaigns, Chinese property owners were again bearing a disproportionate share of both the police and judicial assault on vice in the metropolis and the blame for the spread of such practices among the white population. Although the reports of white Londoners' participation in Chinatown gambling were more widespread in this case, there was contradicting evidence as well. Inspector Mann's memorandum belied the press hysteria over white women's addiction to Chinese gambling on two very significant points. He reported that the gambling houses shut down at 10 pm, while the author of the *Evening News*'s exposé on "the lure of Puk-a-poo" claimed that white women did not even begin to appear in the district until 9 pm. It was around this time of the night, on the other hand, that the cafés where much of the reported social contact between white girls and Chinese or "coloured" men took place opened for business. Mann also reported that Chinese gambling houses, far from being exclusively committed to puk-a-poo, frequently conducted games of dice and fan-tan, neither of which had been associated with white women or interracial social contact. Most significantly, police raids on Chinese gaming houses failed to produce white suspects, or at least none that were ever later charged in East End police courts. Participation in puk-a-poo, however, did not require the player to be present in the gaming house at the time of the drawing. The small paper playing tickets were cheap to produce, easy to conceal, and quickly disposed of. Although neither Mann's report nor the dearth of white defendants disproves the reports that women's "addiction" to puk-a-poo and their concurrent "fascination" with Chinese men had become prevalent social problems in the East End, they certainly cast doubt upon the dramatic assertions made by the Poplar borough council and in press reports.

Even beyond white women's involvement, the alleged popularity of Chinese gambling among "all and sundry" in Chinatown, the open defiance of the law by Chinese proprietors, and the "huge fortunes" reportedly amassed by them were all serious concerns to the Metropolitan Police.[104] Mann and his superiors were willing to employ all legal measures available—and even to adapt those previously unavailable for such offenses—in order to close the Chinese establishments. But the same judicial system that facilitated their efforts was also occasionally employed by Chinese residents to protect themselves against both prosecution and persecution. Despite the barriers of language and culture, some Chinese residents proved adept at using the courts and their knowledge of the law, as the Sunday-opening strategy of gaming house organizers demonstrated. Those arrested on gambling charges, when they had the means to do so, sometimes successfully availed themselves of legal representation. When Wong Kaie Chong was tried at the Thames Police Court with maintaining an unlawful gaming establishment, his barristers—whom the Police Superintendent reported were "men of colour"—were able to convince the magistrate, Forbes Lankester, to dismiss the case.[105] Inspector Mann, who had used undercover police observation to establish that Wong was one of the two proprietors, was dismayed, as was William Horwood, the Commissioner of Police, who asserted that Lankester's decision was "a wrong one."[106] A series of communications followed between Scotland Yard and the Home Office discussing how, in future cases, to more effectively prosecute suspected Chinese gaming house proprietors.

Chinese residents also employed the courts against the police themselves. In November 1920, the King's Bench heard a suit brought by Chong Shui against Sergeant Culling of the Metropolitan Police. Chong, through his solicitor and an interpreter, claimed that Culling had extorted £22 from him on the premise that he was conducting a raid, and also that the officer had assaulted him by pushing him down the stairs, breaking his leg in the process. Culling, in his defense, denied all of the charges and insisted that he was "only doing his duty under the Defence of the Realm Act."[107] The plaintiff, he further explained, had sustained the injury by jumping out of the window, and the money had been taken by another Chinese man in the confusion.[108] Culling's defense also cited his fifteen years of honorable service as a policeman and brought in a medical examiner to testify that the injuries sustained by Chong were consistent with a fall from a window rather than down a set of stairs. Culling's experience and strong record of arrests in Limehouse, however, were the focus of a harsh cross-examination by Chong's solicitor, who alleged that Culling had a history of blackmailing Chinese residents.

The contradicting witness testimony and ambiguous evidence in the trial left no clear conclusion as to the guilt or innocence of the defendant. Had Culling abused his power and taken advantage of the climate of fear in Chinatown, a climate that his own determined pursuit of Chinese offenders had fostered, for pecuniary gain? Or were Chong and his witnesses, one of whom was himself awaiting deportation on an opium possession charge, using the courts to take revenge upon a police officer that they believed had persecuted them? In his closing comments, the presiding justice, Clement Bailhache, told the jury that the case was "of very unusual character and of great importance" since at stake was the reputation of the Metropolitan Police, "of which all Englishmen, and especially Londoners, were proud."[109] Bailhache also cautioned them to prioritize the protocols of the law over any animosity they might feel against the plaintiff on account of his race. "We in England," the justice declared, "prided ourselves in giving even-handed justice to strangers within our gates as well as to our own people—though we might sometimes feel that those strangers were too numerous." Whether intentionally or not, Bailhache's comments both reaffirmed the status of the Chinese as perennial "strangers" in London (one witness had been resident for eight years) and firmly associated their very small population with the larger issues of immigration and alien residency in the metropolis. His comments about Culling, on the other hand, cast him as a representative of an honorable institution that was not only quintessentially English but was also a particular point of pride for Londoners. Such considerations notwithstanding, the jury found in favor of the plaintiff.

The successful contestation of police prosecutions in the Wong Kaie Chong and Chong Shui cases were exceptions to the broader trend. Such efforts were ultimately of little avail in the face of concerted judicial and police action, especially when the trial of every Chinese suspect was being portrayed in the popular press as part of an epic battle against an internationally financed attempt to corrupt the women and children of London. In early October, the *Daily Express*—a paper that, established in 1900 as a competitor to the *Daily Mail*, had first become popular through its coverage of imperial affairs—printed an extensive report on the most recent Chinatown scandal.[110] The Chinese men conducting gambling in the East End, the story claimed, were part of a "Chinese syndicate . . . backed by powerful, if mysterious, influences. Its object is the propagation of vice. It is succeeding all too well."[111] At the center of this international "syndicate of vice" was a character that could have stepped straight out of a Sax Rohmer novel, a "Chinese Moriarity" that served as "the master agent of the London branch."[112] And yet, for all his power and exoticism, this villain, like Rohmer's Sin Sin Wa, concealed himself in the guise of "a humble merchant" of Limehouse. The police, the

Express wrote, were well aware of this dire network and its sinister mastermind and, "reinforced by far-reaching magistrates" who were willing to deport Chinese offenders, they were prepared to face the threat.

But against whom, ultimately, were magistrates and police to employ their powers? This was a particularly vital issue for London's Chinese residents, since judicial and police authority vis-à-vis resident aliens still retained much of its wartime potency. Despite repeated insistences by Chinese residents that only a few among them were involved in gambling or selling opium and that it was largely the demands of white women that were fueling the spread of these habits in the East End, police investigations, magistrates' statements, and press reports continued to portray the entire district as one in which vice of one sort or another was rampant in every property owned by a Chinese resident.[113] By portraying the criminal activities of Chinatown as a conspiracy and the Chinese master criminal as a "humble merchant," the *Daily Express* and other papers cast suspicion upon almost all the Chinese men of the district, and made the group that would have been, had they been British, the most respectable, instead the most suspect of all. The alleged natural affinity of the Chinese for deception and disguise, a reputation that had emerged at least in part from the chronic inability (or unwillingness) of Britons to distinguish between individual Chinese men, only further blurred the line between the guilty and the innocent.

The Metropolitan Police, encouraged by their superior officers and the Poplar borough council, supported by local magistrates, and repeatedly goaded by the London popular press, threw a wide net around the Chinese residents of the East End. Undercover investigations, clandestine observation, sudden raids, mass arrests, and exemplary deportations became commonplace. In September and October, scores of Chinese men were arrested in anti-gambling and anti-opium raids, and East End magistrates recommended deportation on at least a dozen separate occasions.[114] Officer Culling, who would later be accused of extortion and assault, was a key figure in at least one case. At the conclusion of that Thames Police Court trial, the magistrate imposed a £100 fine, the largest ever assessed in a London opium conviction, against Tam Kow for allowing his premises to be used for the purpose of smoking opium.[115] Among those recommended for deportation on gambling charges was Mok Sing, who had been arrested earlier in Culling's impromptu raid and who would later, while awaiting the execution of his sentence, serve as a witness for the plaintiff in the Chong Shui suit. At Mok's Thames Police Court trial,

Inspector Mann added interracial sexuality and the corruption of a young white girl to the defendant's other alleged acts of immorality.[116]

The effects of the latest campaign against Chinese "vice" and "the frantic problem" of interracial sexuality were dramatically highlighted the following January when the conviction of Doe Foon, who had been found guilty of keeping a disorderly house and recommended for deportation in October 1920, came up for appeal in the London Sessions. Sir Ernest Wild, the noted advocate, defended Doe Foon by pointing to his long residency in England (twenty years) and by insisting that his deportation would harm his English wife as well.[117] During his defense of his client, Wild lambasted Cairns for using his courtroom as a forum to encourage racial antipathy. Cairns's statements, he argued, in conjunction with the recent press hysteria, had devastated the Chinese population of the East End. "As a result of the action of the magistrate and the Press," he told the justices, assembled audience, and newspaper representatives, "the population of the Chinese colony at Limehouse has been reduced from 4,000 to 300. The remedy is worse than the disease, for in the place of these Chinamen, who were perfectly well-conducted citizens, the houses have been taken over by people of another nationality, who are very much worse than the people they replace."[118] Wild concluded his speech, which would be reprinted in both the East End press and in the *Times*, with a warning to Cairns and any other magistrate who might use their judgment seat "to coin phrases for the newspapers." The *Times*'s coverage of the trial, which appeared under the headline "Chinese Exodus from Limehouse," reported that the chairman of the sessions, in rare departure from common practice, refused to confirm the recommendation for Doe Foon's deportation.[119]

Cairns, ever outspoken, was not content to receive Wild's aspersions without response. In his opinion, the judicial and police campaign had admirably achieved its goals by staunching Chinese vice, female immorality, and the anathema of interracial sexuality in Chinatown. "Worse than the disease!" he exclaimed the following day to a reporter from the *East End News*, "in my opinion, the daily parade of white girls charged with disorderly behaviour has ended. The appeals of heartbroken parents whose daughters were lured to Chinatown has ended. The charges of playing puk-a-pu, having relation to gambling are ended [*sic*]. The charges of opium smoking are ended. These are my experiences."[120] Cairns cited police reports as confirmation of this, relating to the reporter that "a divisional inspector of police" had told him "the Limehouse problem was solved, and that Pennyfields was like a country village," The editors of the *News*, however, were less sanguine that police raids, arrests, and exemplary deportations had brought a full measure of law and order and had expunged the unsavory alien presence from the district. "So far as Pennyfields being like 'a country village,'" their story concluded, "it would be interesting to know where Mr. Cairns has seen a country village resembling it—not in England, for certain."[121]

Cairns, in any event, had been little deterred from his campaign against Chinese vice and interracial sexuality by Wild's acerbic comments. In July 1921, he was given another opportunity to put a close on unfinished business. Three years previously, his colleague, Frederick Mead, had labeled Ada Ping You the "high priestess of . . . unholy rites." For her role in organizing opium smoking parties in the West End and for her alleged contribution to the tragic death of Billie Carleton, Mead had sentenced her to five months hard labor. But Henry Rooth, another of his colleagues, had been lenient with her Chinese husband, Len Ping You, insisting that it was unfair to treat him harshly for practicing the Chinese "national vice" of opium smoking. By the time of her husband's second trial in 1921, Ada Ping You was dead, Rooth was preparing to be transferred from the Thames Police Court, and most importantly, the attitudes of East End magistrates, police, and the press toward Chinese residents had hardened considerably.[122] When Len Ping You, who had been seized in a police raid on his Limehouse home, was convicted for possessing opium utensils and for allowing his premises to be used for opium smoking, Cairns did not hesitate to bring the full force of the law to bear. Having been informed by the police witness that Ping You was "one of the principals in the opium traffic in the Chinese colony," Cairns recommended him for deportation twice.[123]

Chapter 7

Epilogue
The Ghosts of Chinatown

Even as East End magistrates and police were shutting down cafés where interracial social contact reportedly took place, raiding Chinese gambling houses, and deporting the Chinese men accused of running them, international pressure was growing for Britain to bring its domestic narcotics laws into line with the stipulations of the 1912 international Hague Opium Convention. The incorporation of the latter into the Treaty of Versailles, combined with the growing public anxiety over gender and vice in the wake of the Billie Carleton affair, gave Sir Malcolm Delevingne of the Home Office the political momentum he needed to expand the state's power vis-à-vis the trade in illicit narcotics.[1] The reported growth of narcotics addiction in the empire also helped spur this change.[2] On September 1, 1920, the Dangerous Drugs Act made permanent the wartime emergency powers regulating narcotics.[3] Building on the foundation of DORA 40b, the act absolutely prohibited the importation of prepared opium; prohibited, except under license, the import, export, or manufacture of raw opium, cocaine, morphine, and heroin; and raised the maximum penalties for violation of these statutes to six months' imprisonment and a fine of £200.

Following the passage of the Dangerous Drugs Act, the legal campaign against narcotics use and the public scandals over Chinese and black men who allegedly used "dope" to seduce young white women continued to mount, reaching a climax in 1922–24 with the trials of "Brilliant" Chang and Edgar Manning. Chang, a Chinese restaurateur and a prominent figure in West End nightlife, was implicated in the death, by cocaine overdose, of the jazz club dancer Freda Kempton in March 1922. Although police were initially unable to convict him, the incident spawned a police and media frenzy that rivaled the one following the Billie Carleton affair. Tales of Chinese drug barons proliferated in the press and in the newest medium of public culture, the cinema. The "dope" film genre was popularized among British audiences by Birmingham director Jack Graham-Cutts's movie, *Cocaine* (1922).[4] *Cocaine* retold the Kempton incident in the most salacious possible manner, with Flora le Breton playing a guileless ingénue who is seduced into drug slavery through the machinations of a Chinese criminal syndicate.[5] The banning of the film, which was released two months after Kempton's death, by the British Board of Censors only added to the sensation it had created.[6]

Following the Kempton scandal and the release of *Cocaine*, British anti-narcotics laws were strengthened once again with the Dangerous Drugs and Poisons (Amendment) Act of 1923, which expanded police search powers and raised the maximum penalties to £1000 and ten years' imprisonment with hard labor.[7] Britain, once the laggard in the regulation of the international narcotics trade, was fast becoming its leader in Europe.[8] The effects on the policing of the illicit narcotics trade in Britain were substantial, with arrests and prosecutions for both opium and cocaine increasing dramatically in 1923.[9] When police finally did convict Chang on cocaine charges in April 1924, he felt the full weight of the harsher regulations. The so-called "Dope King" of Limehouse was sentenced in the Central Criminal Court to fourteen months' imprisonment and recommended for deportation.[10] In a related case, Lily Brentano, a Limehouse resident and alleged associate of Chang's, was arrested and sentenced to six months' hard labor after a West End policeman witnessed her behaving in a "suspicious manner" with two other women.[11]

Chang's arrest and imprisonment prompted a brief resurgence of public interest in Limehouse, a district whose media prominence had faded somewhat as London nightlife, and accompanying police attention, coalesced around the West End jazz scene.[12] The year 1923 also witnessed the popular release of the first Fu Manchu film, and Sax Rohmer himself described his delight at seeing "larger than life sized posters [depicting] the leering visage and clutching hands of the Devil Doctor" all over London.[13] The new wave of visitors seeking "adventure and experience" in Chinatown in the mid-1920s was reported as far afield as Canadian newspapers.[14] Arrests for opium and gambling in the district continued intermittently until the outbreak of the World War II, but by the late-1920s, police and journalists alike were declaring that the days of Chinatown as an exotic locale of vice, crime, and decadence were over. The Dangerous Drugs Act of 1923 and the concerted efforts of police, according to such accounts, had spelled the end of the sensation. Beneath the judicial campaign against Chinese gambling and narcotics use in the East End, the discouragement of Chinese settlement London had been carried out in more subtle ways as well. In 1923, the London County Council passed a resolution giving preference to British subjects in council dwellings, and the Poplar borough council followed suit by refusing to accept Chinese tenants in its rehousing schemes.[15]

The *Daily Express* and the *Evening Standard* reported lurid stories of Chinatown opium raids well into the late 1920s (see Fig. 7.1), and negative portrayals of Chinese men on the London stage were so widespread that they prompted an official protest from the Chinese Legation in 1928.[16] But by the end of the decade, the pendulum of official reports and journalistic depictions of Chinese residents in the East End had once again swung back toward portrayals of them as law-abiding and relatively harmless, even as other groups were assuming greater prominence in the public discourse on dangerous aliens.[17] The fading of the public sensation over Limehouse Chinatown and the

Figure 7.1. Chee Kong Tong lodge and newspaper advertising placards, Limehouse, c. 1927. (Courtesy of the Tower Hamlets Local History Library and Archive.)

attribution of its newfound respectability to police efforts were also followed by a phase of public retrospection among the magistrates, journalists, and authors who continued to comment on the district. Some began to question if the reputation of the area for crime and debauchery had ever been justified in the first place. Articles in several of the newspapers where the stories of Chinatown's exotic villainy had appeared previously even speculated that such tales had perhaps been manufactured by reporters in search of a story. In his 1930 history of the district, J. G. Birch, the Rector of St. Anne's, likewise insisted that "those who look for the Limehouse of Mr. Thomas Burke simply will not find it."[18] The author's "vivid imagination," he continued, had created something that "may be literature, but it is not Limehouse." James A. Jones of the *Evening News* similarly cautioned readers in 1931 that "if Chinatown means to you the glamour and romance of the East . . . you will be sadly disillusioned."[19]

But whether those writing about the district in the 1930s believed that there was some truth in Chinatown's reputation for vice and decadence, or whether they thought that such accounts had been exaggerations all along, the reciprocal relationship of law, press, and literature remained central to the defining of the neighborhood and its inhabitants in public discourse. It was police accounts, court trials, and magistrates' statements—dramatically retold or reinterpreted in newspapers and popular fiction—that had propagated Chinatown's lurid reputation, and the same sources, it now seemed, were sounding its demise. Jones, who was primarily a court reporter, relied on police accounts to substantiate his story, "Chinatown: The Truth," and Birch quoted Thames Police Court magistrate J. A. R. Cairns as the final word on the banality of Limehouse. Those who went searching for the exotic there, the magistrate had asserted, would find instead "a solid block of English people as English in their tastes and habits, in their patience and loyalty, in their domestic relations and civic responsibilities, as is York or Bristol or Berwick-on-Tweed."[20] In a 1934 article entitled "Chinatown Myth Exploded," the *East London Observer* similarly relied on the police evidence given at a coroner's inquest into the death of Loo Fook, a Chinese Limehouse resident, as a bellwether of the neighborhood's character. During the inquest, the police witness, p.c. Coombe, who had worked in the district for twenty years, insisted that opium smoking had all but disappeared in Chinatown.[21] "And it is supposed to be one of the show places of England," the coroner responded, "there cannot be much to see there." The *Daily Telegraph* titled its article on the same inquest "Limehouse 'Debunked,'" and in it described how Coombe's testimony had "robbed [Limehouse] of its dramatic aspect."[22] "No wonder the novelist has had to change his settings as well as characters, and put his villains into dress suits and Mayfair [i.e. West End] residences," the article concluded.

The attempts by Birch, James, Coombe, and others to downplay the sensationalized reputation of the neighborhood jibes with the recollections of Annie Lai, who married Yuen Lai, a Chinese opium dealer, and lived in the district during the 1920s. Lai insisted that both the dens themselves and the stories of debauchery and seduction in Chinatown had been fictitious all along. Her husband refused to let her use opium initially, she told a reporter for the *Guardian* in 1998, the "den" he ran was simply a large room over a shop, and its Chinese patrons used opium as a mild relaxant and for relief from respiratory illness. As for the tales of sexual license, Lai dismissed them out of hand. Women were banned from her husband's shop when opium was being smoked, she explained, and "there was no sex . . . nothing like that."[23]

Lai's account represents the unique perspective of a British woman whose marriage to a Chinese opium dealer was part and parcel of Chinatown's scandalous reputation. It must be approached with caution, both because it was recorded more than a half-century after the events in question and because Lai demonstrated an acute awareness of the lurid tales that had once been told about a community of which she had been an integral part. But her unromantic memories of Limehouse were supported by a contemporary description written by Lao She (the pseudonym of Shu Ch'ing-ch'un), a Chinese intellectual and novelist who worked as an instructor at the University of London in the 1920s.[24] His semi-autobiographical account of middle-class Chinese life in 1920s London, *Mr. Ma & Son: A Sojourn in London* (1929–30), remains one of the few surviving records written by a London Chinese author in this period. In it, he expressed outrage at the descriptions of Chinese residents that had been spread through "fiction, diaries, and news" by Westerners on voyeuristic jaunts to Chinatown, "the most degrading of all places for Chinese."[25] "Those who write fiction, plays, movies, all describe Chinese on the basis of these myths," Lao wrote, "and all those who read the books, or see the movies or plays—be they children, old ladies, or even Kings of England, have these insane images firmly etched in their minds. Hence Chinese have been made the most treacherous people in the world, the most foul, disgusting, contemptible beasts to walk on two legs!"[26]

Lao, who had spent considerable time studying both cultures, posited a deeper analysis of relations between Britons and Chinese immigrants, one that emphasized the dynamics of imperialism and the powerful impact of both racism and nationalism. "In the twentieth century," he wrote, "the terms 'people' and 'nation' are inextricably linked: people from strong nations are human beings, and those from weak nations, dogs."[27] One result of the West's military and economic domination of China was that even the casual visitor to Chinatown could wantonly construct a villainous image of Chinese immigrants without fear of being gainsaid:

> There's really nothing spectacular there, and the workers aren't engaged in any fantastic activities. It's simply because *Chinese* live there and they want to take a look—because China is a weak country, thus they can casually ascribe a myriad of odious names to the industrious, enduring immigrant Chinese who are simply struggling to eke out a living in a strange place. If there were twenty Chinese living in Chinatown, their accounts would say five thousand; moreover every one of these five thousand yellow devils would certainly smoke opium, smuggle arms, murder people then stuff the corpses under beds, and rape women regardless of age.[28]

Lao She's analysis of the relationship between Chinatown and images of the Chinese in Britain suggests that by the late 1920s, a significant change had taken place in the flow of ideas between empire and metropole, one that would grant the mythology of Chinatown a more powerful and enduring legacy. Instead of images of the Chinese generated in the empire being mapped onto London's Chinese population, portrayals of Chinatown and its residents, according to the author, had become the lens through which the British, and Western observers more generally, viewed the Chinese people as a whole.

By the mid 1930s, Limehouse had changed dramatically—its residents had either departed or assimilated to the best of their ability, and much of the original neighborhood had been demolished when the London County Council had widened Limehouse Causeway in 1934.[29] Even as the Chinese population of Limehouse declined and the reports of arrests and vice slowed to a bare trickle, the negative stereotyping of Chinatown and its residents summarized by Lao She proved to be remarkably persistent. Images of the Chinese as a dire threat to the white race and to the British nation, and of the villainy and immorality of Chinese immigrants, lived on in the tales told of what Chinatown and its denizens had been like during their scandalous heyday.[30] James A. Jones, the court reporter for the *Evening News*, wrote in 1931 that there was "no mystery, by daylight, in the squalid curve of Pennyfields or the drab length of Limehouse Causeway," but he acknowledged the powerful hold still exerted by the neighborhood's lurid reputation.[31] "At night, every doorway, standing open . . . leads in your imagination to an opium den. Every Chinese man, stealing past you with cat-like tread, is a Fu Manchu. Every pale-faced girl is a Broken Blossom."[32] The prejudice against interracial sexuality had not abated either, he wrote, and the only true dramas and tragedies that remained were to be found among the children of such unions. The daughters, in particular, were doomed to "drift about the streets, ostracized by white girls of their own age. They, and not the white wives, are the broken blossoms."

In the 1930s, new forms of mass entertainment accelerated the exchange of negative Chinese stereotypes between Britain, Europe, and the United States. According D. H. Green, one of the pioneering scholars of British research into the dynamics of racial prejudice, film played an especially powerful role in the transmission of the sinister reputation of Chinese immigrants from one generation to the next.[33] Speaking in 1931 under the auspices of the League of Nations, Green described the results of his study of racial prejudice among young children. "A whole body of prejudice had been made definite by the 'dope' films and the films of the Dr. Fu Manchu series," he wrote. [34] "Quite young children referred in their papers to abductions, to floors that gave way, to stealthy attack and secret murder on the part of the Chinese, and appeared to take for granted that such things made up the ordinary life of the Chinese they saw on the streets." Fu Manchu would remain a popular figure in films, novels, short stories, comics, radio, television, and even children's cartoons in Britain, the United States, Australia, and Canada for decades to come.[35]

The menacing reputation of Limehouse Chinatown and its residents far outlived the district itself. When what remained of the post-Blitz neighborhood was scheduled for demolition in the mid-1950s, the *Times* printed a romanticized retrospective claiming that the abduction of young white girls, smuggling, opium smoking and cocaine use, and all "the old customs, vices, and crimes" had been rampant there well into the 1930s.[36] Writing his autobiography twenty years later, Louis Heren (b. 1919), the noted journalist and chronicler of East End life in the 1920s and 1930s, distinctly recalled the district's evil repute. "Beyond New Park and well to the east was Limehouse," he wrote, "where we never went but knew to be filled with Chinese Tong men and opium dens. (We read in the *News of the World* of beautiful young society girls becoming addicts there, just like in du Maurier's *Trilby*.)"[37] For Heren and his boyhood friends, the lurid stories of

Limehouse and the negative stereotypes of Chinese men circulated in popular culture had become the reality—a reality frightening enough to discourage them from ever visiting the neighborhood itself. These representations, spawned in law, press, literature, and film, proved to be far more resilient than the people and places that had once inspired them were. Long after the tides of migration, war, and urban renewal had swept away "the fog-bound labyrinth of Limehouse," the "ghosts of Chinatown" lingered on.[38]

Notes

Chapter 1

1. The two oldest and most popular of the Chinese puzzle games in the West are the tangram and the sliding-block puzzle.
2. Marian Bower and Leon Lion, *The Chinese Puzzle: An Original Play in Four Acts*, acting ed. (New York: Samuel French, 1919); *Times* (London), July 12, 1918, 9. The play received critical acclaim and was adapted for the screen the following year. *Times* (London), October 13, 1919, 10.
3. Robert Bickers, *Britain in China: Community, Culture, and Colonialism, 1900–1949* (Manchester: Manchester University Press, 1999), 35–36; Hugh Brogan, *The Life of Arthur Ransome* (London: Jonathan Cape, 1984), 293.
4. Review of *The Chinese Puzzle*, by Arthur Ransome, and *Explaining China*, by John Earl Baker, *Journal of the Royal Institute of International Affairs* 7, no. 1 (January 1928): 57.
5. *Times* (London), September 10, 1877, 4.
6. *The Seaman: The Official Organ of the International Seafarers and the National Sailors' and Firemen's Union* 4 (May 1908).
7. A point emphasized in John Seed's recent article, "Limehouse Blues: Looking for Chinatown in the London Docks, 1900–1940," *History Workshop Journal* 62 (2006): 68–69. See also Colin Holmes, "The Chinese Connection," in *Outsiders and Outcasts: Essay in Honour of William J. Fishman*, ed. Geoffrey Alderman and Colin Holmes (London: Duckworth, 1993), 85.
8. Thomas C. Holt draws on the work of Henri Lefebvre in his argument that race was "mutually constituted . . . in the global and the everyday." Thomas C. Holt, "Marking: Race, Race-Making, and the Writing of History," *American Historical Review* 100, no. 1 (February 1995): 10.
9. For China serving as a role model for the British Empire in the nineteenth century, see Barry Milligan, *Pleasures and Pains: Opium and the Orient in Nineteenth-Century British Culture* (Charlottesville, VA: University Press of Virginia, 1995), 52. Philippa Levine describes the barriers that the British erected around themselves in the imperial context in *The British Empire: Sunrise to Sunset* (Harlow, U.K.: Pearson Longman, 2007), 126–27. Colin Mackeras discusses the general evolution of Western opinion on China in *Western Images of China* (Hong Kong:

Oxford University Press, 1989) and in his edited anthology, *Sinophobes and Sinophiles: Western Views of China* (Oxford: Oxford University Press, 2000).

10. The figure of "John Chinaman" is generally attributed to the American satirist and political cartoonist Thomas Nast, who began depicting the image in the 1860s. But the term and image had both appeared previously in the British press, most prominently in the pages of the *Times* (1840) and, later, in *Punch* (1857). "John Bull" had its origins in British satirist John Arbuthnot's depictions of Whig magnates in 1712. By the mid-nineteenth century, the rotund male figure bedecked in a Union Jack had come to represent the British everyman, just as "John Chinaman," with his "coolie" jacket and queue, was establishing himself as the most common image of Chinese men in the U.S. and British press.
11. David Northrup, *Indentured Labor in the Age of Imperialism, 1834–1922* (Cambridge: Cambridge University Press, 1995). Chinese workers were also essential to the agricultural labor force in European imperial territories in the nineteenth century.
12. Lynn Pan, *Sons of the Yellow Emperor: A History of the Chinese Diaspora* (New York: Kodansha International, 1990), 90.
13. "Coolie" has its immediate origins in the Hindi word *qūlī*, meaning "laborer." The original source is most likely the Tamil word *kuli*, which means "wages." Northrup, *Indentured Labor*, 60. The Chinese word *kŭlí*, which is a transcription of the Hindi, means "bitterly hard (use of) strength."
14. Seed, "Limehouse Blues," 79.
15. Rozina Visram, *Ayahs, Lascars, and Princes: Indians in Britain 1700–1947* (London: Pluto, 1986), 38–39.
16. *Old Bailey Proceedings Online (OBP)*, *http://*www.oldbaileyonline.org, September 1800 trial of William Rayner and Charles Moren, t18000917–29.
17. In 1851, the official tally of China-born residents in London stood at 110. Ng Chee Choo, *The Chinese in London*, published MA thesis, University of London (London: Oxford University Press, 1968), 5.
18. Ibid., 6. By 1891, the number of officially recorded China-born resident aliens had risen to 302.
19. Mid-century accounts discuss a second, smaller Chinese community in the East End neighborhood of Bluegate Fields (St. George's-in-the-East), but references to it had ceased by the turn of the century.
20. Poverty, unsanitary conditions, and violence between Chinese seamen and among Lascar seamen in the East End had attracted official attention on several occasions in the early nineteenth century. Michael Fisher, *Counterflows to Colonialism: Indian Travelers and Settlers in Britain, 1600–1857* (New Delhi: Permanent Black, 2004), 172–73. For a broader view of anti-immigrant sentiment in the prewar period, see Colin

Holmes, *John Bull's Island: Immigration and British Society, 1871–1971* (London: Macmillan, 1988), 65–85.

21. Henry Mayhew, *London Labour and the London Poor, vol. 4* (London: Griffin, Bohn, 1861–62; New York: Dover, 1968) 232–33. Citations are to the Dover edition.
22. Count E. Armfelt, "Oriental London," in *Living London*, ed. George R. Sims (London: Cassell, 1901–3), 84; George A. Wade, "The Cockney John Chinaman," *London Illustrated Magazine*, July 1900, 302.
23. Walter Besant, *East London* (London: Chatto and Windus, 1901), 205–6. Pan, *Sons of the Yellow Emperor*, 86–87.
24. Joseph Charles Parkinson, "Lazarus, Lotus Eating," in *Places and People, Being Studies from Life* (London: Tinsley Bros., 1869), 36–37, reprinted from *All the Year Round* 15 (May 12, 1866).
25. Mayhew, *London Labour*, 232–33.
26. George A. Wade insisted, in his 1900 account, that "in this Chinese portion of the East End, there are no women from China." Wade, "John Chimaman," 302. Census statistics contradict this assessment, however, indicating that there were two dozen present in London in 1901 and nearly a hundred there by 1921. Choo, *Chinese in London*, 11.
27. Mayhew, *London Labour*, 232–33; Parkinson, *Places and People*, 28; Joseph Salter, *The East in the West; or Work Amongst the Asiatics and Africans in London* (London: S. W. Partridge, 1895), 35.
28. Armfelt, "Oriental London," 86.
29. Parkinson, *Places and People*, 21.
30. Wade, "John Chinaman," 307.
31. Ross G. Forman, "Peking Plots: Fictionalizing the Boxer Rebellion of 1900," *Victorian Literature and Culture* 27 (1998): 19–48; Paul A. Cohen, *History in Three Keys: The Boxers as Event, Experience, and Myth* (New York: Columbia University Press, 1997), 191–97.
32. The postcolonial critique rightly insists that any examination of race must take into account both the power dynamics inherent in European racial discourse and the ways that racial "others" responded to and contested these dynamics. Edward Said, *Orientalism* (New York: Vintage, 1978); Gayatri Spivak, "Can the Subaltern Speak?" in *Marxism and the Interpretation of Culture*, ed. Cary Nelson and Larry Grossberg (Chicago: University of Chicago Press, 1988), 271–313; Dipesh Chakrabarty, *Rethinking Working-Class History: Bengal 1890–1940* (Princeton, NJ: Princeton University Press, 1989); Ranahit Guha, Gayatri Spivak, and Edward Said, eds., *Selected Subaltern Studies* (Oxford: Oxford University Press, 1989); Partha Chatterjee, *The Nation and Its Fragments: Colonial and Postcolonial Histories* (Princeton, NJ: Princeton University Press, 1993). In the British context, Laura Tabili has emphasized black workers' contestation of racial subordination in interwar Britain. Laura Tabili, *"We Ask for British Justice": Workers and Racial Difference in Late Imperial Britain* (Ithaca, NY: Cornell University Press, 1994), 2–5.

33. Terence Gomez and Gregor Benton, *Chinese in Britain: Economy, Transnationalism, and Identity* (New York: Palgrave Macmillan, 2008).
34. Important early works include Douglas A. Lorimer, *Colour, Class, and the Victorians* (Leicester, U.K.: Leicester University Press, 1978); Nancy Leys Stepan, *The Idea of Race in Science: Great Britain 1800–1960* (Hamden, CT: Archon Books, 1982).
35. This concept of race and its linkages with the social, cultural, economic, and political dynamics of empire in the nineteenth century animates much of the recent scholarship on these subjects. In the British context, see Paul Rich, *Race and Empire in British Politics* (Cambridge: Cambridge University Press, 1986); Tabili, *British Justice*; Anne McClintock, *Imperial Leather: Race, Gender, and Sexuality in the Colonial Contest* (New York: Routledge, 1995); Mrinalini Sinha, *Colonial Masculinity: The "Manly Englishman" and the "Effeminate Bengali" in the Late Nineteenth Century* (Manchester: Manchester University Press, 1995); and Zine Magubane, *Bringing the Empire Home: Race, Class, and Gender in Britain and Colonial South Africa* (Chicago: University of Chicago Press, 2004).
36. For work on the subject after World War II, see Paul Gilroy, "*There Ain't No Black in the Union Jack": The Cultural Politics of Race and Nation* (Chicago: University of Chicago Press, 1987), and Kathleen Paul, *Whitewashing Britain: Race and Citizenship in the Postwar Era* (Ithaca, NY: Cornell University Press, 1997).
37. Prominent examples of this scholarship include Ron Ramdin, *The Making of the Black Working Class in Britain* (Aldershot, U.K.: Gower, 1987); Tabili, *British Justice* and "Women 'of a Very Low Type': Crossing Racial Boundaries in Imperial Britain," in *Gender and Class in Modern Europe*, ed. Laura Frader and Sonya O. Rose (Ithaca, NY: Cornell University Press 1996); Gretchen Holbrook Gerzina, ed., *Black Victorians/Black Victoriana* (New Brunswick, NJ: Rutgers University Press, 2003); Antoinette Burton, *At the Heart of Empire: Indians and the Colonial Encounter in Late Victorian Britain* (Berkeley and Los Angeles: University of California Press 1998); Shompa Lahiri, *Indians In Britain: Anglo-Indian Encounters, Race and Identity 1880–1930* (London: Frank Cass, 2000); Visram, *Ayahs, Lascars, and Princes*; Jonathan Schneer, *London 1900: The Imperial Metropolis* (New Haven, CT: Yale University Press, 1999), chap. 8 and 9; Paul Deslandes, "'The Foreign Element': Newcomers and the Rhetoric of Race, Nation, and Empire in 'Oxbridge' Undergraduate Culture, 1850–1920," *Journal of British Studies* 37, no. 1 (January 1998): 54–90; Marika Sherwood, "Lascar Struggles against Discrimination in Britain 1923–1945: The World of N. J. Upadhyaya and Surat Alley," *The Mariner's Mirror* 90, no. 4 (November 2004): 438–55.
38. Holmes, "The Chinese Connection," 71. James Watson made a similar assertion previously ("The Chinese, Hong Kong Villagers in the British

Catering Trade," in James Watson, ed., *Between Two Cultures: Migrants and Minorities in Britain* (Oxford: Blackwell, 1977), 181).

39. The former referred to the Middle East and the latter to China, Japan, and SE Asia. Said, *Orientalism*, 1.
40. For the difficulties involved in applying Said's theories in the Chinese context, see Simon Leys, ed., *The Burning Forest* (New York: Holt, Rinehart & Winston, 1985). For a recent response, see Chen Xiaomei, *Occidentalism: A Theory of Counter-Discourse in Post-Mao China* (New York: Oxford University Press, 1995). Homi K. Bhabha identifies some of the weaknesses of "Orientalism" as a theoretical approach to colonial discourse in "The Other Question: Homi K. Bhabha Reconsiders the Stereotype and Colonial Discourse," *Screen* 24, no. 6 (1983), 23–25.
41. Dominic LaCapra succinctly outlines some of the major issues encountered in the study of race in his introduction to *The Bounds of Race: Perspectives on Hegemony and Resistance* (Ithaca, NY: Cornell University Press, 1991), 1–4.
42. Laura Tabili discusses the importance of grounding and contextualizing racial dynamics in social relations and the pitfalls of relying on "intolerance, bigotry, and ignorance" as givens and therefore as sufficient explanations alone for racism. Laura Tabili, "The Construction of Racial Difference in Twentieth-Century Britain: The Special Restriction (Coloured Alien Seamen) Order, 1925," *Journal of British Studies* 33, no. 1 (January 1994): 55–56. She further develops and expands this argument in *"We Ask for British Justice": Workers and Racial Difference in Late Imperial Britain* (Ithaca, NY: Cornell University Press, 1994).
43. Bhabha explores this complex process in "The Other Question." Joan W. Scott also argues that both race and gender are constructed categories and therefore cannot be naturalized. Joan W. Scott, "Gender: A Useful Category of Historical Analysis," *The American Historical Review* 91, no. 5 (December 1986): 1053–75.
44. The majority of scholarship on "whiteness" has emerged from American labor history. David Roediger, *The Wages of Whiteness: Race and the Making of the American Working Class* (London: Verso, 1991); Noel Ignatiev, *How the Irish Became White* (New York: Routledge, 1995). For "whiteness" in Britain, see Alastair Bonnett, "How the British Working Class Became White: The Symbolic (Re)formation of Racialized Capitalism," *Journal of Historical Sociology* 11 (1998): 316–40.
45. According to Anne McClintock, "race, gender, and class are not distinct realms of experience, existing in splendid isolation from each other . . . rather they come into existence *in and through* relation to each other—if in contradictory and conflictual ways." McClintock, *Imperial Leather*, 5. For the relationship between class and race, see Jonathan Hyslop, "The Imperial Working Class Makes Itself 'White': White Labourism in Britain, Australia, and South Africa Before the First World War," *The Journal of Historical Sociology* 12, no. 4 (December 1999): 398–421. See also

Linda Colley, *Britons: Forging the Nation, 1707–1837* (New Haven, CT: Yale University Press, 1992), 6; Ruth Lindeborg, "The 'Asiatic' and the Boundaries of Victorian Englishness," *Victorian Studies* 37, no. 3 (1994): 381–404; Benedict Anderson, *Imagined Communities: Reflections on the Origins and Spread of Nationalism* (London: Verso, 1983); Homi K. Bhabha, ed., *Nation and Narration* (London: Routledge, 1990); and Robert J. C. Young, *Postcolonialism: An Historical Introduction* (Malden, MA: Blackwell, 2001).

46. For a discussion of the methodological pitfalls of "whiteness" as an analytical category, see Eric Arnsen, "Whiteness and the Historians' Imagination," *International Labour and Working-Class History* 60 (Fall 2001): 3–32.
47. I am particularly conscious of Antoinette Burton's assertion that Britain itself served as "an imperial contact zone." Burton, *Heart of Empire*, 1. This relationship in the modern period is also examined in Catherine Hall and Sonya O. Rose, eds., *At Home with the Empire: Metropolitan Culture and the Imperial World* (Cambridge: Cambridge University Press, 2006); Andrew Thompson, *The Empire Strikes Back: The Impact of Imperialism on Britain from the Mid-Nineteenth Century* (Harlow, U.K.: Pearson Education, 2005); John M. MacKenzie, *Propaganda and Empire: The Manipulation of British Public Opinion, 1880–1960* (Manchester: Manchester University Press, 1984); Schneer, *London 1900*; Richard Price, "One Big Thing: Britain, Its Empire, and Their Imperial Culture," *Journal of British Studies* 45, no. 3 (July 2006): 602–27.
48. Kathleen Wilson, "Introduction: histories, empires, modernities," in *A New Imperial History: Culture, Identity, and Modernity in Britain and the Empire, 1660–1840*, ed. Kathleen Wilson, (Cambridge: Cambridge University Press, 2004), 1. See Antoinette Burton, "Introduction: On the Inadequacy and the Indispensability of the Nation," in *After the Imperial Turn: Thinking with and Through the Nation*, ed. Antoinette Burton (Durham, NC: Duke University Press, 2003) for a comprehensive assessment of work in this field. For a recent study of Europe's broader impact on Chinese culture and society, and for Britain's particular role in this context, see James Hevia, *English Lessons: The Pedagogy of Imperialism in Nineteenth-Century China* (Durham, NC: Duke University Press, 2003).
49. David Feldman and Gareth Stedman Jones, eds., *Metropolis London: Histories and Representations since 1800* (London: Routledge, 1989); Judith Walkowitz, *City of Dreadful Delight: Narratives of Danger in Late Victorian London* (Chicago: University of Chicago Press, 1992); Ellen Ross, *Love and Toil: Motherhood in Outcast London* (New York: Oxford University Press, 1993); Susan Pennybacker, *A Vision for London: Labour, Everyday Life, and the LCC Experiment* (London: Routledge, 1995); Deborah Epstein Nord, *Walking the Victorian Streets: Women, Representation and the City* (Ithaca, NY: Cornell University Press, 1995); Lynda Nead, *Victorian Babylon: People, Streets, and Images in Nineteenth-Century London*

(New Haven, CT: Yale University Press, 2000); Simon Joyce, *Capital Offenses: Geographies of Class and Crime in Victorian London* (Charlottesville, VA: University Press of Virginia, 2003); Seth Koven, *Slumming: Sexual and Social Politics in Victorian London* (Princeton, NJ: Princeton University Press, 2004).

50. For a social history of the former, see Maria Lin Wong, *Chinese Liverpudlians: A History of the Chinese Community in Liverpool* (Birkenhead, U.K.: Liver Press, 1989).
51. Wade, "John Chinaman," 301.
52. Judith Walkowitz, *Prostitution and Victorian Society: Women, Class and the State* (Cambridge: Cambridge University Press, 1980); Carolyn Conley, *The Unwritten Law: Criminal Justice in Victorian Kent* (New York: Oxford University Press, 1991); A. James Hammerton, *Cruelty and Companionship: Conflict in Nineteenth-Century Married Life* (London: Routledge, 1992); George Behlmer, "Summary Justice and Working-Class Marriage in England, 1870–1940," *Law and History Review* 12, no. 2 (Fall, 1994): 229–76; Ginger Frost, *Promises Broken: Courtship, Class, and Gender in Victorian England* (Charlottesville, VA: University Press of Virginia, 1995); Margot Finn, "Working-Class Women and the Contest for Consumer Control in Victorian County Courts," *Past and Present* 161, no. 1 (November 1998): 116–54; Gail Savage, "'The Magistrates Are Men': Working-Class Marital Conflict and Appeals from the Magistrates' Court to the Divorce Court after 1895," in *Disorder in the Courts: Trials and Sexual Conflict at the Turn of the Century*, ed. George Robb and Nancy Erber (New York: NYU Press, 1999), 231–49.
53. Specifically, in *The Report on Lascars and Other Asiatic Seamen, 1814–15* and *The First Report from the Committee on the State of the Police in the Metropolis, 1817*. Choo, "Chinese in London," 16–17; Fisher, *Counterflows to Colonialism*, 172–73.
54. Shompa Lahiri, "Contested Relations: The East India Company and Lascars in London," in *The Worlds of the East India Company*, ed. H. V. Bowen, Margaret Lincoln, and Nigel Rigby (Woodbridge, U.K.: Boydell, 2002), 178–79.
55. Levine, *The British Empire*, 114.
56. Ronald Hyam, *Britain's Imperial Century, 1815–1914, 3rd ed.* (Cambridge: Cambridge University Press, 2002), 76–77.
57. For the broader relationship between law and literature in Britain, see Shani D'Cruze, *Crimes of Outrage: Sex, Violence, and Victorian Working Women* (Dekalb, IL: Northern Illinois University Press, 1998); Margot Finn, "Victorian Law, Literature and History: Three Ships Passing in the Night," *Journal of Victorian Culture* 7, no. 1 (2002): 134–46; Hal Gladfelder, *Criminality and Narrative in Eighteenth-Century England: Beyond the Law* (Baltimore: Johns Hopkins University Press, 2001). See also Gillian Spraggs, *Outlaws and Highwaymen: The Cult of the Robber in England from the Middle Ages to the Nineteenth Century* (London: Pim-

lico, 2001); Donna T. Andrew and Randall McGowan, *The Perreaus and Mrs. Rudd: Forgery and Betrayal in Eighteenth-Century London* (Berkeley and Los Angeles: University of California Press, 2001).

58. Nayan Shah, *Contagious Divides: Epidemics and Race in San Francisco's Chinatown* (Berkeley and Los Angeles: University of California Press, 2001); Mary Ting Yi Lui, *The Chinatown Trunk Mystery: Murder, Miscegenation, and Other Dangerous Encounters in Turn-of-the-Century New York City* (Princeton, NJ: Princeton University Press, 2005); Andrew Gyory, *Closing the Gate: Race, Politics, and the Chinese Exclusion Act* (Chapel Hill, NC: University of North Carolina Press, 1998). For the legal historiography, see Richard Cole and Gabriel Chin, "Emerging from the Margins of Historical Consciousness: Chinese Immigrants and the History of American Law," *Law and History Review* 17, no. 2 (Summer 1999): 325–64.
59. The analysis of a nineteenth-century global "white labor" discourse, for example, has provided very useful insights, as demonstrated in a recent article by Matthew Guterl and Christine Skwiot, "Atlantic & Pacific Crossings: Race, Empire, and the 'Labor Problem' in the Nineteenth Century," *Radical History Review* 91, no. 1 (Winter 2005): 40–61.
60. For some pertinent examples of how the models of cultural history can be usefully applied to the study of race, nation, and empire, see Bhabha, *Nation and Narration*; Nicholas Thomas, *Colonialism's Cultures: Anthropology, Travel and Government* (Princeton, NJ: Princeton University Press, 1994); McClintock, *Imperial Leather*; Paula M. Krebs, *Gender, Race, and the Writing of Empire: Public Discourse and the Boer War* (Cambridge: Cambridge University Press, 1999); Ann Laura Stoler, *Haunted by Empire: Geographies of Intimacy in North American History* (Durham, NC: Duke University Press, 2006). For a more general overview of the methodology, see Victoria E. Bonnell and Lynn Hunt, eds., *Beyond the Cultural Turn: New Directions in the Study of Society and Culture* (Berkeley and Los Angeles: University of California Press, 1999).

Chapter 2

1. First Opium War, 1839–42, and Second Opium War, 1856–60. See, for example, "A Lesson to John Chinaman," in *Punch*, May 9, 1857, 185.
2. The importation of Chinese indentured laborers to British Guiana in 1853 to make up for the labor shortfall that followed the emancipation of slaves there in 1834 had set the precedent for their use in South Africa. Alan Adamson, "The Impact of Indentured Immigration on the Political Economy of British Guiana," in *Indentured Labour in the British Empire 1834–1920*, ed. Kay Saunders (London: Croom Helm, 1984); David Northrup, *Indentured Labor in the Age of Imperialism, 1834–1922* (Cambridge: Cambridge University Press, 1995); Persia Campbell,

Chinese Coolie Emigration to Countries within the British Empire (New York: Negro Universities Press, 1923), 1–26.

3. Walton Look Lai, *Indentured Labor, Caribbean Sugar: Chinese and Indian Migrants to the British West Indies, 1838–1918* (Baltimore: Johns Hopkins University Press, 1993), 38.
4. In it, R. K. Douglas, professor of Chinese at King's College, London, asserted that "the Chinese set little or no value upon truth." R. K. Douglas, "No Value in Truth," in *Sinophiles and Sinophobes: Western Views of China*, ed. Colin Mackerras (Oxford: Oxford University Press, 2000), 70. The twenty-five volumes of the ninth edition of the *Encyclopedia* were published between 1875–89.
5. Montagu Williams, *Round London: Down East and Up West* (London: Macmillan, 1892), 77.
6. Ibid., 78. The only case recorded in this period that even remotely fits Williams's description was the 1878 Central Criminal Court trial of thirteen Chinese seamen for assault on an East End lodging-house keeper, unlawful assembly, and disturbing the peace. There was no mention of any weapons or of any injury being done to anyone besides the complainant. Montagu Williams, who appeared as counsel for the defense, suggested that his clients should plead guilty and then could be "got rid of" on the first ship bound for China. This suggestion was followed by the adjudicating magistrate. *Times* (London), March 18, 1878, 11.
7. Williams, *Round London*, 77.
8. The growth of anti-Chinese sentiment among working-class Australians would have significant long-term consequences for Anglo-Chinese relations across the British Empire. By the pre–World War I period, as Jonathan Hyslop argues, an "imperial working class" and its shared identity of "whiteness" had bridged geographical distance and regional peculiarities to unite workers in Australia, South Africa, and Britain. "The development of labour identity," he concludes, "was inextricably tangled with notions of race." Jonathan Hyslop, "The Imperial Working Class Makes Itself 'White': White Labourism in Britain, Australia, and South Africa Before the First World War," *Journal of Historical Sociology* 12, no. 4 (December, 1999): 399. See also Alastair Bonnett, "How the British Working Class Became White: The Symbolic (Re)Formation of Racialized Capitalism," *Journal of Historical Sociology* 11, no. 3 (September 1998): 318.
9. Robert A. Hutteback, *Racism and Empire: White Settlers and Colored Immigrants in the British Self-governing Colonies, 1830–1910* (Ithaca, NY: Cornell University Press, 1976), 60.
10. Ibid., 15.
11. Specifically, The Chinese Immigration Act of 1855 (Vic no. 39) (Huttenback, *Racism and Empire*, 61–62; Lake and Reynolds, *Drawing the Global Colour Line*, 20–21). The Lambing Flat riots (1860–61) in New South Wales were instrumental in securing the passage of the Chinese

Immigration Regulation and Restriction Act. Ann Curthoys, "Liberalism and Exclusionism: A Prehistory of the White Australia Policy," in *Legacies of White Australia: Race, Culture, and Nation*, ed. Laksiri Jaya Suriya, David Walker, and Jan Gothard (Crawley, Perth: University of Western Australia Press, 2003), 19.

12. Hyslop, "Imperial Working Class," 406.
13. "Australian Radical History: Maritime Strike of 1878–1879," *Anarchist Age Weekly Review* 286 (February 10–16, 1998).
14. Official census records from 1861, for example, put the Chinese population of Victoria at 24,732, down from an estimated 35,000 in 1856. Huttenback, *Racism and Empire*, 67. C. P. Hodges, in his report to the Parliament of Victoria , put the number of Chinese in Victoria in 1859 at 46,000. *Times* (London), August 6, 1880, 5. The total population of Australia was roughly 2.25 million at this time.
15. *Times* (London), August 6, 1880, 5.
16. Helen Grace, "A Practical Man: Portraiture between Word And Image," *Continuum: The Australian Journal of Media & Culture* 6, no. 2 (1991): 858.
17. *Hansard Pariliamentary Debates*, 3rd ser., v. 326, 5th volume of the session, 15 May, 1888, col. 333. Discussion followed on 8 June 1888, cols. 1503–1522. See also Curthoys, "Liberalism and Exclusionism," 15.
18. Lawrence Elwin Neame, *The Asiatic Danger in the Colonies* (London: Routledge, 1907), 75.
19. *Times* (London), May 22, 1888, 11.
20. *Oxford Dictionary of National Biography* (*DNB*), online ed., s.v. "Sir George Smyth Baden-Powell."
21. *Times* (London), May 26, 1888, 10.
22. Marilyn Lake, "The White Man under Siege: New Histories of Race in the Nineteenth Century and the Advent of White Australia," *History Workshop Journal* 58 (2004): 50.
23. Ibid.
24. Ibid., 53.
25. Robert Travers, *Australian Mandarin: the Life and Times of Quong Tart* (Kenthurst, AU: Kangaroo Press, 1981), 170.
26. Ibid., 41.
27. *Times* (London), June 2, 1888, 5.
28. Mark Hearn, "Rose Summerfield's Gospel of Discontent: a Narrative of Radical Identity in Late Nineteenth Century Australia," *Labour History* 87 (May 2004): 71.
29. Such leaders included Peter Whiteside, who subsequently became the president of the Witwatersrand Trades and Labour Council; James Briggs, who would become the president of the Pretoria Trades Council; and Bendingo-born Robert Burns Waterston, who would later be deported by Jan Smuts for his "Unionist" agitation. Hyslop, "The Imperial Working Class," 408.

30. *Trades Union Congress, Annual Report*, 1886, 17 [TUC Library, London Metropolitan University].
31. James Jupp, *The Australian People: An Encyclopedia of the Nation, its People and their Origins*, 2nd ed. (Cambridge: Cambridge University Press, 2002), 203.
32. *Times* (London), May 13, 1890, 11.
33. *Times* (London), May 28, 1890, 4.
34. Ibid.
35. Curthoys, "Liberalism and Exclusionism," 35–36.
36. *DNB*, online ed., s.v. "Philip William May."
37. M. P. Sheil, *The Yellow Danger* (London: Grant Richards, 1898).
38. As the *Times* reviewer wrote "[Sheil] must certainly expect us to laugh, but we laugh with him rather than at him." *Times* (London), September 13, 1898, 13.
39. Jeremy Martens, "A Transnational History of Immigration Restriction: Natal and New South Wales, 1896–97," *Journal of Imperial and Commonwealth History* 34, no. 3 (2006): 333.
40. Hyslop, "Imperial Working Class," 406.
41. Peter Richardson, *Chinese Mine Labour in the Transvaal* (London: Macmillan, 1982), 22–23. At the conclusion of the Boer War in 1902, the two Boer Republics, the Orange Free State and the South African Republic (Transvaal), had been annexed by Britain as crown colonies. J. D. Omer-Cooper, *History of Southern Africa*, 2nd ed. (London: James Curry, 1994), 148–51.
42. Alfred Milner to Sir E. H. Walton, April 8, 1903, *The Milner Papers, v. 2: South Africa 1899–1905*, ed. Cecil Headlam (London: Cassell, 1933), 461.
43. Paula Krebs, *Gender, Race, and the Writing of Empire: Public Discourse and the Boer War* (Cambridge: Cambridge University Press, 1999), 29–30.
44. Alfred Milner in Headlam, *The Milner Papers*, 349. Excerpted from Cmd. 1895, June 2, 1903, 37–44, cf. Sir Lionel Philipps, "Transvaal Problems."
45. Campbell, *Chinese Coolie Emigration*, 171–72.
46. Milner to Dr. J. E. Moffat, April 1, 1903, *The Milner Papers*, 460.
47. Ibid.
48. See Richardson, *Chinese Mine Labour*; Gary Kynoch, "Controlling the Coolies: Chinese Mineworkers and the Struggle for Labor in South Africa, 1904–1910," *International Journal of African Historical Studies* 36, no. 2 (2003): 309–29, and "'Your Petitioners are in Mortal Terror': The Violent World of Chinese Mineworkers in South Africa, 1904–1910," *Journal of Southern African Studies* 31, no. 3 (September 2005): 53–46.
49. *Times* (London), December 14, 1903, 16.

50. One of the few attempts to bring opium prominently into the public discussion was quickly and quietly squelched by Winston Churchill. *Times* (London), November 16, 1906, 6.
51. Elaine Katz, "White Workers' Grievances," *The South African Journal of Economics* 42, v. 2 (June 1974): 148–49.
52. Campbell, *Chinese Coolie Emigration*, 177.
53. The penalty for "illegal introduction" was £100 per worker.
54. The Chinese were allowed relative freedom of movement within the compounds, which ranged from 300 to 1,000 acres in size. Dispatch from Lord Selborne to Mr. Lyttleton, October 7, 1905. Colonial Office, *Further Correspondence Relating to the Transvaal Mines*, Cd. 2786.
55. Richardson, *Chinese Mine Labour*, chap. 7.
56. Draft of the Labour Importation Ordinance of 1904, as outlined in the *Times* (London), January 7, 1904, 3.
57. Leonard Thompson, *A History of South Africa* (New Haven, CT: Yale University Press, 2001), 118, 121.
58. Kevin Grant, *A Civilized Savagery: Britain and the New Slaveries in Africa, 1884–1926* (New York: Routledge, 2005), 89.
59. *Hansard Parliamentary Debates*, 4th ser., vol. 129, 1st volume of the session, February 16, 1904, col. 1565; *Times* (London), February 19, 1904, 6.
60. *Times* (London), February 20, 1904, 6, and February 26, 1904, 6.
61. *Hansard Parliamentary Debates*, 4th ser., vol. 129, 1st volume of the session, February 12, 1904, cols. 1158–76.
62. *Times* (London), February 8, 1904, 8.
63. *Times* (London), February 11, 1904, 10.
64. *Hansard Parliamentary Debates*, 4th ser., vol. 129, 1st volume of the session, February 16, 1904, col. 1502.
65. In April 1908, Crewe would succeed Victor Bruce, the Earl of Elgin, as Colonial Secretary.
66. *Times* (London), March 25, 1904, 8.
67. *The Chinese Labour Ordinance: A Speech Delivered by Mr. J. Fletcher Moulton, K.C., M.P. in the House of Commons on March 21st, 1904* (London, 1904), 6 [BL].
68. Grant, *Civilized Savagery*, 89.
69. *Times* (London), February 20, 1904, 6.
70. Grant, *Civilized Savagery*, 91. Grant examines the discourse on "Chinese slavery" as part of a broader anti-slavery discourse in British politics at the time.
71. *The Great Demonstration to Protest against the Introduction of Chinese Labour to South Africa under Conditions of Slavery, Illustrated Official Programme and Guide* (London: Twentieth Century Press, 1904) [BL].
72. Thomas Naylor, *Yellow Labour: The Truth About the Chinese in the Transvaal* (London, 1904), 6.

73. *Times* (London), December 26, 1904, 3; Richardson, *Chinese Mine Labour*, 166.
74. *Times* (London), November 14, 1905, 8.
75. The letter was also signed by John Edward Seely, a veteran of the Boer War who had left the Conservative Party in May 1904 over the issue of "Chinese slavery." *DNB*, online ed., s.v. "John Edward Bernard Seely, first Baron Mottistone."
76. *Times* (London), December 8, 1905, 9.
77. Krebs, *The Writing of Empire*, 44; Koss, *Rise and Fall of the Political Press*, 1, 83.
78. Kynoch, "Mortal Terror," 543. Among the Chinese workers themselves, however, the rate of violent crime was much higher. Colonial Office, *Further Correspondence Relating to the Transvaal Mines*, Cd. 2819, February 1906.
79. Lord Selborne to Mr. Lyttleton, September 18, 1905. Colonial Office, *Further Correspondence Relating to the Transvaal Mines*, Cd. 2786.
80. Omer-Cooper, *Southern Africa*, 152; Campbell, *Chinese Coolie Emigration*, 206.
81. 401 seats in total. Walter Arnstein, *Britain Yesterday and Today, 1830 to the Present*, 8th ed. (Boston: Houghton Mifflin, 2001), 223.
82. Ross G. Forman, "Randy on the Rand: Portuguese African Labor and the Discourse on 'Unnatural Vice' in the Transvaal in the Early Twentieth Century," *Journal of the History of Sexuality* 11, 4 (2002): 592.
83. J. A. S. Bucknill, the architect of the report, would later serve as the Attorney-General for Hong Kong from 1912–14.
84. *Times* (London), November 15, 1906, 7.
85. Kynoch, "Controlling the Coolies," 538. Kynoch has emphasized that highly questionable methods were employed during the course of the investigation.
86. Richardson, *Chinese Mine Labour*, 184.
87. *Times* (London), January 26, 1911, 5.
88. Nor were the implications ignored in the United States. Harold Wright, review of *An Experiment in Alien Labor*, by E. George Payne, *Economic Journal* 22, no. 86 (June 1912), 270.
89. Tabili, *British Justice*, 84.
90. *Times* (London), July 18, 1910, 9.
91. Campbell, *Coolie Immigration*, 82.
92. Richardson, *Chinese Mine Labour*, 104; Kynoch, "Mortal Terror," 534.
93. The campaign against Chinese seamen presaged, by more than a decade, a more widespread and concerted interwar campaign against black seamen working aboard British ships. Tabili, *British Justice*, 88–93.
94. *The Seaman* 4 (February 1908), 3.
95. Ibid. By 1911, according to the parliamentary *Census of Seamen*, the number of Chinese working in British shipping, but not necessarily in domestic shipping, would rise to 4,595. J. P. May, "The Chinese in Brit-

ain, 1860–1914," in *Immigrants and Minorities in British Society*, ed. Colin Holmes (London: Allen & Unwin, 1996), 115.

96. According to Board of Trade figures, there were 38,425 Lascar and 34,906 "foreign" sailors working in British domestic shipping in 1906, as compared to 4,384 Chinese sailors. *The Seaman* 4 (February 1908), 5.
97. The number of "foreign" and "Lascar" sailors in 1891 had been 21,322 and 23,884, respectively. *The Seaman* 4 (February 1908), 5.
98. Tabili, *British Justice*, 91.
99. *The Seaman* 4 (February 1908), 8.
100. *The Seaman* 3 (January 1908), 9.
101. *Times* (London), March 5, 1908, 14.
102. *The Seaman* 5 (March 1908), 6.
103. Ibid., 2.
104. *Instructions to Superintendents of Marine Mercantile Offices: Engagement of Chinese Seamen and the Language Test*, Board of Trade, Marine Department, April 1914, 5.
105. In 1907, of the 590 Chinese seamen who had signed on at Poplar, 190 (32 percent) had declared Hong Kong or Singapore as their birthplace. By March 1908, 162 of the 192 (84 percent) that had signed on there had made similar declarations. *The Seaman* 5 (March 1908), 1908, 4.
106. *The Seaman* 5 (March 1908), 4.
107. Ibid.
108. *The Shipping Gazette*, excerpted in *The Seaman*, 4 (February 1908), 3. The use of the moniker "Sin," in one form or another, was common in stereotypes of Chinese men. "Ah Sin," a play on "I sin," was popularized by Bret Harte's poem, "The Heathen Chinee" (1870). The satire inherent in "Wun Lung" needs no further elaboration. Both names had previously appeared as mockeries of Chinese immigrants during the debate over Chinese labor in South Africa (*Morning Leader*, February 24, 1904, 3).
109. *The Shipping Gazette*, excerpted in *The Seaman*, 4 (February 1908), 3.
110. *The Seaman* 4 (February 1908), 3; Tabili, *British Justice*, 87. Shipowners would, in a later period, make the same argument with regard to black seamen (ibid., 53). That the same argument was made with regard to both Chinese and black seamen suggests that this rhetoric was more of a tool to justify *not* employing white seamen than a reason *for* employing African or Asian seamen.
111. Joseph Havelock Wilson, quoted in *Reynolds's Newspaper*, excerpted in *The Seaman* 4 (February 1908), 1908, 3.
112. *The Seaman* 4 (February 1908), 1908, 3.
113. *The Seaman* 5 (March 1908), 3.
114. There were 21,583 Lascars on British ships in 1911, according to the Parliamentary *Census of the Sea* (May, "Chinese in Britain," 115).
115. *The Seaman* 5 (March 1908), 1908, 3.

116. Merchant Shipping Act 1894 (57 & 58 Vict., c. 60), s. 3.
117. *The Seaman* 5 (March 1908), 1908, 3.
118. Ibid.
119. According to census records, the number of China-born aliens residing in London in 1911 was only 247, up from 120 in 1901. Although the population of Chinese aliens in England and Wales remained quite small overall, it did rise measurably, according to census figures, from 387 in 1901 to 1,319 in 1911. Ng Chee Choo, *The Chinese in London* (London: Oxford University Press, 1968), 7. The Merseyside (Liverpool and Birkenhead) population, though still remaining small, also saw a measurable increase, from 76 in 1901 to 403 in 1911. Maria Lin Wong, *Chinese Liverpudlians: A History of the Chinese Community in Liverpool* (Birkenhead, United Kingdom: Liver Press, 1989), 4.
120. *Register of Seamen's Lodging Houses*, PH/REG/1/19 [LMA].
121. *The Seaman* 7 (May 1908), 3.
122. Ibid.
123. Ibid.
124. *The Seaman* 8 (June 1908), 3.
125. *East End News*, June 5, 1908.
126. *The Seaman* 8 (June 1908), 3.
127. One of Chang Ahon's boardinghouses was immediately adjacent to the police station on the West India Dock Road, and the contingent that applied to crew the *Strathness* was housed in his establishment at No. 42 Oriental Street, Pennyfields, where they would take shelter later when pursued by an angry mob of white seamen (*The Seaman* 8 [June 1908]). When Wilson later claimed in Parliament that Chinese "crimps" had organized the *Zambezi* and *Strathness* expeditions, he was likely referring to Chang. *Times* (London), May 14, 1908, 6; *East End News*, May 15, 1908.
128. *The Seaman* 8 (June 1908), 3.
129. For the racialized images of masculinity in the debates over the employment of black seamen, see Tabili, *British Justice*, 53–54.
130. The account pointed out that this entrance was "close to the Wade Arms, in which Mr. John Burns and others had their headquarters when they organized the great strike for the dockers' tanner." *The Seaman* 8 (June 1908), 3.
131. *East End News*, June 5, 1908
132. *Times* (London), May 14, 1908, 6.
133. *The Seaman* 9 (July 1908), 6.
134. *Times* (London), June 15, 1908, 12.
135. *East London Observer*, April 10, 1909. As indicated earlier in this chapter, however, official London County Council statistics do not support this assessment.
136. Ibid.

137. Buxton was a key figure both in East London, whose constituency he served as Poplar's representative (Liberal) to Parliament from 1886 to 1914, and in the Colonial Office, where he held an undersecretary position from 1892–95. Buxton's desire to maintain his popularity among his East End constituency was crucial in his decision to support, counter to party lines, the Aliens Bill of 1905. *DNB*, online ed., s.v. "Sydney Charles Buxton, Earl Buxton."
138. *Times* (London), April 29, 1910, 14. The NSFU would not see any substantial success in their attempts to legally exclude Chinese seamen from British ships until 1919, when the National Maritime Board made the preference for British subjects over "non-British Chinese and 'Alien Coloured' seamen" official policy. Tabili, *British Justice*, 93–94.
139. *East London Advertiser*, November 20, 1909.
140. Sax Rohmer (Arthur Ward), *The Mystery of Dr. Fu Manchu* (London, 1913), 15.

Chapter 3

1. John Seed's analysis of census data assesses the 1911 Chinese population of London and Limehouse at 247 and 101, respectively. John Seed, "Limehouse Blues: Looking for Chinatown in the London Docks, 1900–40," *History Workshop Journal* 62 (2006): 63.
2. "Report on Miss Robinson's Allegations re: Chinamen," by Inspector McIntyre of the Public Control Department, London County Council, March 24, 1911, 47, HO45/139147/18 [TNA].
3. Seed, "Limehouse Blues," 63; Maria Lin Wong, *Chinese Liverpudlians: A History of the Chinese Community in Liverpool* (Birkenhead, United Kingdom: Liver Press, 1989), 4.
4. J. P. May, "The Chinese in Britain, 1860–1914," in *Immigrants and Minorities in British Society*, ed. Colin Holmes (London: Allen & Unwin, 1978), 115.
5. Laura Tabili, *"We Ask for British Justice": Workers and Racial Difference in Late Imperial Britain* (Ithaca, NY: Cornell University Press, 1994), 87.
6. May, "Chinese in Britain," 115. In 1906, there were 38,425 Lascars employed on ships registered in the British Isles and 119,612 seamen from Great Britain. *The Seaman* 3 (January 1908), 5.
7. *Times* (London), January 17, 1911, 13.
8. *Times* (London), June 16, 1911, 8.
9. Ann Dummet and Andrew Nicol, *Subjects, Citizens, Aliens and Others: Nationality and Immigration Law* (London: Weidenfeld and Nicolson, 1990), 165.
10. Ibid.
11. Tabili, *British Justice*, 88.

12. *Times* (London), July 10, 1913, 15.
13. The NSFU used a smaller version of the same image, with no caption, in their 1912 anti-Chinese campaign. It is this third iteration that is reproduced in Tabili, *British Justice*, 89.
14. *The Morning Leader*, January 25, 1904.
15. *Times* (London), June 16, 1911, 8.
16. Campbell Balfour, "Captain Tupper and the 1911 Seamen's Strike in Cardiff," *Morgannwg: Transactions of the Local Glamorgan History Society* 14 (1970): 66.
17. Ibid., 74.
18. *Times* (London), July 21, 1911, 7; Dummet and Nicol, *Subjects, Citizens*, 165.
19. The history of public concern with Chinese laundries in Britain, despite their small number and their possible threat to white labor in the same sector, dated back to the 1890s. Colin Holmes, *John Bull's Island: Immigration and British Society, 1871–1971* (London: Macmillan), 78.
20. *Times* (London), May 8, 1911, 3.
21. *East End News*, May 26, 1911. Although all three sailors were of Scandinavian (Finnish) background, they were Russian subjects.
22. Ibid.
23. *Times* (London), May 8, 1911, 3.
24. *Old Bailey Proceedings Online, http:// www.oldbaileyonline.org*, June 1911 trial of August Sepp, t19110627-10.
25. Herman Scheffauer, "The Chinese in England: A Growing National Problem," *The London Magazine*, June 1911, 465 in HO45/139147/39.
26. In contrast to the British legal system, in Qing China, trials were often mere formalities and the guilt of any particular suspect would have been established through a confession, often extracted by beatings and torture, before they ever stepped foot in the courtroom. Jonathan D. Spence, *The Search for Modern China, 2nd ed.* (New York: W. W. Norton, 1999), 124.
27. *East End News*, May 26, 1911.
28. Christopher Munn, *Anglo-China: Chinese People and British Rule in Hong Kong, 1841–1880* (Richmond, UK: Curzon, 2001), 16.
29. Ibid., 17.
30. A tendency noted earlier by Count E. Armfelt in his contribution to *Living London*. Count E. Armfelt, "Oriental London," in *Living London*, ed. George R. Sims (London: Cassell, 1901–3), 84.
31. *Hansard Parliamentary Debates*, 4th ser., vol. 129, 1st volume of the session, February 12, 1904, col. 1159; Spence, *Modern China*, 124.
32. Herman Scheffauer, "The Chinese in England: A Growing National Problem," *The London Magazine*, June 1911, 465 in HO45/11843/139147/39.

33. Jennifer Davis, "A Poor Man's System of Justice: The London Police Courts in the Second Half of the Nineteenth Century," *The Historical Journal* 27, 2 (1984): 309–35
34. *Times* (London), April 15, 1912, 3.
35. What had begun as a military rebellion against Qing Manchu rule had escalated into a full-blown Chinese nationalist revolution in 1911.
36. *East End News*, April 16, 1912.
37. For the operation of this dynamic in the policing of New York City's Chinatown in the same period, see Mary Ting Yi Liu, *The Chinatown Trunk Mystery: Murder, Miscegenation, and Other Dangerous Encounters in Turn-of-the-Century New York City* (Princeton, NJ: Princeton University Press, 2005), 188.
38. *Times* (London), April 29, 1912, 5.
39. During one of the trials that emerged out of the different incidents, one police officer pointed out that the weapons used by some of the assailants were "well known among the Boxers." *East London Advertiser*, April 20, 1912.
40. *East End News*, April 16, 1912
41. In 1900, the Reuters Hong Kong correspondent had reported that "it was widely believed throughout China that the 'Boxers' are merely a branch of the White Lily or Triad Secret Society. This may very well be so, for it is a well-known fact that one-half of the secret societies of China are in reality merely outlying branches of this great parent organization." *Times* (London), August 30, 1900, 4. Whether the "White Lily" (aka "White Lotus"), as a diffuse sectarian tradition, had any connection at all to the Boxer Rebellion is debated by historians, but the portrayal of it as a cohesive society with focus on criminal activity was a misrepresentation. Paul A. Cohen, *History in Three Keys: The Boxers as Event, Experience, and Myth* (New York: Columbia University Press, 1997), 30, 38–39.
42. *East London Advertiser*, May 4, 1912.
43. *East End News*, April 16, 1912.
44. Ibid.
45. *East London Advertiser*, May 4, 1912.
46. *East End News*, April 30, 1912.
47. *East End News*, May 7, 1912.
48. *Aliens Act 1905, s. 3, Ia*; *Times* (London), Jan. 11, 1911, 10. The charges of assault and felonious wounding leveled at several of the participants in the May incidents would therefore not have qualified for such an order. The charges of "affray," however, and the use of firearms, depending upon the circumstances and the decision of the magistrate, might have.
49. By the terms of the Aliens Act of 1905, a court could only recommend expulsion in cases where the individual in question had been convicted of a crime serious enough to merit a sentence of imprisonment or upon a conviction for vagrancy. Dummet and Nicol, *Subjects, Citizens*, 104–5.

50. The exact number of London Chinese residents informally expelled by the East London magistrates in May is hard to determine, but one report explained that the eleven men convicted by Dickinson in the Thames Police Court would join the "fifteen Chinamen [already] sent on their way . . . and others were going to sea." *East London Advertiser*, May 4, 1912.
51. *Times* (London), March 18, 1878, 11.
52. "The Expulsion of Aliens," *Justice of the Peace*, May 18, 1912, 233.
53. 1911 census figures indicated that half of all the Chinese living in Limehouse were merchant seamen. Seed, "Limehouse Blues," 66.
54. Chandak Sengoopta, *Imprint of the Raj: How Fingerprinting was Born in Colonial India* (Basingstoke, UK: Macmillan, 2003), 128–34.
55. John Rowland, *The Finger-Print Man: The Story of Sir Edward Henry* (London: Lutterworth, 1959), 54.
56. Gerald Lambourne, *The Fingerprint Story* (London: Harrap, 1984), 58, 63.
57. Rowland, *The Finger-Print Man*, 95–96.
58. Melanie Yap and Dianne Leong Man, *Colour, Confusion and Concessions: The History of the Chinese in South Africa* (Hong Kong: Hong Kong University Press, 1996), 45, 113, 139.
59. *Memorandum for the Inspector*, Collector of Customs, Port Adelaide, December 19, 1908; *Minute Paper*, Customs and Excise Office, South Australia, March 15, 1909 (National Archives of Australia, accessed online, http://vrroom.naa.gov.au).
60. Rowland, *The Finger-Print Man*, 99.
61. Yap and Man, *Colour, Confusion and Concessions*, 135–68. Ironically, it was the Chinese imperial government itself that had first employed individual finger marks as a means to identify criminals in the nineteenth century.
62. *East End News*, May 7, 1912 and April 30, 1912.
63. Ibid.
64. H. L. Cancellor, *The Life of a London Beak* (London: Hurst and Blackett, 1930), 65.
65. *Daily Telegraph*, June 26, 1920. Alan Palmer, *The East End: Four Centuries of London Life* (New Brunswick, NJ: Rutgers University Press, 2000), 108.
66. Interviews with Leslie Heng, Connie Hoe, and Leslie Hoe, "'Whispers of Time': An Oral History of the London Chinese," Chinese National Healthy Living Centre (2005), http: //www.riverculturesfestival.co.uk. Hong Kong and the surrounding area also included populations of Hakka and Teochow, though it is not clear to what degree, if any, they were represented among Chinese residents of London.
67. The Blue Funnel Line, whose China route included both cities, had been instrumental in the growth of the Chinese community in Liverpool, where the company was based. Wong, *Chinese Liverpudlians*, 3.

68. For a detailed account of "Tong" violence in San Francisco, see Richard H. Dillon, *The Hatchet Men: The Story of the Tong Wars in San Francisco's Chinatown* (New York: Van Rees, 1962).
69. *Daily Sketch*, May 3, 1934; *East End News*, January 27, 1928; Louis Heren, *Growing Up Poor in London* (London: Hamish Hamilton, 1973), 16.
70. Spence, *Modern China*, 252–53.
71. Paula Krebs, *Gender, Race, and the Writing of Empire: Public Discourse and the Boer War* (Cambridge: Cambridge University Press), 43; Stephen Koss, *The Rise and Fall of the Political Press in Britain* (London: Hamish Hamilton, 1984), 76. The Harmsworth brothers were also the proprietors of the *Observer*, the *Evening News*, the *Weekly Dispatch*, and as of 1908, the *Times* (London).
72. Herman Scheffauer, "The Chinese in England: A Growing National Problem," *London Magazine*, June 1911, 465 in HO45/11843/139147/39 (hereafter, Scheffauer, "Chinese in England," pt. 1).
73. Herman Scheffauer, "The Chinese in England: A Growing National Problem," *London Magazine*, July 1911, 651 in HO45/11843/139147/39 (hereafter, Scheffauer, "Chinese in England," pt. 2).
74. Scheffauer, "Chinese in England," pt. 2, 654.
75. Scheffauer, "Chinese in England," pt. 1, 478.
76. Scheffauer, "Chinese in England," pt. 2, 645.
77. Ibid., 651.
78. Ibid., 648.
79. Scheffauer, "Chinese in England," pt. 2, 650.
80. Scheffauer, "Chinese in England," pt. 1, 466.
81. Scheffauer, "Chinese in England," pt. 2, 657.
82. Scheffauer, "Chinese in England," pt. 1, 478; Scheffauer, "Chinese in England," pt. 2, 654.
83. "Report on Miss Robinson's Allegations re: Chinamen," by Inspector McIntyre of the Public Control Department, London County Council, Home Office Papers, March 24, 1911, 48, HO45/11843/139147/18.
84. Persia Campbell, *Chinese Coolie Emigration to Countries within the British Empire* (New York: Negro Universities Press, 1923), 51. The population of British Columbia at the time, roughly 50,000, was split almost evenly between white and indigenous peoples.
85. *Times* (London), September 21, 1907, 6.
86. *Report of the Royal Commission on Chinese and Japanese Immigration* 1902, excerpted in *Times* (London), September 21, 1907, 6.
87. Ibid.
88. This was, of course, a reference to the goldfields where many Chinese immigrants hoped to make their fortune. Australia, in a similar vein, was often referred to in Chinese communities as "New Gold Mountain."

89. Anon., *The Oriental Canker in Canada* (alt. title, *The Yellow Peril in Canada*) (1912), 27 [BL].
90. *Times* (London), May 20, 1914, 3.
91. Campbell, *Coolie Immigration*, 37.
92. *Times* (London), April 6, 1914, 8.
93. *Times* (London), April 7, 1914, 7.
94. *Ibid.*
95. *Times* (London), May 22, 1914, 7
96. *Times* (London), May 23, 1914, 7, and May 25, 1914, 18
97. *Times* (London), April 3, 1914, 7. The Taiping Rebellion (1850–64) was an anti-Manchu uprising that began in southern China but eventually progressed northwards as far as Nanjing, which Taiping forces captured and occupied in 1853. Spence, *Modern China*, 171–91.
98. Henan and Anhui Provinces are in east central China, lying roughly between the cities of Xi'an to the west and Nanjing to the east.
99. *Times* (London), April 13, 1914, 8.
100. Paul Reed, "Murder, Charges, Dispositions, Commutations, and Executions, Canada, 1879 to 1960," *Statistics Canada*, Section Z: Justice, Canada's National Statistics Agency, http://www.statcan.ca/english/freepub/11-516-XIE/sectionz/sectionz.htm.
101. Its significance for a similar trend in Canada itself is discussed in Karen Dubinsky and Adam Giverts, "'It Was Only a Matter of Passion': Masculinity and Sexual Danger," in *Gendered Pasts: Historical Essays in Femininity and Masculinity in Canada*, ed. Kathryn McPherson, Cecilia Morgan, and Nancy M. Forrestel (Oxford: Oxford University Press, 1999), 65–79.
102. Ibid., 77.
103. *Times* (London), November 28, 1913, 12.
104. *Ibid.*
105. "Sax Rohmer" was the pseudonym employed by Arthur Henry Sarsfield Ward.
106. Sax Rohmer, *The Mystery of Dr. Fu Manchu* (London: Cassell, 1913; London: Allison & Busby, 2000), 15 (citations are from the 2000 edition).
107. Ibid., 75.
108. Ibid., 15.
109. For a detailed discussion of the relationship between the Fu Manchu novels and modernism, see Urmila Seshagiri, "Modernity's (Yellow) Perils: Dr. Fu Manchu and English Race Paranoia," *Cultural Critique* 62 (2006): 162–94.
110. Foreshadowing the technological horrors of World War I, Fu Manchu employed both poison gas and biological weapons in his war on the white race. Rohmer, *The Mystery of Dr. Fu Manchu*, 189–90.

111. Cay Van Ash and Elizabeth Sax Rohmer, *Master of Villainy: A Biography of Sax Rohmer* (Bowling Green, OH: Bowling Green University Popular Press, 1972), 75.
112. "I made my name on Fu Manchu because I know nothing about the Chinese," he told his biographer, "I know something about Chinatown. But that is a different matter." Ibid., 72.
113. As Colin Holmes points out, from the perspective of historical analysis, Rohmer's sincerity on this score is of far less importance than his undoubted success in propagating anti-Chinese stereotypes to a broad and enthusiastic reading audience. Colin Holmes, "The Chinese Connection," in *Outsiders and Outcasts: Essays in Honor of William J. Fishman*, ed. Jeffrey Alderman and Colin Holmes (London: Duckworth, 1990), 89.
114. Van Ash and E. Rohmer, *Master of Villainy*, 26.
115. Ibid., 73.
116. Ibid., 74.
117. Ibid.
118. Frank Mott, *A History of American Magazines, 1885–1905, vol. 4* (Cambridge, MA: Harvard University Press, 1957), 471.
119. Rohmer, *The Mystery of Dr. Fu Manchu*, 75.
120. Ibid., 47.
121. Ibid., 137. "Few Londoners know London," his narrator tells us, "there are haunts in the very heart of the metropolis whose existence is unsuspected by all but the few; places unknown even to the ubiquitous copy-hunting pressman."
122. Daniel Pick, *Svengali's Web: The Alien Enchanter in Modern Culture* (New Haven, CT: Yale University Press, 2000), 2–5; Judith Walkowitz, *City of Dreadful Delight: Narratives of Sexual Danger in Late-Victorian London* (Chicago: University of Chicago Press, 1992), 191–93.
123. Rohmer, *The Mystery of Dr. Fu Manchu*, 97. The author described Fu Manchu as being "serpentine," "lean," and "cat-like," but also "hypnotic" and capable of capturing the will of women.
124. Rohmer, *The Mystery of Dr. Fu Manchu*, 118.
125. Seshagiri, "Modernity's (Yellow) Perils," 176. Rohmer granted the Chinese, both in London and in China itself, a unity that transcended cultural, ethnic, and political divisions.
126. Thomas Metcalf, "Imperial Towns and Cities," in *The Cambridge Illustrated History of the British Empire*, ed. P. J. Marshall (Cambridge: Cambridge University Press, 1996), 229–30
127. Rohmer, *The Mystery of Dr. Fu Manchu*, 107.
128. Ibid., 190.
129. Robert Bickers, *Britain in China: Community, Culture, and Colonialism 1900–1949* (Manchester: Manchester University Press, 1999), 53.

130. The U.S. Congress subsequently banned opium in 1905, restricted the use and sale of opiates with the 1906 Pure Food and Drugs Act, and outlawed the importation of opium and opiates in 1909.
131. For a fuller account of the British government's commitment to maintaining the trade in opium, see J. B. Brown, "The Politics of the Poppy: The Society for the Suppression of the Opium Trade, 1874–1916," *Journal of Contemporary History* 8, no. 3 (July 1973): 97–111.
132. *Times* (London), July 1, 1908, 9.
133. The immediate catalyst of the campaign was King's 1908 parliamentary report, *The Need for the Suppression of Opium Traffic in Canada*.
134. The Aboriginals Protection and Restriction of the Sale of Opium Act (1897) and the Opium Amendment Act (1906) were two key pieces of legislation in this regard. *The Australasian Medical Gazette*, July 20, 1906, 347; *Times* (London), June 18, 1908, 4.
135. Margaret Tart, *The Life of Quong Tart: or How a Foreigner Succeeded in a British Community* (Sydney: W. W. Maclardy, 1911).
136. This attitude was replicated in Liverpool, where, according to Colin Holmes, "even the police did not regard opium-smoking among the Chinese as a significant social problem." Holmes, "The Chinese Connection," 77.
137. Virginia Berridge, "East End Opium Dens and Narcotic Use in Britain," *The London Journal* 4, no. 1 (1978): 16.
138. Virginia Berridge and Edward Griffiths, *Opium and the People: Opiate Use in Nineteenth-Century England* (New York: St. Martin's, 1981), 189
139. *Trades Union Congress, Annual Reports*, Minutes of the Annual Meeting, September 8, 1916, 329.
140. Spence, *Modern China*, 253–54, 276. For a discussion of earlier Qing efforts at prohibition, see David Bello, *Opium and the Limits of Empire: Drug Prohibition in the Chinese Interior, 1729–1850* (Cambridge, MA: Harvard University Press, 2005).
141. *Times* (London), May 9, 1911, 10.
142. Berridge, "East End Opium Dens," 8.
143. Ibid., 15. In 1909, for example, a group of Liverpool Chinese residents petitioned the Home Office to institute a complete ban on the sale and smoking of opium in Britain, a stance that exceeded even that taken by the Society for the Suppression of the Opium Trade.
144. For a thorough analysis of depictions of opium in nineteenth-century British literature, see Barry Milligan, *Pleasures and Pains: Opium and the Orient in Nineteenth-Century British Culture* (Charlottesville, VA: University Press of Virginia, 1995).
145. Charles Dickens, *The Mystery of Edwin Drood* (1870; repr., Oxford: Oxford University Press, 1998), 1; Milligan, *Pleasures and Pains*, 86–94.
146. Dickens, *Drood*, 2.

147. Milligan identifies this dynamic in the portrayal of Opium addiction in Charles Dickens's *Mystery of Edwin Drood* (1870). Milligan, *Pleasures and Pains*, 13, 84–85, 100–1.
148. "Miniature Orients within the heart of the British Empire," according to Milligan. Ibid., 13. Andrew Blake argues that the enshrinement of the East End as a "racialized other" dates back to the 1870s and its portrayal as "Darkest England." Andrew Blake, "Foreign Devils and Moral Panics: Britain, Asia, and the Opium Trade," in *The Expansion of England: Race, Ethnicity and Cultural History*, ed. Bill Schwarz (London: Routledge, 1996), 253.
149. Rohmer, *The Mystery of Dr. Fu Manchu*, 40.
150. Ibid., 31
151. Milligan, *Pleasures and Pains*, 83–84. Berridge, "East End Opium Dens," 13–15.
152. Lynn Pan, *Sons of the Yellow Emperor: A History of the Chinese Diaspora* (New York: Kodansha International, 1990), 86–88.
153. *Times* (London), June 22, 1907, 7.
154. *East London Advertiser*, December 28, 1907.
155. Virginia Berridge argues that the "West End opium" smoker and the concurrent fears of "middle-class degeneracy" was a "new facet of the contemporary presentation of the opium den," and points to Wilde's *Dorian Grey* as a prime example. Berridge, "East End Opium Dens," 15.
156. *East London Advertiser*, December 28, 1907.
157. *Times* (London), November 25, 1914, 6.
158. Joseph Salter, *The East in the West; or Work among the Asiatics and Africans in London* (London: S. W. Partridge, 1895), 45.
159. *East London Advertiser*, December 28, 1907.
160. "The intrusion of inquisitive strangers," his story asserted, "has too often been followed by an outcry in the Press, by routings-out of peaceful households, and fierce measures of reform." *Times* (London), November 25, 1914, 6.
161. *Times* (London), November 28, 1913, 7.
162. Koss, *Political Press*, 1.
163. *Daily Graphic*, August 2, 1913, 218.
164. By 1911, the proportion of British Chinese residents in London and Liverpool that were employed in seafaring was only 36 percent, down from 61 percent in 1901. Ng Chee Choo, *The Chinese in London* (Oxford: Oxford University Press, 1968), 10.
165. *East London Advertiser*, July 4, 1914.

Chapter 4

1. The act, which applied to all aliens (not merely those of enemy nations), gave the Home Secretary almost unrestricted power to refuse entry or to

deport any alien whose presence in the nation he deemed to be contrary to the public interest. Ann Dummet and Andrew Nicol, *Subjects, Citizens, Aliens and Others: Nationality and Immigration Law* (London: Weidenfeld & Nicholson, 1990), 107.

2. The most serious and widespread of these incidents were the riots following the sinking of the ocean liner *Lusitania* by a German U-boat in 1915. Nicoletta Gullace, "Friends, Aliens, and Enemies: Fictive Communities and the Lusitania Riots of 1915," *Journal of Social History* 39, no. 2 (2005): 345–67.
3. The British-supported Japanese invasion of Shangdong in late 1914 represented a new nadir in the in the history of Anglo-Chinese diplomatic relations. Jonathan Spence, *The Search for Modern China*. 2nd ed. (New York: W. W. Norton, 1999), 281.
4. *Times* (London), October 21, 1915, 7.
5. Lee's execution was actually carried out on January 1, 1916, but his trial and sentencing took place in 1915, hence my employment of statistics from that year as context.
6. In other instances of domestic homicide in England, where passion was often seen as the root cause of violence, a conviction for manslaughter, which carried a lesser sentence, was common. David Taylor, *Crime, Policing, and Punishment in England, 1750–1914* (New York: Palgrave, 1998), 29.
7. *Times* (London), October 21, 1915, 7.
8. Lee's employment of a mediator conformed closely to the patterns by which conflicts concerning loss of "face" (*tiou lien*) were typically resolved in Chinese communities. Martin C. Yang, *A Chinese Village: Taitou, Shangtung Province* (New York: Columbia University Press, 1945), 168.
9. Other Chinese men arrested in Limehouse had also, on occasion, been found in possession of police whistles.
10. *Times* (London), November 18, 1915, 3.
11. Martin Wiener, *Men of Blood: Violence, Manliness, and Criminal Justice in Victorian England* (Cambridge: Cambridge University Press, 2004), 239.
12. Gail Savage, "'The Magistrates Are Men': Working-Class Marital Conflict and Appeals from the Magistrates' Court to the Divorce Court after 1895," in *Disorder in the Court: Trials and Sexual Conflict at the Turn of the Century*, ed. George Robb and Nancy Erber (New York: NYU Press 1999), 240–41.
13. *Oxford Dictionary of National Biography* (*DNB*), online ed., s.v. "Charles John Darling, first Baron Darling"; s.v. "William Wilberforce Harris Greathed."
14. *Times* (London), December 6, 1921, 4.
15. Derek Walker-Smith, *The Life of Lord Darling* (London: Cassell, 1938), 178.

16. Albert Lieck, *Bow Street World* (London: Robert Hale, 1938), 97.
17. *Justice of the Peace*, December 25, 1915, 616.
18. *Times* (London), December 7, 1915, 3.
19. Ibid.
20. *Justice of the Peace*, December 25, 1915, 616.
21. Lieck, in his memoirs, was more direct in his assessment. When it came to defendants who did not speak English, he wrote, "some police court cases are conducted very laxly." Lieck, *Bow Street World*, 97.
22. *Justice of the Peace Reports*, April 22, 1916, 167.
23. Ibid.
24. They were recently brought to bear, for example, in Privy Council Appeal No. 41/1992, *Radhakrishnan Kunnath v. the State*.
25. All told, from 1900–30, seven Chinese men were executed for murder in England, and the victims in four of those cases were other Chinese men.
26. *East London Observer*, May 27, 1916.
27. *East End News*, May 28, 1916.
28. Ibid. Kai's specific answer was that he had been "near the Old Bailey," a statement that elicited laughter from the court.
29. Ibid.
30. *East End News*, June 2, 1916.
31. *DNB*, online ed., s.v. "Robert Younger, Baron Blanesburgh."
32. *East End News*, June 2, 1916.
33. Ibid.
34. For a broader discussion of the relationship between masculinity and national power in wartime, see Joanna Bourke, *Dismembering the Male: Men's Bodies, Britain and the Great War* (Chicago: University of Chicago Press, 1996); Nicoletta Gullace, *Blood of Our Sons: Men, Women, and the Renegotiation of Citizenship during the Great War* (New York: Palgrave Macmillan, 2002), 73–74, 101.
35. The rising official concern over the transmission of venereal disease, the impetus to control working-class women's and black colonial soldiers' sexuality, and the alleged moral threats posed by the Indian and black soldiers in the Western Theater are examined in Philippa Levine, "Battle Colours: Race, Sex, and Colonial Soldiery in World War I," *Journal of Women's History* 9, no. 4 (1998): 104–30.
36. *Times* (London), March 6, 1915, 5.
37. Ibid.
38. A "Division" was the British equivalent of a police precinct.
39. *East London Advertiser*, November 27, 1915.
40. Ibid.; *East End News*, June 27, 1916.
41. Virginia Berridge, "East End Opium Dens and Narcotic Use in Britain," *The London Journal* 4, no. 1: 16; Marek Kohn, *Dope Girls: the Birth of the British Drug Underground* (London: Granta, 1992), 44. The parent legislation—the Defense of the Realm Act—was passed on August 8, 1914.

42. One notable exception was the Russian immigrants who fell under the stipulations of the Military Service (Conventions with Allied States) Act of 1917. Sascha Auerbach, "Negotiating Nationalism: Jewish Conscription and Russian Repatriation in London's East End," *Journal of British Studies* 44 (July 2007): 609–18.
43. *Times* (London), May 12, 1916, 5.
44. Major-General Sir Francis Lloyd to Sir Edward Henry regarding the drugging of soldiers, December 31, 1915, MEPO 2/1698 [TNA].
45. Kohn, *Dope Girls*, 65–66.
46. Dummet and Nicol, *Subjects, Citizens, and Aliens*, 104.
47. Kohn, *Dope Girls*, 65–66.
48. "Minutes of the Interdepartmental Conference on the Restriction of the Opium Traffic," June 19, 1916, HO 45/10500 [TNA].
49. *Times* (London), July 29, 1916, 5.
50. *Times* (London), November 1, 1932, 14, and December 1, 1950, 8; *DNB*, online ed., s.v. "Sir Malcolm Delevingne"; Kohn, *Dope Girls*, 42–44.
51. "Raids on Chinese Opium Houses," June 30, 1917, HO 45/24683/311604/28.
52. "Opium Smugglers at Liverpool," June 21, 1916, HO 45/24683/311604/11; Dummet and Nicol, *Subjects, Citizens, and Aliens*, 107.
53. "Chinese Suspected of Opium Smuggling," August 12, 1916, HO 45/24683/311604/12; *Evening Times*, August 17, 1916.
54. "Chinese Convicted of Infringing Regulation 40B (3&4) Opium," August 18, 1916, HO 45/24683/311604/14.
55. *Evening Express*, August 18, 1916.
56. "Opium Smugglers at Liverpool," June 21, 1916, HO 45/24683/311604/11.
57. Thomas Burke, *Out and About: A Note-Book of London in War-Time* (London: Allen & Unwin, 1919), 86.
58. *Times* (London), August 24, 1918, 3.
59. Deputation to the President of the Board of Trade (Sir Auckland Geddes), February 6, 1920, *Trades Union Congress Annual Reports* (hereafter *TUC Annual Reports*).
60. Jonathan Seed, "Limehouse Blues: Looking for Chinatown in the London Docks, 1900–40," *History Workshop Journal* 62 (2006): 75.
61. *Times* (London), June 10, 1916, 3; *East End News*, June 13, 1916; Seed, "Limehouse Blues," 75. According to the acting police superintendent of London's K Division, as of July 1916, there were 1,062 Chinese aliens registered there. "Registration of Chinese Seamen," MEPO 2/1962/988692/2.
62. *East London Observer*, June 15, 1916.
63. In contrast to "Asiatic" seamen, "coloured" British seamen, who were generally drawn from various parts of the empire, were paid at the same

rates as white seamen, though the jobs they were assigned aboard ship were usually of a lower paying category. Laura Tabili, *"We Ask for British Justice": Workers and Racial Difference in Late Imperial Britain* (Ithaca, NY: Cornell University Press, 1994), 42–44.

64. *Daily Telegraph*, October 3, 1916. The Sailor's Home, which aided seamen who had suffered shipwrecks or other misfortunes, was opened by the The British and Foreign Sailors' Society in 1835. http://www.portcities.org.uk/london, maintained by the National Maritime Museum and the Royal Observatory, Greenwich.
65. *Daily Telegraph*, October 3, 1916.
66. *TUC Annual Reports*, Minutes of the Annual Meeting, September 8, 1916, 328.
67. The National Union of Ship's Stewards, Cooks, Butchers and Bakers represented service personnel working aboard British merchant ships.
68. *TUC Annual Reports*, September 8, 1916, 329.
69. Ibid.
70. Ibid.
71. Ibid.
72. Ibid. Sexton had also been a key figure in the organization of working-class demonstrations against "Chinese labour" in South Africa. James Sexton, *Sir James Sexton, Agitator: The Life of the Docker's M.P.* (London: Faber & Faber, 1936), 34.
73. *TUC Annual Reports*, September 8, 1916, 329.
74. Ibid., 330.
75. *Times* (London), September 11, 1916, 5.
76. Ibid.
77. *Daily Telegraph*, October 3, 1916.
78. Ibid.
79. *Liverpool Courier*, September 15, 1916.
80. Brian Fawcett, "The Chinese Labour Corps in France 1917–1922," *Journal of the Royal Asiatic Society, Hong Kong Branch* 40 (2000): 33–111. France would bring over a similar number, bringing the full total of Chinese laborers employed on the front to nearly 200,000.
81. *Times* (London), April 23, 1919, 14.
82. *DNB*, s.v. "Sir Edward Richard Henry, baronet."
83. *Times* (London), December 29, 1917, 8.
84. Ibid.
85. *The War Illustrated*, July 27, 1918; November 9, 1918; and December 15, 1917. *The War Illustrated*, published from 1914–18, was a popular magazine aimed largely at working-class readers.
86. *Times* (London), December 29, 1917, 8. For a discussion of the replication of imperial dynamics of racial subordination in the British use of black and Indian troops during WWI, see Tabili, *British Justice*, 15–29.

87. Cay Van Ash and Elizabeth Sax Rohmer, *Master of Villainy: A Biography of Sax Rohmer* (Bowling Green, OH: Bowling Green University Popular Press, 1972), 26.
88. Ibid., 102.
89. *East London Advertiser*, May 21, 1910. King had been before the courts on one other previous occasion in order to seek a divorce from his wife, a white British woman, on the grounds of her alleged adultery with another Chinese man. *Times* (London), March 18, 1911, 3.
90. The storyline of *The Yellow Claw* and the plots of Dr. Fu Manchu would be linked in a later novel, *The Golden Scorpion* (1919).
91. Sax Rohmer, *The Yellow Claw* (London: Methuen, 1915; New York: McBride, Nast, 1915), 278.
92. Ibid., 101.
93. Ibid., 248.
94. Ibid., 244.
95. Ibid., 171.
96. The link between opium and espionage had been highlighted in the British press coverage of the sensational Ullmo Affair of 1907, when a French naval officer attempted to sell military secrets to the Germans while under the influence of opium. *Times* (London), November 16, 1907, 5.
97. Rohmer, *Yellow Claw*, 172. The theme of aristocratic decay and its association with drug addiction had been prevalent in the works Robert Louis Stevenson, Arthur Conan Doyle, and Oscar Wilde as well. Andrew Blake, "Foreign Devils and Moral Panics: Britain, Asia, and the Opium Trade," in *The Expansion of England: Race, Ethnicity, and Cultural History*, ed. Bill Schwarz (London, 1996), 254. In Dickens's *The Mystery of Edwin Drood* (1870), the moral degradation of white Britons, both male and female, had been similarly described as facilitating their domination by Oriental villains. Barry Milligan, *Pleasures and Pains: Opium and the Orient in Nineteenth-Century British Culture* (Charlottesville, VA: University Press of Virginia, 1995), 94–95.
98. Rohmer, *Yellow Claw*, 146.
99. Ibid., 283.
100. Ibid., 191, 288.
101. Ibid., 253.
102. The furnishings of Mr. King's apartment in the Cave of the Golden Dragon are "markedly Chinese—and—feminine." Rohmer, *Yellow Claw*, 387. The Cave itself is administered on a daily basis by Ho-Pin, a dandified Chinese maître d'hôtel. In contrast, even Rohmer's moral female protagonist, the partner of Gaston Max, possesses "a face of masculine vigor" and an "athletic figure." Ibid., 86.
103. Just as one protagonist in the first Fu Manchu novel asserted, "East and West may not intermingle." Sax Rohmer, *The Mystery of Dr. Fu Manchu* (London: Methuen, 1913), 136.

104. Gaston Max is himself French, although he speaks with an American accent. All other major characters working against the King syndicate are English, Scottish, or French. As with the villains in the Fu Manchu stories, King and his henchmen are drawn largely from regions where Britain exercised significant imperial authority.
105. Rohmer, *Yellow Claw*,184.
106. Ibid., 191.
107. Ibid., 376.
108. Between November 1914 and April 1916, the British government executed eleven men for spying and treason. Another thirteen were executed in Ireland for their roles in the Easter Uprising.
109. Rohmer, *Yellow Claw*, 364.
110. *Times* (London), January 10, 1921, 8.
111. Rohmer, *Yellow Claw*, 392.
112. Bourke, *Dismembering the Male*, 13.
113. Kohn, *Dope Girls*, 62–63; Berridge, "Opium Dens," 16–21.
114. Burke, *Limehouse Nights* (London: Grant Richards, 1917; Freeport, NY: Books for Libraries Press, 1969), 19, 45, 56, 51, 104, 26–27, 309–10 (citations are from the 1969 edition).
115. Thomas Burke, *Son of London* (London: Herbert Jenkins, 1946), 219; Seed, "Limehouse Blues," 77.
116. "The word 'Chinatown,' which once carried a perfume of delight, is now empty of meaning save as indicating a district of London where Chinamen live." Burke, *Out and About*, 35.
117. Burke, *Limehouse Nights*, 41.
118. Seed, "Limehouse Blues," 78.
119. Anne Witchard, "Aspects of Literary Limehouse: Thomas Burke and the 'Glamorous Shame of Chinatown,'" *Literary London: Interdisciplinary Studies in the Representation of London* 2 (2004), 2.
120. For recent scholarship on how literature and journalism helped shape the experience of Victorian Londoners with regard to gender, class, and morality, see Judith Walkowitz, *City of Dreadful Delight: Narratives of Danger in Late Victorian London* (Chicago: University of Chicago Press, 1992); Deborah Epstein Nord, *Walking the Victorian Streets: Women, Representation and the City* (Ithaca, NY: Cornell University Press, 1995); Lynda Nead, *Victorian Babylon: People, Streets, and Images in Nineteenth-Century London* (New Haven, CT: Yale University Press, 2000); Simon Joyce, *Capital Offenses: Geographies of Class and Crime in Victorian London* (Charlottesville, VA: University Press of Virginia, 2003).
121. Burke, *Out and About*, 46, and *Limehouse Nights*, 16.
122. Describing the "real" 1917 Limehouse in *Out and About*, Burke wrote that the casual social mixing of races and the visible presence of white girls were still prominent features of the neighborhood, "but the whole thing was very decorous and war-timish." Burke, *Out and About*, 37.

123. Robert Bickers, *Britain in China: Community, Culture, and Colonialism, 1900–1949* (Manchester: Manchester University Press, 1999), 44.
124. Burke, *Limehouse Nights*, 238.
125. Witchard, "Literary Limehouse," 2.
126. Burke, *Limehouse Nights*, 41.
127. For a broader discussion of "respectability" in working-class culture, see Ellen Ross, "'Not the Sort That Would Sit on the Doorstep': Respectability in Pre-World War I London Neighborhoods," *International Labor and Working Class History* 27 (Spring 1985): 39–59; Anna Davin, *Growing Up Poor: Home, School, and Street in London, 1870–1914* (London: Rivers Oram, 1996); Peter Bailey, *Popular Culture and Performance in the Victorian City* (Cambridge: Cambridge University Press, 1998), 30–46.
128. Burke, *Limehouse Nights*, 30.
129. Ibid., 64–66.
130. Ibid., 80.
131. Ibid., 302.
132. Ibid., 300, 302.
133. Ibid., 308–10.
134. Ibid., 311.
135. Witchard, "Literary Limehouse," 2.
136. Burke, *Out and About*, 41, 47.
137. *East End News*, June 1, 1917.
138. *Times* (London), June 26, 1917, 3.
139. *East End News*, June 29, 1917.
140. *East End News*, October 12, 1917. Deportation recommendations were approved in the vast majority of cases, so it is safe to conclude that most, if not all, of these defendants were eventually deported. From 1905–11, for example, the Secretary of State for the Home Department rejected only 116 (less than 5 percent) of the 2,378 recommendations made by various courts across Britain. *Justice of the Peace*, March 16, 1912, 126.
141. *East End News*, January 18, 1918.
142. *East End News*, March 9, 1917. The prosecution asserted that it was the efforts by Chinese seamen to organize their labor that had triggered the violence. *East End News*, May 4, 1917.
143. The Recorder of London, Sir Forrest Fulton. *East End News*, May 4, 1917.
144. "Chinese Going from London to Cardiff," September 27, 1916, MEPO 2/1692/988692/6.
145. "Registration of Chinese," Memo from E. N. Cooper, H. M. Inspector of Aliens, March 10, 1916, MEPO 2/1692/988692/2.
146. "Chinese Going from London to Cardiff," September 27, 1916, MEPO 2/1692/988692.
147. "Chinese Seamen," June 30, 1917, MEPO 2/1692/988692/7.

148. "Regulations Concerning the Importation of Chinese," July 1918, HO 45/11843/139147/113.
149. Jill Pellew, "The Home Office and the Aliens Act, 1905," *The Historical Journal* 32, no. 2 (June, 1989): 374.
150. "Chinese Crew of the *T.S.S. War Soldier*," December 3, 1918, HO 45/11843/139147/124.
151. "Deportation from America of Chinese Seamen Who Have Deserted from British Ships," November 27, 1919, HO 45/11843/139147/123.
152. "Chinese Colony in East London," November 18, 1918, HO 45/11843/139147/119.

Chapter 5

1. Lucy Bland, "White Women and Men of Colour: Miscegenation Fears in Britain after the Great War," *Gender and History* 17, no. 1 (April 2005), 33.
2. For an excellent discussion of the relationship between the urban geography of race and that of gender in the American context, see Mary Ting Yi Lui, *The Chinatown Trunk Mystery: Murder, Miscegenation, and Other Dangerous Encounters in Turn-of-the-Century New York City* (Princeton, NJ: Princeton University Press, 2004).
3. For further discussion of nineteenth-century literary descriptions of white women and Chinese "vice" in the East End, see Barry Milligan, *Pleasures and Pains: Opium and the Orient in Nineteenth-Century British Culture* (Charlottesville, VA: University Press of Virginia, 1995), 85–97.
4. William Gibson, Sr., was originally from Scotland, but he had emigrated to Australia in 1882. Sally O'Neill, "Gibson, William (1842?–1918)," *Australian Dictionary of Biography*, vol. 8, (Melbourne: Melbourne University Press, 1981), 656–57.
5. This case is also discussed, briefly, in Colin Holmes, "The Chinese Connection," in *Outsiders and Outcasts: Essays in Honour of William J. Fishman*, ed. Geoffrey Alderman and Colin Holmes (London: Duckworth, 1993), 80.
6. *Times* (London), August 15, 1918, 3.
7. The Poisons and Pharmacy Act of 1908 (8 Edw. VII, c. 55).
8. *Times* (London), August 24, 1918, 3.
9. Terry Parssinen, *Secret Passions, Secret Remedies: Narcotic Drugs in British Society, 1820–1930* (Philadelphia: Institute for the Study of Human Issues, 1983), 135.
10. Ibid.
11. *Times* (London), August 15, 1918, 3, and August 24, 1918, 3.
12. Colin Holmes refers to such journalistic juxtapositions as the "drip" technique. Holmes "Chinese Connection," 87. Other scholars have

mentioned public anxiety and official concern over the West End, middle-class opium smoker in previous decades. Virginia Berridge, "East End Opium Dens and Narcotic Use in Britain," *The London Journal* 4, no. 1 (1978): 2–28, 15; Milligan, *Pleasures and Pains*, 103–17.

13. *Times* (London), August 24, 1918, 3.
14. Ibid.
15. For a recent discussion of morphine addiction in late-Victorian Britain, see Susan Ziegler, "'How Far am I Responsible?': Women and Morphinomania in Late-Nineteenth-Century Britain," *Victorian Studies* 48, no. 1 (Autumn 2005): 59–81.
16. The process required, for example, access to organic solvents and familiarity with their use. Opium could be refined into a state suitable for injection, however, through less complicated and expensive means. My thanks to Dr. Colin Burns, Department of Chemistry, East Carolina University, for sharing with me his knowledge of organic chemistry and for explaining the mechanism by which raw opium is refined into morphine and heroin. Dr. Burns has no known connections to Chinatown.
17. Much of the final product had been also exported to China, where morphine use had been offered as an alternative to opium smoking and had shored up India's export economy as the direct opium trade to China had gone into decline. Parssinen, *Secret Passions*, 144–52. Parssinen estimates that the amount of morphine exported from Britain to China in 1911–13 and 1919–20 was 275,000–300,000 ounces per year and was double that during the wartime period.
18. *Times* (London), February 5, 1916, 3; February 11, 1916, 3; May 29, 1918, 3.
19. Parssinen, *Secret Passions*, 79–105.
20. *Times* (London), August 15, 1918, 3.
21. Carleton had taken several different drugs in the twenty-four hours preceding her death, and there was some debate during the trial over whether it was cocaine or veronal that had ultimately been responsible for her death. Marek Kohn, *Dope Girls: The Birth of the British Drug Underground* (London: Granta, 2001), 96–97.
22. *Times* (London), December 4, 1918, 3; December 13, 1918, 3; January 3, 1919, 2; January 10, 1919, 5; January 17, 1919, 4; January 24, 1919, 4; January 25, 1919, 3; February 1, 1919, 3; April 5, 1919, 12; April 8, 1919, 7.
23. Evidence of her crime, he told the court, came from "a large number of witnesses, some of whom are trustworthy and others not." *Times* (London), December 21, 1918, 5.
24. *Times* (London), December 21, 1918, 5.
25. Ibid.
26. Ibid.
27. Ibid.
28. *Times* (London), December 14, 1918, 5.

29. De Veulle lived on Dover Street, just two blocks north of Buckingham Palace.
30. *Times* (London), December 21, 1918, 5.
31. Ibid.
32. Ibid.
33. *Times* (London), July 24, 1918, 2.
34. *Times* (London), December 21, 1918, 5.
35. These two possible interpretations of Ada Ping You were emblematic of the debate over women's agency that had occupied a prominent place in wartime discussions of gender roles and expectations. For recent discussions of changing roles and images of working-class women during WWI, see Deborah Thom, *Nice Girls and Rude Girls: Women Workers in World War I* (London: I. B. Tauris, 1998); Nicoletta Gullace, *"The Blood of Our Sons": Men, Women, and the Renegotiation of British Citizenship during the Great War* (New York: Palgrave Macmillan, 2002).
36. Kohn, *Dope Girls*, 87.
37. *Times* (London), July 24, 1918, 2
38. *Times* (London), January 3, 1919, 2.
39. *Times* (London), December 21, 1918, 5.
40. *Times* (London), January 11, 1919, 3.
41. *World's Pictorial News*, March 22, 1925, cited in Kohn, *Dope Girls*, 67.
42. *Times* (London), December 21, 1918, 5.
43. *Times* (London), December 13, 1918, 3.
44. *Times* (London), December 21, 1918, 5.
45. *Times* (London), December 13, 1918, 3.
46. Laura Tabili, "Outsiders in the Land of Their Birth: Exogamy, Citizenship, and Identity in War and Peace," *Journal of British Studies* 44, no. 4 (October 2004): 801.
47. Philipa Levine, "Sexuality, Gender, and Empire," in *The Oxford History of the British Empire, Companion Series: Gender and Empire*, ed. Philipa Levine (Oxford: Oxford University Press, 2004), 140.
48. Kohn, *Dope Girls*, 88.
49. *Times* (London), February 26, 1919, 7.
50. *Times* (London), December 13, 1918, 3; January 3, 1919, 2; December 14, 1918, 5; December 21, 1918, 5.
51. Burke was openly derisive of the press's romanticizing of the "glamorous shame" of Chinatown in the aftermath of the Carleton affair. Thomas Burke, *Out and About: A Note-Book of London in War-Time* (London: Allen & Unwin, 1919), 47.
52. Stephen Koss, *The Rise and Fall of the Political Press in Britain* (London: Hamish Hamilton, 1984), 205.
53. Although identified as "Len Ping You" in his Thames Police Court trial, the *Daily Chronicle* story and much subsequent coverage of the Carleton case omitted his Anglicanized first name and referred to him merely as "Lo Ping" or "Lo Ping You."

54. *Daily Chronicle*, December 14, 1918.
55. Judith Walkowitz, *City of Dreadful Delight: Narratives of Danger in Late Victorian London* (Chicago: University of Chicago Press, 1992), 197.
56. *The Star*, January 9, 1919.
57. Similar claims would appear in the *Daily Mail* in the wake of the Carleton scandal. Kohn, *Dope Girls*, 105.
58. *The Star*, January 9, 1919.
59. *Times* (London), December 16, 1918, 5, and February 1, 1919, 3.
60. Kohn, *Dope Girls*, 106–9.
61. In addition to press accounts cited earlier, other eyewitness reports directly contradicted the sensationalized portrayal of the dens. Berridge, "Opium Dens," 8–9. In contrast to Liverpool, New York City, San Francisco, and Vancouver, there is no known photographic record of a London opium den.
62. *Daily Telegraph*, January 23, 1919.
63. Ibid.
64. *Times* (London), January 30, 1919, 3.
65. Ibid.
66. Ibid.
67. *Times* (London), December 31, 1918, 5.
68. *Times* (London), December 16, 1918, 5.
69. *Times* (London), February 26, 1919, 7.
70. Most notably in the stories of a Chinese "Moriarity" and a "vast syndicate of vice" based in Limehouse, and in the portrayals of the Chinese restaurateur "Brilliant" Chang as a "Dope King." Seed, "Limehouse Blues," 70; Kohn, *Dope Girls*, 125–31; "In the Grip of the Yellow Fangs: Chinese Secret Society of Dope, Debauchery, and Death," *John Bull*, December 23, 1922, 10.
71. Cay Van Ash and Elizabeth Sax Rohmer, *Master of Villainy: A Biography of Sax Rohmer* (Bowling Green, OH: Bowling Green University Popular Press, 1972), 111.
72. Sax Rohmer, *Dope: A Story of Chinatown and the Drug Traffic*. London: Cassell, 1919; New York, McBride, 1919.
73. Ibid., 113.
74. Kohn, *Dope Girls*, 113.
75. Rohmer, *Dope*, 112, 284, 325.
76. Ibid., 109.
77. For a recent discussion of the complex racial differences between the Celts and Anglo-Saxons propagated in British public discourse, see Michael de Nie, "A Medley Mob of Irish-American Plotters and Irish Dupes': The British Press and Transatlantic Fenianism," *Journal of British Studies* 40, no. 2 (April 2001): 233–36. Donald MacRaild provides a more general description of anti-Irish imagery in *Irish Migrants in*

Modern Britain, 1750–1922 (New York: Palgrave MacMillan, 1999), 155–84.

78. Rohmer himself was an example of this ethnic reconciliation. He was of Irish parentage, but he had been born in Birmingham and had adopted a pseudonym drawn from the Saxon language (sax = "blade," rohmer = "roamer"). Van Ash and E. Rohmer, *Master of Villainy*, 13.
79. Rohmer, *Dope*, 109. For a discussion of the transformative power of opium in Dickens, see Milligan, *Pleasures and Pains*, 96–97.
80. Rohmer, *Dope*, 161.
81. Ibid., 126, 120.
82. Women's particular vulnerability to seduction by an "alien enchanter" was also a central aspect of the Svengali controversy. Daniel Pick, *Svengali's Web: The Alien Enchanter in Modern Culture* (New Haven, CT: Yale University Press), 8–9.
83. Rohmer, *Dope*, 90.
84. Ibid., 137.
85. For the Victorian views of women as being more susceptible to suggestion than men were, see Pick, *Svengali's Web*, 65.
86. Rohmer, *Dope*, 95. Victorian portrayals of drug addiction were similarly gendered, and emphasized women's loss of self-control. Ziegler, "Women and Morphinomania," 73–76.
87. Rohmer, *Dope*, 366.
88. Colin Holmes, *John Bull's Island: Immigration and British Society, 1871–1971* (Basingstoke: Macmillan, 1988), 111–12.
89. Journalists also referred to the area in question as "Pennyfields" at times.
90. Thomas Burke, *Out and About*, 42–43.
91. Ibid., 47
92. Burke's *Limehouse Nights* would experience a revival of its popularity with the cinematic interpretation of "The Chink and the Child" in D.W. Griffith's *Broken Blossoms* (released in Britain in 1920).

Chapter 6

1. A "moral panic" involves the identification of a threat to the social body, the erecting of barricades to protect society from this threat, the demonization of the threatening group or individual, and the promulgation of fictitious solutions in the form of laws and well-publicized arrests. The concept, originally drawn from Stanley Cohen's sociological study, has been refined by Stuart Hall and Simon Watney—who have emphasized the active role of the media in shaping such events for specific audiences—and employed by Judith Walkowitz in *City of Dreadful Delight: Narratives of Danger in Late Victorian London* (Chicago: University of Chicago Press, 1992), 121. See also Simon Watney, *Policing Desire:*

Pornography, AIDS and the Media (Minneapolis: University of Minnesota Press, 1989); Stuart Hall et al., *Policing the Crisis: Mugging, the State and Law and Order* (London: Palgrave Macmillan, 1978); Stanley Cohen, *Folk Devils and Moral Panics: The Creation of the Mods and Rockers* (London: MacGibbon and Kee, 1972).

2. By 1921, they represented only 23 percent of the officially recorded, China-born population of London (which totaled 711). Ng Chee Choo, *The Chinese in London* (Oxford: Oxford University Press, 1968), 6, 12.
3. By 1919, it is estimated that there were fourteen Chinese-owned businesses in Limehouse, whereas in 1911, there had been nine, and in 1906, only one. John Seed, "Limehouse Blues: Looking for Chinatown in the London Docks, 1900-40," *History Workshop Journal* 62 (2006): 65.
4. Michael Rowe, "Sex, 'Race,' and Riot in Liverpool, 1919," *Immigrants and Minorities* 19, no. 2 (July 2000): 53–70; Jacqueline Jenkinson, "The 1919 Riots," in *Racial Violence in Britain in the Nineteenth and Twentieth Centuries*, ed. Panikos Panayi (Leicester, U.K.: Leicester University Press, 1996), 93–111; Roy May and Robin Cohen, "The Interaction between Race and Colonialism: A Case Study of the Liverpool Race Riots of 1919," *Race And Class* 16, no. 2 (1974): 111–26. "Black" is an inexact term, but it remains the standard in current scholarly usage. The term is not capitalized here in order to maintain parity with the use of the term "white" throughout.
5. Alan O'Day, "Varieties of Anti-Irish Behaviour in Britain, 1846–1922," in *Racial Violence in Britain in the Nineteenth and Twentieth Centuries*, ed. Panikos Panayi (Leicester, U.K.: Leicester University Press, 1993), 29; David Feldman, "The Importance of Being English: Jewish Immigration and the Decay of Liberal England," in *Metropolis London: Histories and Representations since 1800*, ed. David Feldman and Gareth Stedman Jones (London: Routledge, 1989), 56–57.
6. Although it should be noted that prejudice remained particularly acute against recent Russian Jewish immigrants, a group that had grown substantially in the later decades of the nineteenth century and who continued to stand out from the more established Anglo-Jewry of the East End. Jamie Bronstein, "Rethinking the 'Readmission': Anglo-Jewish History and the Immigration Crisis," in *Singular Continuities: Tradition, Nostalgia, and Identity in Modern British Culture*, ed. George Behlmer and Fred Leventhal (Stanford, CA: Stanford University Press, 2000), 38–39.
7. Jenkinson, "1919 Riots," 95.
8. *Daily Chronicle*, May 29, 1919.
9. Jenkinson, "1919 Riots," 94. Reports on the issue of interracial sexuality in London had begun to appear in the *Times* and to be commented upon in London police court cases in early 1919. *Times* (London), February 25, 1919, 5.

10. Jenkinson, "1919 Riots," 92; Andrea Murphy; *From the Empire to the Rialto—Racism and Reaction in Liverpool, 1918–1948* (Birkenhead, U.K.: Liver Press, 1995), ix–x; Rowe, "Sex, 'Race,' and Riot," 59.
11. Joanna Bourke, *Dismembering the Male: Men's Bodies, Britain, and the Great War* (Chicago: University of Chicago Press, 1996); Lucy Bland, "White Women and Men of Color: Miscegenation Fears in Britain after the Great War," *Gender and History* 17, no. 1 (April 2005): 37.
12. Sascha Auerbach, "Negotiating Nationalism: Jewish Conscription and Russian Repatriation in London's East End, 1916–1918," *Journal of British Studies* 46, no. 3 (July 2007): 598.
13. Robert Holland, "The British Empire and the Great War, 1914-1918" in *The Oxford History of the British Empire, Volume IV: The Twentieth Century*, ed. Judith Brown and Wm. Roger Louis (Oxford: Oxford University Press, 1999), 115–37.
14. Laura Tabili, "Women 'of a Very Low Type': Crossing Racial Boundaries in Imperial Britain," in *Gender and Class in Modern Europe*, ed. Laura Frader and Sonya Rose (Ithaca, NY: Cornell University Press, 1996), 173; Wm. Roger Louis, "Introduction," 2–3; and Stephen Constantine, "Migrants and Settlers," 183, both in *The Oxford History of the British Empire*; P. J. Marshall, "An Empire under Threat, 1870–1918," in *The Cambridge Illustrated History of the British Empire*, ed. P. J. Marshall (Cambridge: Cambridge University Press, 1996[0]), 39, 60.
15. Such was the case with the depiction of black men in Cardiff as well. Kenneth Little, *Negroes in Britain: A Study of Racial Relations in English Society* (London: Routledge and Kegan Paul, 1948), 80–81; *Times* (London), November 4, 1919, 17.
16. *The Star*, June 17, 1919.
17. Rowe, "Sex, 'Race,' and Riot," 61. This was the claim made by a deputation from the local branch of the Discharged and Demobilized Soldiers' and Sailors' Deputation to the Bethnal-green Borough Council in September 1919. *Times* (London), September 26, 1919, 7.
18. John Seed's analysis of census data reveals that from 1911 to 1921, the Chinese population of England, London, and Limehouse grew from 1,120 to 2,419, 247 to 711, and 101 to 337, respectively. The proportion of London's Chinese residents who lived in Limehouse had also grown, from roughly a third in 1911 to one-half in 1921. Seed, "Limehouse Blues," 63.
19. In 1921, 21.2 percent of the population of Poplar was living in conditions of more than two people per room. "Public Housing in Poplar: The Inter-War Years," *Survey of London, v. 43 and 44: Poplar, Blackwall, and the Isle of Dogs*, ed. Hermione Hobhouse (London: The Athlone Press, University of London,1994), http://www.british-history.ac.uk/report.
20. *East End News*, June 20, 1919.
21. Ibid.

22. By the 1920s, 25 percent of the officially recorded Chinese residents of London lived in the West End boroughs of Westminster, St. Pancras, and St. Marylebone. Seed, "Limehouse Blues," 64.
23. *East End News*, June 26, 1919.
24. Ibid.
25. *Times* (London), July 1, 1919, 4.
26. *Times* (London), April 16, 1919, 11; July 1, 1919, 4; July 17, 1919, 11; November 19, 1919, 11.
27. May and Cohen, "Liverpool Race Riots," 122.
28. Ibid., 124.
29. Robert Huttenback, *Racism and Empire: White Settlers and Colored Immigrants in the British Self-Governing Colonies, 1830-1910* (Ithaca, NY: Cornell University Press, 1976), 20; Bland, "Miscegenation Fears," 37.
30. Tabili, "Women 'of a Very Low Type,'" 168–69. See also the extensive discussion in Philip D. Morgan and Sean Hawkins, eds., *Black Experience and the Empire, Companion Series to the Oxford History of the British Empire* (Oxford: Oxford University Press, 2004).
31. J. A. R. Cairns, *The Loom of the Law*. 2nd ed. (London: Hutchinson, 1922), 216.
32. *Instructions to Superintendents of Marine Mercantile Offices: Engagement of Chinese Seamen and the Language Test*, Board of Trade, Marine Department, April 1914, 4–5 [TNA].
33. May and Cohen, "Liverpool Race Riots," 119; Rowe, "Sex, 'Race,' and Riot," 62–64; Jenkinson, "The 1919 Riots," 102; Tabili, *British Justice*, 136–37.
34. *Times* (London), July 1, 1919, 4.
35. Estimates of the total number of black men who were repatriated by 1921 range from 2–3,000 out of a total overall population of roughly 20,000. May and Cohen, "Liverpool Race Riots," 120; Rowe, "Sex, 'Race,' and Riot," 64; Jenkinson, "The 1919 Riots," 103–7; Winston James, "The Black Experience in Twentieth-Century Britain," in *Black Experience and the Empire, Companion Series to the Oxford History of the British Empire*, ed. Philip D. Morgan and Sean Hawkins (Oxford: Oxford University Press, 2003), 357.
36. The 1920s witnessed a sharp rise in the number of Chinese women living in London. The male-female ratio of China-born born aliens in the metropolis dropped from nearly 8:1 in 1921 (627 to 84) to less than 2:1 in 1921 (729 to 465). Choo, *Chinese in London*, 11.
37. Tabili, "Women 'of a Very Low Type,'" 166–67; Bland, "Miscegenation Fears," 36.
38. In February, one East End policewoman had painted a very different picture. In bringing charges of against a 21-year-old English girl for "soliciting a coloured man in the street," the officer claimed that such offences

were becoming "very common in East London." *Times* (London), February 25, 1919, 5.

39. *Times* (London), January 30, 1919, 2.
40. *Times* (London), September 8, 1919, 7.
41. Ibid.
42. *Times* (London), September 15, 1919, 7.
43. H. L. Cancellor, *The Life of a London Beak* (London: Hurst and Blackett, 1930), 109. Cancellor also described him, inaccurately, as being Japanese.
44. Ibid.
45. Ibid., 113.
46. Ibid.
47. *Times* (London), September 22, 1919, 7.
48. *Times* (London), December 9, 1921, 7.
49. *Times* (London), July 21, 1920, 6.
50. *Evening Standard*, February 24, 1920.
51. *Times* (London), November 8, 1919, 4.
52. This practice was introduced by a Chinese witness in 1804. *Old Bailey Proceedings Online* http://www.oldbaileyonline.org, December 1804 trial of Ann Alsey and Thomas Gunn, t18041205-56. My thanks to Dr. Michael Fisher, Department of History, Oberlin College, for directing me to this particular case.
53. Paul Marshall, "The Lord Chamberlain and the Containment of Americanization in the British Theater of the 1920s," *The New Theater Quarterly* 19 (2003): 381–94.
54. *Times* (London), June 10, 1920, 14. The film adaptation of the play would star Warner Oland as Charlie Yong. Oland would later be cast as Dr. Fu Manchu in *The Mysterious Fu Manchu* (1929) and in *The Return of Fu Manchu* (1930).
55. Ibid.
56. *Daily Telegraph*, June 26, 1920.
57. This effort eventually culminated in the 1934 founding of the Chung Hwa School and Club in Pennyfields, which combined educational and philanthropic activities focusing on "the poor Sino-British families in East London." *Appeal for Funds for the New Club House* [pamphlet], Chung Hwa School and Club, London, 1936 [THLHLA].
58. This mirrored the views on children of black-white unions (Tabili, *British Justice*, 146).
59. According to the article, "something like forty children and fifty adults" had promptly signed up for the language program. *Daily Telegraph*, June 26, 1920.
60. Thomas Burke claimed that the performance of cultural difference was common among Chinese businessmen in Chinatown. Thomas Burke, *Out and About: A Note-Book of London in War-Time* (London: Allen & Unwin, 1919), 44–45.

61. Interviews with Leslie Heng, Connie Hoe, and Leslie Hoe, "'Whispers of Time': An Oral History of the London Chinese," Chinese National Healthy Living Centre (2005), http: //www.riverculturesfestival.co.uk; Alan Palmer, *The East End: Four Centuries of London Life* (New Brunswick, NJ: Rutgers University Press, 2000), 108.
62. *Daily Telegraph*, June 26, 1920.
63. An Act for better preventing Thefts and Robberies, and for Regulating Places of Entertainment, and Punishing Persons keeping Disorderly Houses 1751 (25 Geo. II, c. 36); Dagmar Kift, *The Victorian Music Hall: Culture, Class, and Conflict* (Cambridge: Cambridge University Press, 1996), 146–48. The specific charge was that Doe allowed prostitutes to loiter in his eating-houses.
64. Leslie Moran, *The Homosexual(ity) Law* (London: Routledge, 1996), 229.
65. *East End News*, October 5, 1920.
66. *Times* (London), October 4, 1920.
67. J. A. R. Cairns, *The Sidelights of London* (London: Hutchinson, 1923; New York: Henry Holt, 1924), 50 (citations are to the 1924 edition).
68. Cairns, *Loom of the Law*, 220.
69. Cancellor, *London Beak*, 65.
70. Ibid., 66.
71. Ibid., 67.
72. Ibid., 64.
73. Ibid.
74. *Daily Mail*, October 5, 1920.
75. *Evening News*, October 4, 1920.
76. *Times* (London), October 6, 1920, 7.
77. Janine Booth, "A Different Sort of Labour Council," *Workers Liberty* 66 (January 2001), http://archive.workersliberty.org/wlmags/wl66/janine.htm.
78. *Evening News*, October 5, 1920.
79. Dummet and Nicol, *Subjects, Citizens, Aliens*, 107; Aliens Restriction (Amendment) Act 1919, (9 & 10 Geo. V, c. 92); Colin Holmes, *John Bull's Island: Immigration and British Society, 1871–1971* (Houndsmills, U.K.: Macmillan, 1988), 113.
80. Auerbach, "Negotiating Nationalism," 615–18.
81. *Times* (London), October 6, 1920, 7. It was also referred to as "puck-apu," "puckapoo," or "puck-a-pue."[0] The correct transliteration is "pák kòp piú," which means "white pigeon ticket." The name originated from the practice, when the game was introduced in China, of using messenger pigeons to carry the game tickets and winning numbers between the locales where the lottery was being conducted. Stewart Culin, "Gambling Games of the Chinese in America," *Series in Philology Literature and Archeology* 1, no. 4 (Philadelphia: University of Pennsylvania Press, 1891): 7–8.

82. *Evening News*, October 5, 1920.
83. *Evening News*, October 5, 1920.
84. Ibid.
85. *Daily Express*, October 1, 1920.
86. Deborah Thom, *Nice Girls and Rude Girls: Women Workers in World War I* (London: I.B. Tauris, 2000); Angela Woollacott, *On Her Their Lives Depend: Munitions Workers in the Great War* (Berkeley and Los Angeles: University of California Press, 1994).
87. *Evening News*, October 7, 1920.
88. In 1914, opium could be bought over the shop counter for 18 shillings and 6 pence for a four-ounce tin. By the mid-1920s, opium in Chinatown cost 2 shillings for a "tiny little packet." Annie Lai, Bob Little, Pippa Little, "Chinatown Annie: The East End Opium Trade 1920–1935: The Story of a Woman Opium Dealer," *Oral History Journal* 14, no. 1 (1986): 21, 28.
89. For descriptions of a similar dynamic in the United States, see Mary Ting Yi Lui, *The Chinatown Trunk Mystery: Murder, Miscegenation, and Other Dangerous Encounters in Turn-of-the-Century New York City* (Princeton, NJ: Princeton University Press, 2005), 5.
90. *Evening News*, October 6, 1920.
91. Ibid.
92. The London County Council elections of 1919 had brought "striking gains" for Labour in the borough councils of Poplar, Hackney, and Bethnal Green. Alan Palmer, *The East End: Four Centuries of London Life* (New Brunswick, NJ: Rutgers University Press, 2000), 125).
93. *Evening News*, October 5, 1920.
94. Ibid.
95. *Evening News*, October 7, 1920.
96. *Evening News*, October 6, 1920. Census records reveal that significant clusters of Chinese residents were to be found in these areas by the 1920s. Seed, "Limehouse Blues," 64.
97. *Daily Graphic*, October 7, 1920.
98. Report of Superintendent, K Division, on the raids on No. 10 Limehouse Causeway, October 23, 1920, *Memorandum on Chinese Gaming Houses*, Records of the Metropolitan Police, MEPO 2/2285 (hereafter, *Chinese Gaming*) [TNA]; *Evening News*, October 5, 1920.
99. *Evening News*, October 5, 1920.
100. "Re: Execution of Search Warrants under the Gaming Acts on Sunday," October 21, 1920, *Memorandum on Gaming Houses Conducted by Chinese*, Records of the Metropolitan Police, MEPO 2/2275 (hereafter, *Gaming Houses*).
101. Mann referred specifically to the Sunday Observance Act, 1677, sec. 6, "which enacts that a write or warrant cannot be executed on Sunday except for treason, felony, or breach of the peace." *Gaming Houses.*
102. Ibid.

103. "Warrants, Execution on Sunday," October 2, 1920, *Gaming Houses.*
104. Ibid.
105. The two barristers were D. A. Majid and Chen Alloy. Report of Superintendent, K Division, on the raids on No. 10 Limehouse Causeway, October 23, 1920, *Chinese Gaming.*
106. W. Horwood to the Home Office, November 8, 1920, *Chinese Gaming.*
107. *Times* (London), November 9, 1920, 5.
108. *Times* (London), November 10, 1920, 5.
109. Ibid.
110. Glenn R. Wilkinson, *Depictions and Images of War in Edwardian Newspapers* (New York: Palgrave Macmillan, 2003), 11.
111. *Daily Express*, October 1, 1920.
112. Ibid.; Seed, "Limehouse Blues", 70.
113. "Nearly every house displays Chinese signs," the *Evening News* reported, "and is a café or boarding-house at 8pm." *Evening News*, October 5, 1920.
114. *Times* (London), October 6, 1920.
115. *East End News*, October 8, 1920.
116. *Times* (London), October 15, 1920.
117. *East End News*, January 18, 1921.
118. *East London Advertiser*, January 22, 1921. Wild was referring to the growing population of Russian Jewish immigrants.
119. According to the Chairman, Mr. Lawrie, this decision was based on the appellant's "past good character and the fact that he had married an Englishwoman." Caught between the two evils of allowing a supposed abettor of interracial social contact to remain in London and pauperizing a white British woman, Lawrie chose the former course. *Times* (London), January 15, 1921, 5.
120. *East End News*, January 18, 1921.
121. Ibid.
122. Ada Ping You had died of tuberculosis shortly after her release from prison. Marek Kohn, *Dope Girls: The Birth of the British Drug Underground* (London: Granta, 2001), 116. Rooth was officially transferred to Lambeth Police Court in December 1921. *Times* (London), December 9, 1921, 7.
123. *Times* (London), July 30, 1921, 7.

Chapter 7

1. Terry Parsinnen, *Secret Passions, Secret Remedies: Narcotic Drugs in British Society, 1820—1930* (Philadephia: Institute for the Study of Human Issues, 1983), 137.
2. Ibid., 161.
3. Dangerous Drugs Act, 1920 (10 and 11 Geo. V, c. 46).

4. Marek Kohn, *Dope Girls: The Birth of the British Drug Underground* (London: Granta, 2001), 134. Alfred Hitchcock would serve as an apprentice under Graham-Cutts the following year.
5. For a more complete description of the film's plot and characters see Kohn, *Dope Girls*, 134–37.
6. *Times* (London), May 13, 1922, 5.
7. Dangerous Drugs and Poisons (Amendment) Act, 1923 (13 & 14 Geo. V, c. 5).
8. Parsinnen, *Secret Passions*, 161.
9. They subsequently declined, by 1924, to a third of their 1923 levels—to roughly 65 convictions for opium and 25 for cocaine. Ibid., 167.
10. *East End News*, April 15, 1924.
11. *East End News*, May 6, 1924.
12. The focus of the second set of high-profile cases involving race, narcotics, and interracial sexuality was Edgar Manning, a black musician who was convicted on cocaine, opium, and firearms charges in April 1922 and again in July 1923, amid much media attention. *Times* (London), July 20, 1923, 9; Virginia Berridge, "The Origins of the English Drug 'Scene' 1890–1930," *Medical History* 32 (1988): 62; Kohn, *Dope Girls*, 150–58.
13. Cay Van Ash and Elizabeth Sax Fohmer, *Master of Villainy: A Biography of Sax Rohmer* (Bowling Green, OH: Bowling Green University Popular Press, 1972), 157.
14. *Montreal Standard*, July 12, 1924.
15. "Public Housing in Poplar: The Inter-war Years," *Survey of London, v. 43 and 44: Poplar, Blackwall, and the Isle of Dogs*, ed. Hermione Hobhouse (London: The Athlone Press, University of London, 1994), http://www.british-history.ac.uk/report.
16. Robert Bickers, "New Light on Lao She, London, and the London Missionary Society, 1921–1929," *Modern Chinese Literature* 8 (1994): 35–36.
17. Prominent among these latter groups were Jews from Eastern Europe and Russia, a group that had borne the brunt of much anti-immigrant sentiment in the prewar and wartime years, and black seamen. Colin Holmes, *John Bull's Island: Immigration & British Society, 1871–1971* (Houndsmills, U.K.: Macmillan, 1988), 140–41; Laura Tabili, *"We Ask for British Justice": Workers and Racial Difference in Late Imperial Britain* (Ithaca, NY: Cornell University Press, 1994).
18. J. G. Birch, *Limehouse Through Five Centuries* (London: The Sheldon Press, 1930), 145. According to Birch, Burke himself had called his Limehouse writings "experiments in the grotesque and arabesque."
19. James A. Jones, "The Life of London's 190,000 Foreigners," *Evening News*, April 11, 1931.
20. Birch, *Limehouse*, 146.

21. *East London Observer*, February 24, 1934. The designation "p.c." indicated that Coombe was a police constable.
22. *Daily Telegraph*, February 19, 1934.
23. *Guardian*, October 29, 1998, 9.
24. Shu Ch'ing-ch'un taught Chinese the School of Oriental Studies (now the School of Oriental and African Studies) from 1924–29 and subsequently returned to China by way of Singapore.
25. C. T. Hsia, the noted scholar of Chinese literature, has compared *Mr. Ma*, in its capacity as a study of racial prejudice, to E. M. Forster's *A Passage to India*. *Bulletin of the School of Oriental and African Studies* (University of London) 46, no. 1 (1983).
26. Lao She (Shu Ch'ing-ch'un), *Mr. Ma and Son: a Sojourn in London* (1929–30), translated into English by Julie Jimmerson (Beijing: Foreign Languages Press, 1991), 15.
27. Lao She, *Mr. Ma*, 15.
28. Ibid.
29. *East End Life*, November 3–9, 1997, 8; *Times* (London), February 15, 1934, 8.
30. John Seed's analysis of official census data reveals a decline from 337 Chinese residents in 1921 to 167 in 1931. "Limehouse Blues: Looking for Chinatown in the London Docks, 1900–1940," *History Workshop Journal* 62 (2006): 63.
31. Jones, "London's 190,000 Foreigners."
32. The latter was a reference to director D. W. Griffith's *Broken Blossoms* (released in Britain in 1920), a film interpretation of Thomas Burke's story, "The Chink and the Child," from *Limehouse Nights* (1917).
33. *Pacific Affairs* 4, no. 3 (March 1931): 243–44.
34. *Times* (London), January 2, 1931, 16.
35. David Walker, *Anxious Nation: Australia and the Rise of Asia, 1850–1939* (St. Lucia, Australia: University of Queensland Press, 1999), 176–80; William F. Wu, *The Yellow Peril: Chinese Americans in American Fiction, 1850–1940* (Hamden, CT: Archon Books, 1982).
36. *Times* (London), August 31, 1955, 10.
37. Louis Heren, *Growing Up Poor in London* (London: Hamish Hamilton, 1973), 16.
38. *East End Life*, November 3–9, 1997, 8.

Bibliography

Archives

Private Organizations

Records of the Trades Union Congress, Trades Union Congress Library, London Metropolitan University, London.

Personal Papers

Sir Edward Richard Henry, Letters to Lord Gladstone, 1906–1913, British Library, London.

Sax Rohmer's Correspondence with the Society of Authors, British Library, London.

Thomas Burke's Correspondence with the Society of Authors, British Library, London.

London Municipal and Local Records

Limehouse Documentary and Photographic Collection, Tower Hamlets Local History Library and Archive, London.

London County Council, Inspection of Seamen's Lodging Houses, 1910–1918, London Metropolitan Archives, London.

Records of the Chung Hwa School and Club, Tower Hamlets Local History Library and Archive, London.

Whispers of Time: An Oral History Record of London's Chinese Community, London Metropolitan Archives, London.

British Government Collections

The National Archives, Kew

HO 45/10500 Restriction of Opium Traffic

HO 45/10813 Restrictions on Cocaine

HO 45/11843 Chinese in London and Liverpool

HO 45/15592 Movement of Chinese Seamen
HO 45/24683 Opium in London and Liverpool
MEPO 2/1692 Registration of Chinese
MEPO 2/1698 Crime, Military, Prostitutes
MEPO 2/2275 Chinese in Limehouse
MEPO 2/2285 Chinese Gaming in Limehouse
MEPO 3/469 Drugs and Smuggling
MEPO 3/1049 Drugs

Government Publications

"Further Correspondence Regarding the Transvaal Labour Question," 1904, Cd. 1899.

"Further Correspondence Regarding the Transvaal Labour Question," 1904, Cd. 1941.

"Further Correspondence Relating to Labour in the Transvaal Mines," 1905, Cd. 2401.

"Further Correspondence Relating to Labour in the Transvaal Mines," 1905, Cd. 2786.

"Further Correspondence Relating to Labour in the Transvaal Mines," 1906, Cd. 2819.

Colonial Office, Papers on Colonial Affairs, South Africa, Chinese Labour in the Transvaal, 1905.

Colonial Office, Papers on Colonial Affairs, South Africa, Naturalization and Immigration, 1907.

Colonial Office Memorandum, "The Opium Question in Hong Kong," 1908.

"Instructions to Superintendents of Marine Mercantile Offices: Engagement of Chinese Seamen and the Language Test," Board of Trade, Marine Department, April 1914.

United Kingdom. *Hansard Parliamentary Debates*, third and fourth series.

Parliamentary Papers

House of Commons Sessional Papers (Woodruff Library of Emory University, Alderman Library of the University of Virginia)

Aliens Act 1905 (5 Edw. VII c. 13)

Merchant Shipping Act 1906 (7 Edw. VII c. 52)

Aliens Restriction Act 1914 (4 & 5 Geo V c. 12)

Aliens Restriction (Amendment) Act 1919 (9 & 10 Geo. V c. 92)

Dangerous Drugs Act 1920 (10 & 11 Geo. V c. 46)

Dangerous Drugs and Poisons (Amendment) Act 1923 (13 & 14 Geo. V c. 5)

Newspapers and Periodicals

Daily Chronicle
Daily Graphic
Daily Mail
Daily News
Daily Sketch
Daily Telegraph
East London Advertiser
East London Observer
East End Life
East End News
Evening News
Evening Standard
Evening Times
Evening Express
Guardian (Manchester)
John Bull
The Justice of the Peace and County, Borough, Poor Law Union and Parish Recorder
The Justice of the Peace Reports
Liverpool Courier
London Illustrated Magazine
London Magazine
Montreal Standard
Morning Leader
News Chronicle
Pictorial Weekly
Punch
Reynolds's Magazine
The Seaman: The Official Organ of the International Seafarers and of the National Sailors' and Firemen's Union
Sphere
Star
Times (London)
The War Illustrated

Primary Sources: Published Books

Anon., *The Oriental Canker in Canada* (alt. title, *The Yellow Peril in Canada*). 1912.

Armfelt, Count E. "Oriental London." In *Living London*, edited by George R. Sims. London: Cassell, 1901–03.

Baedecker's London and its Environs. London: Dulau, 1883.

Beaumont, Joseph. *The New Slavery: An Account of the Indian and Chinese Immigrants in British Guiana*. London: W. Ridgway, 1871.

Besant, Walter. *East London*. London: Chatto and Windus, 1901.

Bowers, Marian and Leon Lion. *The Chinese Puzzle: An Original Play in Four Acts* (acting edition). New York: Samuel French, 1919.

Burke, Thomas. *Nights in Town: A London Autobiography*. London: Allen & Unwin, 1915.

———. *Limehouse Nights*. London: Grant Richards, 1917; New York: McBride, 1917.

———. *Out and About: A Note-Book of London in War-Time*. London: Allen & Unwin, 1919.

———. *Broken Blossoms*. London: Grant Richards, 1920.

———. *The Song Book of Quong Lee*. London: Allen & Unwin, 1920.

———. *Whispering Windows: More Limehouse Nights*. London: Grant Richards, 1921.

———. *Son of London*. London: Herbert Jenkins, 1946.

Cairns, John Arthur Robert. *The Loom of the Law*. London: Hutchinson, 1920.

———. *The Sidelights of London*. London: Hutchinson, 1923; New York: Henry Holt, 1924.

Cancellor, H. L. *The Life of a London Beak*. London: Hurst and Blackett, 1930.

De Quincey, Thomas. *Confessions of an English Opium Eater*. 1821. Reprint, London: Dover, 1995.

Dickens, Charles. *The Mystery of Edwin Drood*. 1870. Reprint, Oxford: Oxford University Press, 1998.

Headlam, Cecil, ed. *The Milner Papers, v. 2: South Africa 1899–1905*. London: Cassell, 1933.

Heren, Louis. *Growing Up Poor in London*. London: Hamish Hamilton, 1973.

Jenkins, John Edward. *The Coolie: His Rights and Wrongs*. New York: Routledge, 1871. Reprint, New York: Ebiron Classics, 2005.

Kinloch-Cooke, Clement. *Chinese Labour (in the Transvaal): A Study of its Moral, Economic, and Imperial Aspects*, rev. ed., London: Macmillan, 1906.

Lieck, Albert. *Bow Street World*. London: Robert Hale, 1938.

Markham, Violet. *The New Era in South Africa*. London: Smith, Elder, 1904.

Mayhew, Henry. *London Labour and the London Poor. vol. I–IV*. London: Griffin, Bohn,1861–62. Reprint, New York: Dover, 1968.

Neame, Lawrence Elwin. *The Asiatic Danger in the Colonies*. London: Routledge, 1907.

Owen, Harold, H. M. Vernon, and Louise Jordan Miln. *Mr. Wu*. 1918. Reprint, New York: Kessinger, 2007.

Parkinson, Joseph Charles. *Places and People, Being Studies from Life*. London: Tinsley Bros, 1869.

Ransome, Arthur. *The Chinese Puzzle*. London: Allen & Unwin, 1927.

Rohmer, Sax (Arthur Henry Sarsfield Ward). *The Mystery of Dr. Fu Manchu.* London: Methuen, 1913. Alternate title, *The Insidious Dr. Fu Manchu.* New York: McBride, 1913; Toronto: McClelland & Goodchild, 1913.

———. *The Yellow Claw.* London: Methuen, 1915; New York: McBride, 1915.

———. *The Si-Fan Mysteries.* London: Methuen, 1917.

———. *Dope: A Story of Chinatown and the Drug Traffic.* London: Cassell, 1919; New York, McBride, 1919.

———. *The Golden Scorpion.* London: Methuen, 1919; New York: McBride, 1920.

Salter, Joseph. *The Asiatic in England: Sketches of Sixteen Years' Work Among Orientals.* London: Seeley, Jackson, and Halliday, 1873.

———. *The East in the West; or Work Amongst the Asiatics and Africans in London.* London: S. W. Partridge, 1895.

Scrutton, Thomas Edward. *The Merchant Shipping Act, 1894, with Notes and References to Decided Cases*, 2nd ed., London: Clowes and Sons, 1895.

Sexton, James. *Sir James Sexton, Agitator: The Life of the Docker's M.P.* London: Faber & Faber, 1936.

Shiel, Matthew Phipps. *The Yellow Danger.* London: Grant Richards, 1898.

Tart, Margaret. *The Life of Quong Tart: or How a Foreigner Succeeded in a British Community.* Sydney: W.W. Maclardy, 1911.

Wilde, Oscar. *The Picture of Dorian Grey.* London: Ward, Lock, 1891.

Williams, Montagu. *Round London: Down East and Up West.* London: Macmillan, 1892.

Primary Sources: Articles, Pamphlets, and Leaflets

Buxton, Sydney. *Chinese Labour: The Transvaal Ordinance Analysed.* London: The Liberal Publication Department, 1904.

The Chinese Labour Ordinance: A Speech Delivered by Mr. J. Fletcher Moulton, K.C., M.P. in the House of Commons on March 21st, 1904. London: The Liberal Publication Department, 1904.

The Great Demonstration to Protest against the Introduction of Chinese Labour to South Africa under Conditions of Slavery, Illustrated Official Programme and Guide. London: Twentieth Century Press, 1904.

Is it Slavery? London: Conservative Central Office, 1906.

National Sailors' and Firemen's Union. *Chinese Labour in British Ships.* London: John Kealey, 1921

Naylor, Thomas. *Yellow Labour: The Truth About the Chinese in the Transvaal.* London, 1904.

Neame, Lawrence Elwin. "Oriental Labor in South Africa." *Annals of the American Academy of Political and Social Science* 34, no. 2, Chinese and Japanese in America (September, 1909): 175–182.

Open Letter to the British Workmen from the Johannesburg Chamber of Trade Regarding Chinese Labour in the Transvaal Gold Mines. Johannesburg, 1906

Rose, Edward. *Uncle Tom's Cabin Up-to-Date or Chinese Slavery in South Africa*. London, 1904.

Scheffauer, Herman. "The Chinese in England: A Growing National Problem," *London Magazine*, June 1911: 465–480 and July 1911: 645–657.

Wade, George A. "The Cockney John Chinaman," *London Illustrated Magazine*, July 1900: 301–307.

Wright, Harold. Review of *An Experiment in Alien Labor*, by E. George Payne. *Economic Journal* 22, no. 86 (June 1912): 268–70.

Films

Griffiths, D. W. *Broken Blossoms: The Yellow Man and the Girl.* United Artists, 1919; New York: Kino Video, 2002, DVD.

Brabin, Charles. *The Mask of Fu Manchu.* MGM, 1932; Burbank, CA:Warner Bros, 2006, DVD.

Poems and Songs

Formby, George, and Jack Cottrell. "Chinese Laundry Blues" (sheet music). London: Chappell & Co., 1932.

Harte, Bret. "The Heathen Chinee." *The Overland Monthly Magazine*, September 1870.

Jerome, William, and Jean Schwartz. "Chinatown, My Chinatown" (sheet music). New York: Jerome H. Remick & Co,1910.

Electronic Resources

Gale, *Times* (London) Digital Archive, 1785–1985

JUSTIS legal archive, http://www.justis.com.

Knapp, Lawrence. The Page of Fu Manchu, hosted by New Jersey Higher Education Network, http://www.njedge.net/~knapp.

The Old Bailey Proceedings Online, 1674–1913, http://www.oldbaileyonline.org.

September 1800 trial of William Rayner, Charles Moren, t18000917-29

September 1800 trial of Mary Bush, Sarah Clarke, Elizabeth Smith, t18000917-106

December 1804 trial of Ann Alsey, Thomas Gunn, t18041205-56

July 1852 trial of Cornelius M'Carthy, t18520705-726

August 1855 trial of Assam, Afuck, Apoi, Ayang, t18550820-788

March 1863 trial of Saqui, t18630302-487

April 1863 trial of Saqui, t18630406-621

August 1870 trial of John Afow, Rwa, t18790805-696

June 1911 trial of August Sepp, t19110627-10
Oxford Dictionary of National Biography, online ed., http://www.oxforddnb.com.

Secondary Sources: Published Books, Articles, Essays, and Reviews

Ackroyd, Peter. *Illustrated London*. London: Chatto & Windus, 2003.

Adamson, Alan. "The Impact of Indentured Immigration on the Political Economy of British Guiana." In *Indentured Labour in the British Empire 1834–1920*, edited by Kay Saunders. London: Croom Helm, 1984.

Alderman, Geoffrey and Colin Holmes eds. *Outsiders and Outcasts: Essays in Honour of William J. Fishman*. London: Duckworth, 1993.

Anderson, Benedict. *Imagined Communities: Reflections on the Origins and Spread of Nationalism*. London: Verso, 1983.

Andrew, Donna T., and Randall McGowan. *The Perreaus and Mrs. Rudd: Forgery and Betrayal in Eighteenth-Century London*. Berkeley and Los Angeles: University of California Press, 2001.

Arnsen, Eric. "Whiteness and the Historians' Imagination." *International Labour and Working-Class History* 60 (Fall 2001): 3–32.

Auerbach, Sascha. "Negotiating Nationalism: Jewish Conscription and Russian Repatriation in London's East End, 1916–1918." *Journal of British Studies* 46, no. 3 (July 2007): 594–620.

"Australian Radical History: the Maritime Strike of 1878–1879." *Anarchist Age Weekly Review* 286 (February 10–16, 1998).

Bailey, Peter. *Popular Culture and Performance in the Victorian City*. Cambridge: Cambridge University Press, 1998.

Baker, John Earl. Review of *The Chinese Puzzle*, by Arthur Ransome. *Journal of the Royal Institute of International Affairs* 7, no. 1 (January 1928): 56–7.

Balfour, Campbell. "Captain Tupper and the 1911 Seamen's Strike in Cardiff." *Morgannwg: Transactions of the Local Glamorgan History Society* 14 (1970): 62–80.

Behlmer, George. "Summary Justice and Working-Class Marriage in England, 1870–1940." *Law and History Review* 12, no. 2 (Fall 1994): 229–76.

Behlmer, George, and Fred Leventhal, eds. *Singular Continuities: Tradition, Nostalgia, and Identity in Modern British Culture*. Stanford, CA: Stanford University Press, 2000.

Bello, David. *Opium and the Limits of Empire: Drug Prohibition in the Chinese Interior, 1729–1850*. Cambridge, MA: Harvard University Press, 2005.

Berridge, Virginia. "East End Opium Dens and Narcotic Use in Britain." *The London Journal* 4, no. 1 (1978): 2–28.

———. "The Origins of the English 'Drug Scene,' 1890–1930." *Medical History* 32 (1988): 51–64.

Berridge, Virginia and Griffith Edwards. *Opium and the People: Opiate Use in Nineteenth-Century England*. London: Allan Lane, 1981.

Bhabha, Homi K. "The Other Question: Homi K. Bhabha Reconsiders the Stereotype and Colonial Discourse." *Screen* 24, no. 6 (1983): 18–36.

———, ed. *Nation and Narration*. London: Routledge, 1990.

Bickers, Robert. "New Light on Lao She, London, and the London Missionary Society, 1921–1929." *Modern Chinese Literature* 8 (1994).

———. *Britain in China: Community, Culture, and Colonialism 1900–1949*. Manchester: Manchester University Press, 1999.

Blake, Andrew. "Foreign Devils and Moral Panics: Britain, Asia, and the Opium Trade." In *The Expansion of England: Race, Ethnicity and Cultural History*, edited by Bill Schwarz. London: Routledge, 1996.

Bland, Lucy. "White Women and Men of Colour: Miscegenation Fears in Britain after the Great War." *Gender and History* 17, no. 1 (April 2005): 29–61.

Bonnell, Victoria E. and Lynn Hunt, eds. *Beyond the Cultural Turn: New Directions in the Study of Society and Culture*. Berkeley and Los Angeles: University of California Press, 1999.

Bonnett, Alastair. "How the British Working Class Became White: The Symbolic (Re)formation of Racialized Capitalism." *Journal of Historical Sociology* 11 (1998): 316–40.

Bourke, Joanna. *Dismembering the Male: Men's Bodies, Britain and the Great War*. Chicago: University of Chicago Press, 1996.

Bowen, H. V., Margaret Lincoln, and Nigel Rigby, eds. *The Worlds of the East India Company*. Woodbridge, U.K.: Boydell & Brewer, 2002.

Broeze, Frank. "Underdevelopment and Dependency: Maritime India during the Raj." *Modern Asian Studies* 18, no. 3 (1984): 429–57.

Bronstein, Jamie. "Rethinking the 'Readmission': Anglo-Jewish History and the Immigration Crisis." In *Singular Continuities: Tradition, Nostalgia, and Identity in Modern British Culture*, edited by George Behlmer and Fred Leventhal. Stanford, CA: Stanford University Press, 2000.

Brogan, Hugh. *The Life of Arthur Ransome*. London: Jonathan Cape, 1984.

Brown, J. B. "The Politics of the Poppy: The Society for the Suppression of the Opium Trade, 1874–1916." *Journal of Contemporary History* 8, no. 3 (July 1973): 97–111.

Brown, Judith, and Wm. Roger Louis. *The Oxford History of the British Empire, Volume IV: The Twentieth Century*. Oxford: Oxford University Press, 1999.

Burton, Antoinette. *At the Heart of Empire: Indians and the Colonial Encounter in Late Victorian Britain*. Berkeley and Los Angeles: University of California Press 1998.

———, ed. *After the Imperial Turn: Thinking with and Through the Nation*. Durham, NC: Duke University Press, 2003.

Campbell, Persia. *Chinese Coolie Emigration to Countries within the British Empire*. New York: Negro Universities Press, 1923.

Chakrabarty, Dipesh. *Rethinking Working-Class History: Bengal 1890–1940.* Princeton, NJ: Princeton University Press, 1989.

Chatterjee, Partha. *The Nation and Its Fragments: Colonial and Postcolonial Histories.* Princeton, NJ: Princeton University Press, 1993.

Choo, Ng Chee. *The Chinese in London* (published M.A. thesis). London: Oxford University Press, 1968.

Cohen, Paul A. *History in Three Keys: The Boxers as Event, Experience, and Myth.* New York: Columbia University Press, 1997.

Cohen, Stanley. *Folk Devils and Moral Panics: The Creation of the Mods and Rockers.* London: MacGibbon and Kee, 1972.

Cole, Richard, and Gabriel Chin. "Emerging from the Margins of Historical Consciousness: Chinese Immigrants and the History of American Law." *Law and History Review* 17, no. 2 (Summer, 1999): 325–64.

Colley, Linda. *Britons: Forging the Nation, 1707–1837.* New Haven, CT: Yale University Press, 1992.

Conley, Carolyn. *The Unwritten Law: Criminal Justice in Victorian Kent.* New York: Oxford University Press, 1991.

Constantine, Stephen. "Migrants and Settlers." In *The Oxford History of the British Empire, Volume IV: The Twentieth Century*, edited by Judith Brown and Wm. Roger Louis. Oxford: Oxford University Press, 1999.

Culin, Stewart. "Gambling Games of the Chinese in America," *Series in Philology Literature and Archeology* 1, no. 4. Philadelphia: University of Pennsylvania Press, 1891.

Curthoys Ann. "Liberalism and Exclusionism: A Prehistory of the White Australia Policy." In *Legacies of White Australia: Race, Culture, and Nation*, edited by Laksiri Jaya Suriya, David Walker, and Jan Gothard. Crawley, Perth: University of Western Australia Press, 2003.

Davin, Anna. *Growing Up Poor: Home, School, and Street in London, 1870–1914.* London: Rivers Oram, 1996.

Davis, Jennifer. "A Poor Man's System of Justice: The London Police Courts in the Second Half of the Nineteenth Century." *The Historical Journal* 27, no. 2 (1984): 309–35.

———. "Prosecutions and their Context: the Use of the Criminal Law in Later Nineteenth-Century London." In *Policing and Prosecution in Britain, 1750–1850*, edited by Douglas Hay and Francis Snyder. Oxford: Oxford University Press, 1989.

D'Cruze, Shani. *Crimes of Outrage: Sex, Violence, and Victorian Working Women.* Dekalb, IL: Northern Illinois University Press, 1998.

De Nie, Michael. "'A Medley Mob of Irish-American Plotters and Irish Dupes': The British Press and Transatlantic Fenianism." *Journal of British Studies* 40, no. 2 (April 2001): 213–40.

Denoon, Donald. *A Grand Illusion: The Failure of Imperial Policy in the Transvaal Colony during the Period of Reconstruction, 1900–1905.* London: Longman, 1973.

Deslandes, Paul. "'The Foreign Element:' Newcomers and the Rhetoric of Race, Nation, and Empire in 'Oxbridge' Undergraduate Culture, 1850–1920." *Journal of British Studies* 37, no. 1 (Jan. 1998): 54–90.

Dillon, Richard H. *The Hatchet Men: The Story of the Tong Wars in San Francisco's Chinatown*. New York: Van Rees, 1962.

Douglas, R. K. "No Value in Truth." In *Sinophiles and Sinophobes: Western Views of China*, edited by Colin Mackerras. Oxford: Oxford University Press, 2000.

Dummett, Ann and Andrew Nicol. *Subjects, Citizens, Aliens and Others: Nationality and Immigration Law*. London: Weidenfeld and Nicolson, 1990.

Fawcett, Brian. "The Chinese Labour Corps in France 1917–1922." *Journal of the Royal Asiatic Society, Hong Kong Branch* 40 (2000): 33–111.

Feldman, David. "The Importance of Being English: Jewish Immigration and the Decay of Liberal England." In *Metropolis London: Histories and Representations since 1800*, edited by David Feldman and Gareth Stedman Jones. London: Routledge, 1989.

Feldman, David, and Gareth Stedman Jones, eds. *Metropolis London: Histories and Representations since 1800*. London: Routledge, 1989.

Finn, Margot. "Working-Class Women And The Contest for Consumer Control In Victorian County Courts." *Past and Present* 161, no. 1 (November 1998): 116–54.

———. "Victorian Law, Literature and History: Three Ships Passing in the Night." *Journal of Victorian Culture* 7, no. 1 (2002): 134–46.

Fisher, Michael. *Counterflows to Colonialism: Indian Travelers and Settlers in Britain, 1600–1857*. New Delhi: Permanent Black, 2004.

Forman, Ross G. "Peking Plots: Fictionalizing the Boxer Rebellion of 1900." *Victorian Literature and Culture* 27 (1998): 19–48.

Frader, Laura, and Sonya O. Rose, eds. *Gender and Class in Modern Europe*. Ithaca, NY: Cornell University Press 1996.

Frost, Ginger. *Promises Broken: Courtship, Class, and Gender in Victorian England*. Charlottesville, VA: University Press of Virginia, 1995.

Gilbert, Pamela K., ed. *Imagined Londons*. Albany, NY: SUNY Press, 2002.

Gilroy, Paul. "*There Ain't No Black in the Union Jack*": *The Cultural Politics of Race and Nation*. Chicago: University of Chicago Press, 1987.

Gladfelder, Hal. *Criminality and Narrative in Eighteenth-Century England: Beyond the Law*. Baltimore: Johns Hopkins University Press, 2001.

Grace, Helen. "A Practical Man: Portraiture between Word And Image." *Continuum: The Australian Journal of Media & Culture* 6, no. 2 (1991) http://wwwmcc.murdoch.edu.au/ReadingRoom/6.2/Grace.html.

Grant, Kevin. *A Civilized Savagery: Britain and the New Slaveries in Africa, 1884–1926*. New York: Routledge, 2005.

Guha, Ranahit, Gayatri Spivak, and Edward Said, eds. *Selected Subaltern Studies*. Oxford: Oxford University Press, 1989.

Gullace, Nicoletta. *Blood of Our Sons: Men, Women, and the Renegotiation of Citizenship during the Great War*. New York: Palgrave Macmillan, 2002.

———. "Friends, Aliens, and Enemies: Fictive Communities and the Lusitania Riots of 1915." *Journal of Social History* 39, no. 2 (2005): 345–67.

Guterl, Matthew, and Christine Skwiot. "Atlantic & Pacific Crossings: Race, Empire, and the 'Labor Problem' in the Nineteenth Century." *Radical History Review* 91, no. 1 (Winter 2005): 40–61.

Gyory, Andrew. *Closing the Gate: Race, Politics, and the Chinese Exclusion Act*. Chapel Hill, NC: University of North Carolina Press, 1998.

Hall, Catherine, and Sonya O. Rose, eds. *At Home with the Empire: Metropolitan Culture and the Imperial World*. Cambridge: Cambridge University Press, 2006.

Hall, Stuart, et al. *Policing the Crisis: Mugging, the State and Law and Order*. London: Palgrave Macmillan, 1978.

Hammerton, A. James. *Cruelty and Companionship: Conflict in Nineteenth-Century Married Life*. London: Routledge, 1992.

Hearn, Mark. "Rose Summerfield's Gospel of Discontent: a Narrative of Radical Identity in Late Nineteenth Century Australia." *Labour History* 87 (May 2004): 65–82.

Hevia, James. *English Lessons: The Pedagogy of Imperialism in Nineteenth-Century China*. Durham, NC: Duke University Press, 2003.

Holland, Robert. "The British Empire and the Great War, 1914–1918." In *The Oxford History of the British Empire, Volume IV: The Twentieth Century*, edited by Judith Brown and Wm. Roger Louis. Oxford: Oxford University Press, 1999.

Holmes, Colin. *John Bull's Island: Immigration and British Society, 1871–1971*. London: Macmillan, 1988.

———. "The Chinese Connection." In *Outsiders and Outcasts: Essays in Honour of William J. Fishman*, edited by Geoffrey Alderman and Colin Holmes. London: Duckworth, 1993.

———, ed. *Immigrants and Minorities in British Society*. London: Allen & Unwin, 1996.

Holt, Thomas C. "Marking: Race, Race-making, and the Writing of History," *American Historical Review* 100, no. 1 (February 1995): 1–20.

Huttenback, Robert. *Racism and Empire: White Settlers and Colored Immigrants in the British Self-Governing Colonies, 1830–1910*. Ithaca, NY: Cornell University Press, 1976.

Hyam, Ronald. *Britain's Imperial Century, 1815–1914*. 3rd ed. Cambridge: Cambridge University Press, 2002.

Hyslop, Jonathan. "The Imperial Working Class Makes Itself 'White': White Labourism in Britain, Australia, and South Africa Before the First World War." *Journal of Historical Sociology* 12, no. 4 (December 1999): 398–421.

Ignatiev, Noel. *How the Irish Became White*. New York: Routledge, 1995.

Jenkinson, Jacqueline. "The 1919 Riots." In *Racial Violence in Britain in the Nineteenth and Twentieth Centuries*, edited by Panikos Panayi. Leicester, U.K.: Leicester University Press, 1996.

Joyce, Simon. *Capital Offenses: Geographies of Class and Crime in Victorian London*. Charlottesville, VA: University Press of Virginia, 2003.

Jupp, James. *The Australian People: An Encyclopedia of the Nation, its People and their Origins*. 2nd ed. Cambridge: Cambridge University Press, 2002.

Katz, Elaine. "White Workers' Grievances." *The South African Journal of Economics* 42, v. 2 (June 1974): 127–56.

Kift, Dagmar. *The Victorian Music Hall: Culture, Class, and Conflict*. Cambridge: Cambridge University Press, 1996.

Kohn, Marek. *Dope Girls: The Birth of the British Drug Underground*. London: Granta, 2001.

Koss, Stephen. *The Rise and Fall of the Political Press in Britain*. London: Hamish Hamilton, 1984.

Koven, Seth. *Slumming: Sexual and Social Politics in Victorian London*. Princeton, NJ: Princeton University Press, 2004.

Kynoch, Gary. "Controlling the Coolies: Chinese Mineworkers and the Struggle for Labor in South Africa, 1904–1910." *International Journal of African Historical Studies* 36, no. 2 (2003): 309–29.

———. "'Your Petitioners are in Mortal Terror:' The Violent World of Chinese Mineworkers in South Africa, 1904–1910." *Journal of Southern African Studies* 31, no. 3 (September 2005): 531–46.

LaCapra, Dominick, ed. *The Bounds of Race: Perspectives on Hegemony and Resistance*. Ithaca, NY: Cornell University Press, 1991.

Lahiri, Shompa. *Indians in Britain: Anglo-Indian Encounters, Race and Identity 1880–1930*. London: Frank Cass, 2000.

———. "Contested Relations: The East India Company and Lascars in London." In *The Worlds of the East India Company*, edited by H. V. Bowen, Margaret Lincoln, and Nigel Rigby. Woodbridge, U.K.: Boydel & Brewer, 2002.

Lai, Annie, Bob Little, and Pippa Little. "Chinatown Annie: The East End Opium Trade 1920–1935: The Story of a Woman Opium Dealer." *Oral History Journal* 14, no. 1 (1986): 18–30.

Lake, Marilyn. "The White Man under Siege: New Histories of Race in the Nineteenth Century and the Advent of White Australia." *History Workshop Journal* 58, no. 1 (2004): 41–62.

Laksiri, Jayasuriya, David Walker, and Jan Gothard, eds. *Legacies of White Australia: Race, Culture, and Nation*. Crawley, Perth: University of Western Australia Press, 2003.

Lambourne, Gerald. *The Fingerprint Story*. London: Harrap, 1984.

Levine, Philippa. "Battle Colours: Race, Sex, and Colonial Soldiery in World War I," *Journal of Women's History*, 9, no. 4 (1998): 104–30.

———, ed. *The Oxford History of the British Empire, Companion Series: Gender and Empire*. Oxford: Oxford University Press, 2004.

———. *The British Empire: Sunrise to Sunset.* Harlow, U.K.: Pearson Longman, 2007.

Leys, Simon, ed. *The Burning Forest.* New York: Holt, Rinehart & Winston, 1985.

Lindeborg, Ruth. "The 'Asiatic' and the Boundaries of Victorian Englishness." *Victorian Studies* 37, no. 3 (1994): 381–404.

Little, Kenneth. *Negroes in Britain: A Study of Racial Relations in English Society.* London: Routledge and Kegan Paul, 1948.

Loomba, Ania. *Colonialism/Postcolonialism.* New York: Routledge, 1998.

Lorimer, Douglas A. *Colour, Class, and the Victorians.* Leicester, U.K.: Leicester University Press, 1978.

Lui, Mary Ting Yi. *The Chinatown Trunk Mystery: Murder, Miscegenation, and Other Dangerous Encounters in Turn-of-the-Century New York City.* Princeton, NJ: Princeton University Press, 2005.

MacKenzie, John M. *Propaganda and Empire: The Manipulation of British Public Opinion, 1880–1960.* Manchester: Manchester University Press, 1984.

Mackeras, Colin. *Western Images of China.* Oxford: Oxford University Press, 1989.

———, ed. *Sinophobes and Sinophiles: Western Views of China.* Oxford: Oxford University Press, 2000.

MacRaild, Donald M. *Irish Migrants in Modern Britain, 1750–1922.* New York: Palgrave MacMillan, 1999.

Magubane, Zine. *Bringing the Empire Home: Race, Class, and Gender in Britain and Colonial South Africa.* Chicago: University of Chicago Press, 2004.

Mansaray, Ayo. "The Alchemy of Mixed Race," *The Global Review of Ethnopolitics* 2, no. 3–4 (March/June 2003): 100–6.

Marshall, Paul. "The Lord Chamberlain and the Containment of Americanization in the British Theater of the 1920s." *The New Theater Quarterly* 19 (2003): 381–94.

Marshall, P. J., ed. *The Cambridge Illustrated History of the British Empire.* Cambridge: Cambridge University Press, 1996.

———. "The Diaspora of the Africans and the Asians." In *The Cambridge Illustrated History of the British Empire*, edited by P. J. Marshall. Cambridge: Cambridge University Press, 1996.

Martin, Ged and Benjamin E. Kline. "British Emigration and New Identities." In *The Cambridge Illustrated History of the British Empire*, edited by P. J. Marshall. Cambridge: Cambridge University Press, 1996.

May, J. P. "The Chinese in Britain, 1860–1914." In *Immigrants and Minorities in British Society*, edited by Colin Holmes. London: Allen & Unwin, 1996.

May, Roy and Robin Cohen. "The Interaction between Race and Colonialism: A Case Study of the Liverpool Race Riots of 1919." *Race and Class* 16, no. 2 (1974): 111–26.

McClintock, Anne. *Imperial Leather: Race, Gender, and Sexuality in the Colonial Contest.* New York: Routledge, 1995.

McDevitt, Patrick. *"May the Best Man Win": Sport, Masculinity, and Nationalism in Great Britain and the Empire, 1880–1935.* New York: Palgrave Macmillan, 2004.

McDonald, Robert A. J. *Making Vancouver: Class, Status, and Social Boundaries, 1863–1913.* Vancouver: University of British Columbia Press, 1996.

McPherson, Kathryn, Cecelia Morgan, and Nancy M. Forrestel, eds. *Gendered Pasts: Historical Essays in Femininity and Masculinity in Canada.* Oxford: Oxford University Press, 1999.

Metcalf, Thomas. "Imperial Towns and Cities." In *The Cambridge Illustrated History of the British Empire*, edited by P. J. Marshall. Cambridge: Cambridge University Press, 1996.

Miers, David. "Gaming Machines in Great Britain: A Century of Change." *Gaming Law Review* 7, no. 2 (Apr 2003): 131–47.

Milligan, Barry. *Pleasures and Pains: Opium and the Orient in Nineteenth-Century British Culture.* Charlottesville, VA: University Press of Virginia, 1995.

Moran, Leslie. *The Homosexual(ity) of Law.* London: Routledge, 1996.

Morgan, Philip D., and Sean Hawkins, eds. *Oxford History of the British Empire, Companion Series: Black Experience and the Empire.* Oxford: Oxford University Press, 2004.

Mott, Frank. *A History of American Magazines, 1885–1905*, v. 4. Cambridge: Harvard University Press, 1957.

Munn, Christopher. *Anglo-China: Chinese People and British Rule in Hong Kong, 1841–1880.* Richmond, U.K.: Curzon, 2001.

Murphy, Andrea. *From the Empire to the Rialto—Racism and Reaction in Liverpool, 1918–1948.* Birkenhead, U.K.: Liver Press, 1995.

Nead, Lynda. *Victorian Babylon: People, Streets, and Images in Nineteenth-Century London.* New Haven, CT: Yale University Press, 2000.

Nelson, Cary, and Larry Grossberg, eds. *Marxism and the Interpretation of Culture.* Chicago: University of Chicago Press, 1988.

Nord, Deborah Epstein. *Walking the Victorian Streets: Women, Representation and the City.* Ithaca, NY: Cornell University Press, 1995.

Northrup, David. *Indentured Labor in the Age of Imperialism, 1834–1922.* Cambridge: Cambridge University Press, 1995.

O'Day, Alan. "Varieties of Anti-Irish Behaviour in Britain, 1846–1922." In *Racial Violence in Britain in the Nineteenth and Twentieth Centuries*, edited by Panikos Panayi. Leicester, U.K.: Leicester University Press, 1993.

Omer-Cooper, J. D. *History of Southern Africa*, 2nd ed. London: James Curry, 1994.

Palmer, Alan. *The East End: Four Centuries of London Life.* New Brunswick, NJ: Rutgers University Press, 2000.

Pan, Lynn. *Sons of the Yellow Emperor: A History of the Chinese Diaspora.* New York: Kodansha International, 1990.

Panayi, Panikos, ed. *Racial Violence in Britain in the Nineteenth and Twentieth Centuries.* Leicester, U.K.: Leicester University Press, 1996.

Paul, Kathleen. *Whitewashing Britain: Race and Citizenship in the Postwar Era.* Ithaca, NY: Cornell University Press, 1997.

Pennybacker, Susan. *A Vision for London: Labour, Everyday Life, and the LCC Experiment.* London: Routledge, 1995.

Pick, Daniel. *Svengali's Web: The Alien Enchanter in Modern Culture.* New Haven, CT: Yale University Press, 2000.

Porter, Bernard. *The Lion's Share.* 3rd ed. Harlow, U.K.: Pearson Education, 1996.

———. *The Absent-Minded Imperialists: Empire, Society, and Culture in Britain.* Oxford: Oxford University Press, 2004

Potter, Simon. *News and the British World: The Emergence of an Imperial Press System, 1876–1922.* Oxford: Oxford University Press, 2003.

Price, Richard. "One Big Thing: Britain, Its Empire, and Their Imperial Culture." *Journal of British Studies* 45, no. 3 (July 2006): 602–27.

Ramdin, Ron. *The Making of the Black Working Class in Britain.* Aldershot, U.K.: Gower, 1987.

Rich, Paul. *Race and Empire in British Politics.* Cambridge: Cambridge University Press, 1986.

Robb, George, and Nancy Erber, eds. *Disorder in the Courts: Trials and Sexual Conflict at the Turn of the Century.* New York: NYU Press, 1999.

Roediger, David. *The Wages of Whiteness: Race and the Making of the American Working Class.* London: Verso, 1991.

Ross, Ellen. "'Not the Sort That Would Sit on the Doorstep': Respectability in Pre-World War I London Neighborhoods." *International Labor and Working Class History* 27 (Spring 1985): 39–59.

———. *Love and Toil: Motherhood in Outcast London.* New York: Oxford University Press, 1993.

Rowe, Michael. "Sex, 'Race,' and Riot in Liverpool, 1919," *Immigrants and Minorities* 19, no. 2 (July 2000): 53–70.

Rowland, John. *The Finger-Print Man: The Story of Sir Edward Henry.* London: Lutterworth Press, 1959.

Said, Edward. *Orientalism.* New York: Vintage, 1978.

Saunders, Kay, ed. *Indentured Labour in the British Empire 1834–1920.* London: Croom Helm, 1984.

Savage, Gail. "'The Magistrates Are Men': Working-Class Marital Conflict and Appeals from the Magistrates' Court to the Divorce Court after 1895." In *Disorder in the Courts: Trials and Sexual Conflict at the Turn of the Century*, edited by George Robb and Nancy Erber . New York: NYU Press, 1999.

Schneer, Jonathan. *London 1900: The Imperial Metropolis.* New Haven, CT: Yale University Press, 1999.

Schwarz, Bill, ed. *The Expansion of England: Race, Ethnicity and Cultural History.* London: Routledge, 1996.

Scott, Joan W. "Gender: A Useful Category of Historical Analysis." *The American Historical Review* 91, no. 5 (December 1986): 1053–75.

Seed, John. "Limehouse Blues: Looking for Chinatown in the London Docks, 1900–1940." *History Workshop Journal* 62 (2006): 58–85.

Sengoopta, Chandak. *Imprint of the Raj: How Fingerprinting was Born in Colonial India*. London: Macmillan, 2003.

Seshagiri, Urmila. "Modernity's (Yellow) Perils: Dr. Fu Manchu and English Race Paranoia." *Cultural Critique* 62 (2006): 162–94.

Shah, Nayan. *Contagious Divides: Epidemics and Race in San Francisco's Chinatown*. Berkeley and Los Angeles: University of California Press, 2001.

Sherwood, Marika. "Lascar Struggles against Discrimination in Britain 1923–1945: The World of N. J. Upadhyaya and Surat Alley." *The Mariner's Mirror* 90, no. 4 (November 2004): 438–55.

Sinha, Mrinalini. *Colonial Masculinity: The "Manly Englishman" and the "Effeminate Bengali" in the Late Nineteenth Century*. Manchester: Manchester University Press, 1995.

Spence, Jonathan D. *The Search for Modern China*. 2nd ed. New York: W. W. Norton, 1999.

Spivak, Gayatri. "Can the Subaltern Speak?" in *Marxism and the Interpretation of Culture*, edited by Cary Nelson and Larry Grossberg. Chicago: University of Chicago Press, 1988.

Spraggs, Gillian. *Outlaws and Highwaymen: The Cult of the Robber in England from the Middle Ages to the Nineteenth Century*. London: Pimlico, 2001.

Stepan, Nancy Leys. *The Idea of Race in Science: Great Britain 1800–1960*. Hamden, CT: Archon Books, 1982.

Tabili, Laura. "The Construction of Racial Difference in Twentieth-Century Britain: The Special Restriction (Coloured Alien Seamen) Order, 1925." *Journal of British Studies* 33, no. 1 (January 1994): 54–99.

———. *"We Ask for British Justice": Workers and Racial Difference in Late Imperial Britain*. Ithaca, NY: Cornell University Press, 1994.

———. "Women 'of a Very Low Type': Crossing Racial Boundaries in Imperial Britain." In *Gender and Class in Modern Europe*, edited by Laura Frader and Sonya O. Rose. Ithaca, NY: Cornell University Press 1996.

———. "Race is a Relationship, And Not a Thing." *Journal of Social History* 37, no. 1 (2003): 125–30.

———. "Outsiders in the Land of Their Birth: Exogamy, Citizenship, and Identity in War and Peace." *Journal of British Studies* 44, no. 4 (October 2004): 796–815.

Taylor, David. *Crime, Policing, and Punishment in England, 1750–1914*. New York: Palgrave, 1998.

Thom, Deborah. *Nice Girls and Rude Girls: Women Workers in World War I*. London: I.B. Tauris, 1998.

Thompson, Andrew. *The Empire Strikes Back: The Impact of Imperialism on Britain from the Mid-Nineteenth Century*. Harlow, U.K.: Pearson Education, 2005.

Thompson, Edward P. *The Making of the English Working Class*. New York: Vintage, 1966.

Van Ash, Cay, and Elizabeth Sax Rohmer. *Master of Villainy: A Biography of Sax Rohmer*. Bowling Green, OH: Bowling Green University Popular Press, 1972.

Visram, Rozina. *Ayahs, Lascars, and Princes: Indians in Britain 1700–1947*. London: Pluto, 1986.

Walker, David. *Anxious Nation: Australia and the Rise of Asia, 1850–1939*. St. Lucia, Brisbane: University of Queensland Press, 1999.

Walker-Smith, Derek. *The Life of Lord Darling*. London: Cassell, 1938.

Walkowitz, Judith. *Prostitution and Victorian Society: Women, Class and the State*. Cambridge: Cambridge University Press, 1980.

———. *City of Dreadful Delight: Narratives of Danger in Late Victorian London*. Chicago: University of Chicago Press, 1992.

Watney, Simon. *Policing Desire: Pornography, AIDS and the Media*. Minneapolis, MN: University of Minnesota Press, 1989.

Ward, W. Peter. *White Canada Forever: Popular Attitudes and Public Policy Toward Orientals in British Columbia*. Montreal: McGill-Queen's University Press, 1978.

Wiener, Martin. *Men of Blood: Violence, Manliness, and Criminal Justice in Victorian England*. Cambridge: Cambridge University Press, 2004.

Wilkinson, Glenn R. *Depictions and Images of War in Edwardian Newspapers*. New York: Palgrave Macmillan, 2003.

Wilson, Kathleen, ed. *A New Imperial History: Culture, Identity, and Modernity in Britain and the Empire, 1660–1840*. Cambridge: Cambridge University Press, 2004.

Witchard, Anne. "Aspects of Literary Limehouse: Thomas Burke and the 'Glamorous Shame of Chinatown.'" *Literary London: Interdisciplinary Studies in the Representation of London* 2 (2004): 1–8, http://www.literarylondon.org/london-journal/september%202004/witchard.html.

Wong, Maria Lin. *Chinese Liverpudlians: A History of the Chinese Community in Liverpool*. Birkenhead, U.K.: Liver Press, 1989.

Woollacott, Angela. *On Her Their Lives Depend: Munitions Workers in the Great War*. Berkeley and Los Angeles: University of California Press, 1994.

Wu, William F. *The Yellow Peril: Chinese Americans in American Fiction, 1850–1940*. Hamden, CT: Archon Books, 1982.

Xiaomei, Chen. *Occidentalism: A Theory of Counter-Discourse in Post-Mao China*. New York: Oxford University Press, 1995.

Young, Robert J. C. *Postcolonialism: An Historical Introduction*. Malden, U.K.: Blackwell, 2001.

Ziegler, Susan. "'How Far am I Responsible?': Women and Morphinomania in Late-Nineteenth-Century Britain." *Victorian Studies* 48, no. 1 (Autumn 2005): 59–81.

Index

Entries in **bold** type refer to maps and figures. Entries in (parentheses) indicate references in footnotes.

24799806R00158

Printed in Great Britain
by Amazon